Decoding the Spiritual Messages
of Everyday Life

Decoding

the

Spiritual Messages

of

Everyday Life

*How Life Shows Us What
We Need to Know*

PAUL DEBELL, M.D.

STERLING ETHOS
An imprint of Sterling Publishing Co., Inc.

New York / London
www.sterlingpublishing.com

STERLING and the distinctive Sterling logo are registered trademarks of
Sterling Publishing Co., Inc.

Library of Congress Cataloging-in-Publication Data
DeBell, Paul.
Decoding the spiritual messages of everyday life / by Paul DeBell.
p. cm.
ISBN 978-1-4027-6712-8
1. Spiritual life. 2. Coincidence—Religious aspects. I. Title.
BL625.93.D42 2009
204'4—dc22
2009002950

2 4 6 8 10 9 7 5 3 1

Published by Sterling Publishing Co., Inc.
387 Park Avenue South, New York, NY 10016
© 2009 by Dr. Paul DeBell
Distributed in Canada by Sterling Publishing
c/o Canadian Manda Group, 165 Dufferin Street
Toronto, Ontario, Canada M6K 3H6
Distributed in the United Kingdom by GMC Distribution Services
Castle Place, 166 High Street, Lewes, East Sussex, England BN7 1XU
Distributed in Australia by Capricorn Link (Australia) Pty. Ltd.
P.O. Box 704, Windsor, NSW 2756, Australia

Design and layout by Adam Bohannon

Manufactured in the United States
All rights reserved

Sterling ISBN 978-1-4027-6712-8

For information about custom editions, special sales, premium and
corporate purchases, please contact Sterling Special Sales
Department at 800-805-5489 or specialsales@sterlingpublishing.com.

CONTENTS

PREFACE

This book is the story of my spiritual journey and the lessons that I have learned. My journey entered a completely new phase twenty-five years ago, around the age of forty, when I started noticing what I now call *spiritual messages*—unmistakable intrusions of unknown forces into my life that I just couldn't explain. These sudden and unlikely coincidences might have seemed to someone else like chance or luck, but they struck me as something more—the kind of thing that people in the past might have considered signs from God. They baffled and intrigued me enough that analyzing them became a kind of hobby.

Since I had lost interest in religion many years before and had no belief in God at the time, I approached them as I would any other experiences that I didn't understand. I set out to discover their meaning using my psychiatric training and my best common sense. The more messages I decoded, the clearer it became. These were not the random effects of poorly understood material forces, but precise lessons forming part of a coherent educational plan that would teach me, and anyone else who would stop and listen, how to get in touch with levels of our minds even deeper than our psychological unconscious and hear the voices of our souls.

Spiritual messages have always existed, breaking through the surface of everyday life to make us momentarily aware of an invisible spiritual dimension. Messages arrive whether we are Hindu, Buddhist, Jewish, Christian, Muslim, or none of the above. They don't seem to care if we are fundamentalists or embrace New Age spirituality, men or women, young or old, Western or Eastern.

They communicate with us whether we are intellectual or emotional, laid-back or high-strung, outgoing or introspective. They guide each of us in a way that is right for us. All we need to do is to learn to decode what they are saying, and that's not always so easy.

As messages have always existed, people have always decoded them. But while people in the past did so largely by considering the effects messages had on their emotions, my messages encouraged me to focus far more on their effects on my *thoughts*. That is to say, while people in the past focused mainly on the transforming power of love in one of its many forms to change their thinking and drive their spiritual development, I, and many others I spoke to, found that our messages induced less strong feelings of love but guided our spiritual development by affecting our rational thinking about events in our everyday life. This different effect, I have come to understand, is true for many of us today because the decisions that we need to make are far more complex and require more information and greater discernment than those of people in the past. As a result, most of us are more rational than people in the past and our knowledge of the world around us is certainly far greater than theirs. Earth is no longer the center of the universe. Science explains far better how the material world works and technology gives us the practical benefits of this knowledge, as when basic sciences, medicine, and psychology work together to come up with more and more effective treatments for our ills every day.

If progress can be made in most other areas of life by taking a more scientific approach to them, then why not in spiritual life? Working with messages has shown me that this is possible. As a psychiatrist for thirty-five years, I have collected and carefully studied my own spiritual messages and hundreds of other people's as well. I've seen how decoding messages can help us get out of tight jams, overcome jealousy, control anger, improve relationships, and live happier, more balanced lives. My goal in this book is to share with you what I have learned about messages and show you how you can use their guidance to make the most of the wide range of opportunities for spiritual growth that exist in your life today.

Decoding spiritual messages is Spirituality 101—the basic course in understanding the spiritual dimension of everyday life—and everyday life is a carefully designed classroom in which we learn to develop our souls. In Part I of this book, I'll introduce you to the ABCs of spiritual messages and show you how to tease out the different effects of messages on your thoughts and feelings by taking the same rational and systematic approach you would to any other experience. Here, you will come to a better understanding of the experiences on which your own beliefs are based. In Part II, you'll discover what messages teach us about the crucial role our attention and intentions play in our spiritual life and how you can use what you learn from decoding messages to enlist spiritual help with everyday problems. Here, you will learn to discern what makes one of your spiritual experiences different from a similar psychological experience.

In Part III, you'll learn how messages help you choose and apply a set of sound spiritual principles and develop your spiritual intelligence—the capacity to understand and fully benefit from the spiritual elements in everyday life. Finally, in Part IV, I will show you how to create a framework for understanding your spiritual development that pulls together what you have learned by decoding messages and orient yourself to whatever task you face in your own life.

To help along the way, I end each chapter with a list of the key points in that chapter and several questions for reflection. Take some time to think about them. Don't feel constrained by my questions; if some other point is more interesting to you, focus on it instead. Before you move on to the next chapter, however, I encourage you to write down your thoughts about the issues raised in the chapter. That's because I have discovered in writing this book that committing what you think to writing is far more illuminating than simply thinking about that topic. Writing down your thoughts forces you to examine how well you really understand something.

You will find that you learn the most from this process by trying to describe your experiences using everyday language as much as possible. Imagine yourself explaining your experiences and beliefs to others who are just as interested in spirituality as you are but have embraced other belief systems. The more you can think of your experiences in normal everyday language, the more you are likely to be able to learn from other people's experiences.

I ask you to first write a brief paragraph that summarizes your conclusions and then explain the evidence on which you base these conclusions in as much detail as you would like. This will help you to highlight in your own mind the elements in your experience that are crucial to you so that both you and those imaginary others can more clearly see those elements and how they connect to your conclusions. Think of your writing as a way not of *arriving* at your conclusions but of *expressing* them. If you do this small exercise at the end of each chapter, I promise you that by the end of the book, you will have a much deeper understanding of your own beliefs than when you began and that it will greatly enrich your everyday life.

The path to God is vital, dynamic, and evolving. To stay on it, we need to decode our own messages and master the challenges that our own life presents. It's not enough to embrace one or another belief system. We need to learn how the spiritual system works and apply that knowledge in our own life. I hope that the steps I have taken will help you decode your own spiritual messages and with their guidance find your own way.

Your experiences and your conclusions are bound to be in some ways similar to and in other ways different from mine, because we have both a common spiritual nature and our own unique selves. I encourage you to add your reflections to mine on a Web site—decodeyourmessages.com—that I have set up for this purpose so that we can all benefit from your experiences and together advance our understanding of the spiritual dimension.

PART I

The ABCs
of Spiritual Messages

CHAPTER I

Opening
the Dialogue

The world we live in is changing rapidly. Every day it grows more complex. We are pushed to keep up with the latest fashions, ideas, and breakthroughs in every area of life. It's the beat of our times and I like it. Yet with each added complexity and each increase in the pace, life becomes more difficult to negotiate, and we can lose sight of the meaning of our existence and drift farther from the core of who we are.

In part, that's because we in modern Western societies have come to value science over spirit, quantifiable evidence over subjective experience. We feel that what we can hold and know physically is more real and valid than what we cannot. We want to know what evidence backs an assertion rather than blindly endorsing an opinion, spiritual or otherwise. As we become more rational in our approach to everything, however, we don't have to turn our backs on the spiritual, because spirituality and science, our inner world and our outer world, are not mutually exclusive.

If at times it seems that way, it's because our understanding of the spiritual dimension is still in its infancy.

Spirituality today is in much the same state that psychology was in at the end of the nineteenth century: poised on the brink of a radical shift in its approach. Before the late 1800s, no one had succeeded in studying the mind scientifically, despite the remarkable success of scientific study in other fields. The "real" sciences gathered information, made observations, developed a theory, and then, through experiments, proved or disproved it. But our thoughts, emotions, and behavior seemed too subjective to be studied by the rigorous new standards of the scientific method. Dreams were considered to be meaningless, chaotic products of disorganized brain activity, just as psychological symptoms such as phobias and compulsions were.

It may be hard for you to imagine that before the revolution in psychology at the end of the nineteenth century, we approached psychology as if it were philosophy. The opinion of the average person on the street was just as valid as that of the most learned psychologist. Neither opinion was based on good objective evidence. Science had not yet been applied to the study of the human mind.

Once psychologists did begin to study human experience scientifically, the field of psychology progressed by leaps and bounds. Today, a reliable body of objective knowledge exists to help us understand our emotions, improve our relationships, solve otherwise perplexing problems, and fulfill our own unique potential. Popular books and magazines take all of these psychological advances and boil them down into simple steps for dealing with the challenges of everyday life so that we can build greater self-esteem, make more money, and have better sex. In effect, the knowledge of psychology has permeated our society and completely altered how we all think of ourselves today.

Seeing all of that progress coming from such humble beginnings gave me the courage to hope. If such progress was possible in psychology as well as in hard sciences like medicine and physics, it could be possible in spirituality too. If science can define laws that govern human emotions, the immune system, and quantum forces by studying their effects, why can't we define the laws governing *spiritual* forces by studying their effects on us? That's when I heard a small inner voice say, *We can*. We don't have to abandon our spiritual inspirations in favor of our more modern but less passionate ways of thinking. Instead, we can use our modern ways of thinking to *enhance* our spiritual life and bring us greater happiness.

We can make this breakthrough by learning to recognize and decipher the feedback we receive from life's deeper dimensions, by decoding what I call the *spiritual messages* that come in response to our everyday actions. We all receive feedback from the nonphysical, or spiritual, dimension, although we don't always recognize it as such. It can come to us in ways that seem miraculous or in ways that seem quite ordinary. In both cases, it weaves itself into the very fabric of our day-to-day lives. It may take us some time to get good at recognizing and deciphering our spiritual feedback, but we can learn it like any other skill. In this book, you'll learn not only how to decode the messages you receive but also how to use what you learn to develop a new level of spiritual intelligence, one that will enable you to take the deeper dimension of life into account in the choices you make every day.

Drawing on my training and thirty-five years of experience as a psychiatrist, I have collected and carefully studied my own and hundreds of other people's spiritual experiences. In so doing, I have become fully convinced that the practice of spirituality does not require us to set aside our powers of reason. To the contrary, our faculties of reasoning and observation, which have advanced so much in the last century, are exactly what we need to decode the spiritual feedback we receive and deepen our understanding of the time-honored truths that lie at the heart of our own traditions.

In short, we stand at a crucial juncture in our evolution where we can no longer afford to look upon spirituality as a subject that is mysterious, counterintuitive, inexplicable, and therefore beyond the reach of our reason. If we do, spirituality will become more and more irrelevant to our concerns as science comes up with better and better explanations for how everything works. Instead, by rising to the challenge and approaching your spiritual life with sound reason and common sense, you can reap the tremendous benefits that come from drawing the resources of your soul into your everyday life. The kind of knowledge you will need for this task won't be gained by simply *reading* this book but by *using* what you read to engage spiritual forces and decipher the personal feedback in its many forms and guises that you receive.

A Tree in the Garden

Most spiritual traditions encourage us to think that everything that happens to us and every choice we make has a spiritual as well as a material meaning. But even if we accept the idea that spiritual forces continually influence what happens in both the physical world and the inner world of our thoughts and feelings, the vast majority of these effects go unnoticed because we are so caught up with everyday demands. Sometimes this other side of life breaks through strongly enough to catch our attention; then we detect what I call a *spiritual message*.

The source of these messages has been described across different traditions and cultures and eras of human existence in many different ways, from an impersonal transcendent force that we interact with as we do the forces of nature to an all-knowing God who seems to step in and personally help us or guide us in knowing what to do next. I prefer to think that there is truth in both of these views—that just as light sometimes acts like a wave and at other times like a particle, so our messages seem at times like the effects of impersonal forces and at others like the effects of a personal will. Regardless of how we experience them, their intrusions into our lives make us aware that there is a transcendent dimension to life, most commonly called a *spiritual dimension*. By recognizing and responding to these messages, we open a dialogue with their source, a dialogue that gradually deepens our perception of reality and reveals to us the reason we are here.

In this chapter, I will describe two different messages—two events, alike on the surface, that initiated two very different spiritual journeys. They will help you see how the main reason we interpret our spiritual experiences so differently is that our messages affect us in ways that reflect our individual characters, backgrounds, and needs. Messages help us engage the spiritual dimension of our *own* everyday lives and guide us on our *own* journeys. But as individualized as each person's messages are, they have key elements in common. Drawing on my knowledge of psychology, I will help you discover these elements so that you will be able to use others' experiences to extend your understanding of your own experiences.

The first example is something that happened to me twenty-five years ago, at a time when I viewed everything "spiritual" as simple superstition. I was on a two-week vacation in Rio de Janeiro with my wife at the time, Isabelle, who was a printmaker and sculptor. We had a large network of Brazilian friends who were emotional, friendly, and naturally sensual. They smiled and laughed a lot. On this vacation, we were staying with our friend Vera, a Brazilian filmmaker. Vera was like many Brazilians I had met, first in New York and then in Rio. Her modern, urban sophistication was sitting atop an organic, sensual, magical view of life. From my perspective, this made her particularly predisposed to being superstitious.

Spirits are as much a part of the lives of Brazilians as the samba. Most of the Brazilians I met told me stories of how spirits had influenced their daily lives or the lives of people they knew, both positively and negatively. When faced with serious problems, my otherwise sophisticated Brazilian friends turned to the priests of

Condonblé, a faith based on the Yoruba religion brought by slaves to Brazil hundreds of years ago that survived by merging African deities with Catholic saints. To me, it seemed completely incongruous that, rather than seeking professional help, my usually rational friends took their problems to people who danced, puffed on big cigars, went into trance, and channeled answers from spirits. Discussions of how they could entertain such a ridiculous approach to their problems made for interesting vacation conversation.

Vera wasn't exactly a follower of Condonblé, nor even a devout Catholic. She did, however, believe in paying attention to how spirits might be influencing her everyday life, particularly when something wasn't going right. She enjoyed telling me about her experiences with the world of spirits, from people who had been cured of cancer to others who had been killed by black magic. She told me of business and personal problems solved by making offerings or following a spirit's advice. She took me to several Condonblé meetings, and I enjoyed them as a tourist enjoys the color that such events add to a vacation. Vera laughed at my skepticism because she could see that to me, a New York psychiatrist, this was all superstition. When she teased me about my narrow psychological view of the world, I gibed back at her about how someone as modern and intelligent as she could hold such primitive beliefs. To her, though, such beliefs were completely rational, because she had seen for herself the positive and negative effects of consulting with these spirits. I was the one who was irrational, she said.

With a mischievous look in her eye, Vera gave me a copy of Carl Jung's essay "Synchronicity" to pry my mind open a bit. I read it on her balcony, looking out at the ocean. To make his argument, Jung presents examples of coincidences in which his inner thoughts seem to synchronize with an external event. For instance, he thinks about a patient he hasn't seen for years and then that person calls for an appointment the next day, or he dreams of something and then sees it happen in real life in just that way. Jung's attitude toward unexplainable coincidences, because it was objective, was more acceptable to my frame of reference than sheer superstition, but I still didn't believe that synchronicity existed, because I hadn't experienced it myself in any way that I couldn't easily chalk up to accident. I could, however, see the value of cultivating intuition and of not being bound by the overly rigid thinking of science.

While reading Jung's essay, I developed a persistent thought: Go to the Botanical Garden and a tree will open the door to the spiritual dimension for you. At first, I dismissed this thought as a bizarre product of my imagination. As Rio is a city of beaches, it was hard to imagine tearing myself away from the white sand and ocean surf, even for a morning. But after reading Jung and listening to Vera, the scientist in me wanted to see what would happen if I actually followed this inspiration. I loved trees but, more than that, I was curious. So I sought out the garden.

It was a warm, humid, windless Sunday morning when Isabelle and I went to the garden with a friend who knew it well. The garden was nestled at the base of one of the steep hillsides that enclose Rio. There were only a few people there, and it was quiet, with the occasional song of a bird adding a touch of magic. As I strolled the paths among the exotic blossoms, waiting for my sign, I could feel the garden's vibrant energy begin to permeate every cell in my body. After years of meditating, I had learned to turn off my thinking mind and become one with the beauty and energy of the plants around me. I entered their world and felt a part of it. I hugged the trees. I put my head against them to listen. I smelled them. I was in heaven.

After an hour or so, though, nothing special had happened, so I gave up and comfortably settled onto a bench across from a scrawny tree with a long Latin name. I wasn't disappointed in the least. I breathed the damp, verdant morning air with great delight.

You've been fooled yet again, I thought with amusement, by your own desire to have a little more magic in your life.

Absentmindedly, I glanced down. Incredibly, at that very moment, a leaf floated down from atop the spindly little tree across the path from me and planted its stem in my loosely closed right hand. I jolted to attention. I understood that this leaf, with its flaming red four-inch blade, had just challenged my entire worldview. If the strange thought that had brought me to this place had been planted in my mind by the same intelligent force that now made this leaf fall into my hand, all of my previous thinking about the nature of the world was quite inadequate. I could have made up the idea to go to the garden, and I could have attributed the fancy acrobatics of that leaf to chance, but that these two things had happened together seemed more than chance.

I was astonished. I had read that such things happened, but this was different. Something mystical *had* actually happened, and to *me*. But *what* had happened? The experience was too concrete for me to dismiss it, but too vague for me to have any idea what to do to understand it better. It made interesting cocktail conversation and not much more.

This experience seems so whimsical that you might wonder what made it worth calling *spiritual*. But one of the most interesting discoveries I've made on my journey is that one cannot know what is spiritual and what is not by the specifics of the event itself. Most people believe something spiritual is at work when they feel that they've been assisted in a difficult situation after calling out for help. They might think something spiritual is happening when they are filled with love. For reasons that will become clear as we go on, a better way to be sure that an event is spiritual is by the inner effects the experience has on your thoughts, effects that guide your overall spiritual development. In my case, the apparently insignificant happening in the garden in Rio that summer morning had a profound effect on me. It started me thinking in ways that gradually but completely changed my life and led to the writing of this book. That's what makes me so sure that it was a spiritual message.

Searching for Meaningful Connections

As I struggled to understand why this experience in Rio had happened to me and what it could possibly mean, an experience that Saint Augustine described in his *Confessions* came to my mind. In some ways it was similar to mine and in other ways quite different. I had read about it twenty years before as a religion major at Oberlin College in the early '60s just before I gave up religion for existentialism in my senior year. Saint Augustine wrote this:

> I probed the hidden depths of my soul and wrung its pitiful secrets from it, and when I mustered them all before the eyes of my heart, a great storm broke within me, bringing with it a great deluge of tears . . . when all at once I heard the sing-song voice of a boy or a girl I cannot say, but again and again it repeated the refrain, "Take it and read, take it and read." At this, I looked up thinking hard whether there was any kind of game in which children used to chant words like these, but I could not remember ever hearing them before. I stemmed my flood of tears and stood up, telling myself that this could only be a divine command to open my book of Scripture and read the first passage on which my eyes should fall. For I had heard the story of Anthony, and I remembered how he had happened to go into a church while the Gospel was being read and had taken it as a counsel addressed to himself when he heard the words, "Go home and sell all that belongs to you. Give it to the poor, and so the treasure you have shall be in heaven; then come back and follow me." By this divine pronouncement, he had at once been converted to you [Jesus].

So I hurried back to the place where Alypius was sitting, for when I stood up to move away, I had put down the book containing Paul's Epistles. I seized it and opened it, and in silence I read the first passage on which my eyes fell: "Not in reveling and drunkenness, not in lust and wantonness, not in quarrels and rivalries, rather, arm yourselves with the Lord Jesus Christ; spend no more thought on nature and nature's appetites." I had no wish to read more and no need to do so. For in an instant, as I came to the end of the sentence, it was as though the light of confidence flooded into my heart and all the darkness of doubt was dispelled.*

The courses of Saint Anthony's, Saint Augustine's, and my own life—like millions of others throughout history in all the major religious traditions—were radically altered by finding a deeper meaning in what, to a detached observer, might seem to be meaningless coincidence. Yet the life-altering changes initiated by our messages led each of us to quite different conclusions that were highly influenced by our own culture and time as well as our character and individual circumstances. Saint Anthony and Saint Augustine immediately became deeply religious, for example, whereas I didn't feel the slightest inclination to do so. Looked at from another angle, however, messages had the same effect on all of us: They launched us on highly personal journeys in which we sought to engage the mysterious forces that had caused our experiences.

When that leaf fell into my hand, I really didn't want to think of it as connected in any way to religion. I was disillusioned by organized religion and allergic to all thoughts of God. Yet it did start me thinking in a different way. It made me want to understand the forces that had caused this to happen and had made people in

---

* Saint Augustine, *Confessions*, trans. R. S. Pine-Coffin (New York: Penguin Books, 1961), pp. 177–78.

the past think of such incidents as spiritual, and I wanted to see what implications, if any, it held for me. All I could do was try to figure it out using the best tool available to me—my everyday reasoning.

While I was trying to make sense of this experience, I realized what I explained at the start of this chapter—that spirituality today is in much the same state that psychology was in during the nineteenth century. I thought that if I looked back on what had enabled psychologists to start studying the mind scientifically when no one had done so before, it might help me study my spiritual experience from a scientific perspective. So I looked back a hundred years at the origins of modern psychology to see what distinctions and connections those pioneering psychologists had made. I was immediately struck by the fact that in his early work, Freud articulated two assumptions that would have to be true for our everyday thoughts, feelings, and actions to be understood in any kind of meaningful way: *psychic determinism* and *the existence of the unconscious*. These hypotheses not only established the basis for the scientific study of the mind but also changed the way you and I think about ourselves today.

The law of psychic determinism described a system of causes and effects in which each thought, feeling, and action was determined by the thoughts, feelings, and actions that preceded it. Any psychological processes that couldn't be understood in terms of these cause-and-effect relationships—for example, dreams or psychological symptoms—were lumped together as being the products of another, deeper level of the mind: the unconscious. The actual meaning of these unconscious processes could be made conscious only with the proper method applied in the right direction with a considerable expenditure of patience and persistence.

In his studies of the mind, Freud adopted an attitude that was different from other psychologists of his time. When he didn't understand something, he wondered what caused it, but he wasn't mystified by it. He assumed there was an answer. If he couldn't find the cause, he assumed that it was because of the limits of his own understanding and that the cause would be discovered in the future. He continued looking for causes in other events that might help explain what he couldn't currently grasp. Each time he found a possible causal relationship, it made it easier to discover others. Eventually, he found enough consistent patterns in a group of his patients to come up with useful ideas about the underlying processes causing their symptoms, which he used to formulate the basis for his treatments.

It's hard to overemphasize what a change Freud's attitude represented and how it has affected the way we experience ourselves today. We no longer see the mind as some dark box that is beyond understanding, but as a place where everything is meaningfully connected, even if we don't yet understand how. We believe, for example, that if we are upset or depressed, there is a cause for it. The cause might be stress or an imbalance in the neurotransmitters in the brain; it might be that we have lost someone dear to us and are going through the same normal stages of bereavement that others do; or it might be that our grieving has become pathological, destined to cripple us unless we take ourselves in hand. Either way, we know that it results from the wholly explicable workings of our minds. And we believe that if we don't understand some aspect of those workings today, people in the future will understand it better. We have a faith in reason and progress that enables us to accept our current limits and not dismiss all of science because we don't understand everything.

As I thought about the revolutionary changes in our understanding of ourselves brought about by the belief in psychic determinism and the existence of the unconscious, I saw that to understand spiritual experience, we would need a parallel construct: *spiritual* determinism and the existence of the *soul*. I saw that our spiritual experiences only appeared to be accidental, coincidental, or disconnected from other events in our lives because we did not yet fully understand the forces that govern such occurrences. Whatever we could not explain about the forces causing Saint Augustine's experience or our own was not inexplicable, just temporarily obscured by our limited understanding. If we carefully investigated such incidents, starting with those in our own lives, we would eventually arrive at a better understanding of the forces that generate spiritual messages and a better understanding of our own souls. It was a wonderful moment. Instead of being in awe of spiritual power, I could wonder *why* it acted in the way it did, knowing that such questions would someday lead to satisfying answers.

Spiritual Experimentation

The explosion in our modern scientific understanding of the world has come from a commitment to experimentation and to gathering evidence according to a predetermined method. We can apply the same experimental approach to our encounters with spiritual reality. It need not be very technical in the beginning. We just need to use good common sense and examine our spiritual hypotheses the same way we do our ideas about other important issues in everyday life.

In our spiritual development, progress is often slow. It wasn't until several years and many messages after the leaf fell into my hands in the garden in Rio that I became convinced that my messages really were teaching me how to rationally understand the forces behind seemingly mysterious events. Then, like a good scientist, I started to set up spiritual experiments to validate or disprove my belief that such forces were real and relevant to my life. To do this, I had to plan an action, predict the outcome of that action, carry out the plan, and then observe the results to see whether they supported my hypothesis—that the spiritual dimension would respond to my action in some clear way.

Following a discussion with some friends about whether it was spiritually important to be charitable to the poor in New York City, where I live, I made a plan to give ten dollars to the first person who asked me for money. I decided that if this was indeed a good thing to do, spiritual forces (if they existed) would respond in the kind of way I might expect from a benevolent higher power that would approve of such an action. To me, it would be an acceptable proof if this power made sure my money got into the hands of someone particularly deserving, rather than the usual kind of panhandler I come across.

So I wasn't pleased when the first person who asked me for money the next morning on my way to work was a shabby, smelly drunk who at that very moment was urinating in a corner of the subway station as I moved past him with the rest of the early-morning rush-hour crowd. I had never seen such a display before, nor have I since. Despite my earlier resolve to give ten dollars to the first person who asked me, I just couldn't walk over and give this man the money. I hurried on in disgust and disbelief.

Feeling a bit confused and thinking that this might all be a big mistake, I walked up the subway steps toward the street, vowing to give my ten-dollar bill to the very next person who asked, no matter what. This time, as if to make sure that I knew that what had happened wasn't a simple coincidence, at the top of the steps I was accosted by a strung-out, disheveled man who was demanding money from everyone as they emerged and shouting insults when they passed him by. This was a more typical city scene than the man urinating in the subway, but still more unsavory than most, so that it too elicited revulsion and disbelief in the hardened New Yorkers rushing past. Again, I just couldn't reach out and hand over the ten-dollar bill I was holding. It was only in the evening, on my way home from work, that I finally succeeded in giving away the money to the third person who approached me.

Although my results were exactly the opposite of what I had predicted, I realized the experiment was even more of a success than I had hoped. I knew beyond a reasonable doubt that "someone" had indeed been "listening" to my thoughts and had responded, even if the response seemed to be a cosmic joke. Suddenly an image flashed into my mind. It was as if I was looking at the scene through the eyes of the source of messages, whoever or whatever that was. I saw myself dressed as a smelly alcoholic. And then it dawned on me: I was just like that alcoholic. I, too, was asking for a handout. I had done little to learn how to interact with the spiritual dimension on its terms, but I was expecting it to respond to me on my terms. I got the message.

Did I expect my experiment to convince anyone but me? Of course not. The goal of this experiment was to provide *me* with evidence that it might be possible to actually capture spiritual forces in action. As the sense of the joke wore off, the pragmatic scientist in me continued on. I began thinking: If spiritual forces could manipulate scenarios in such a clear and graphic way in response to my abstract question about their existence, why couldn't they be enlisted to help us overcome the particular fears, anxieties, and everyday issues that trouble us? Could we find a way to more effectively engage the spiritual forces in our lives so that we could receive specific help with our problems? Could we discover the rules of engagement that govern how they work? After years of studying the spiritual experiences of people from various cultures and lifestyles, I have confirmed that the answer to all such questions is a resounding *yes!*

Over the years, my little bits of evidence have grown until I am now convinced that the material and spiritual parts of our lives are meaningfully connected and dynamically interacting all the time, providing us with a wide range of spiritual feedback in every area of our lives. These connections and interactions affect each of us differently, depending on our characters, interests, situations, culture, time in history, and spiritual understanding. By establishing our personal dialogue with the spiritual dimension, we can hope to take better advantage of its guidance and help in our everyday lives.

Fortunately for us, these dialogues are anything but abstract. They commonly provide down-to-earth, practical benefits that are relevant to our lives, helping us get out of tight jams, overcome jealousy, control anger, and improve relationships. They help us attack the root causes of our daily problems in ways that strengthen our character and at the same time develop our souls. By studying the examples in this book, setting up your own experiments, and putting into practice what you learn, you too will open a dialogue with the source of your messages and use the inspirations you receive to meet the challenges of your everyday life.

How You Can Use This Book

Has anything ever happened to you that you couldn't explain? Do you ever feel guided in your decisions? Do you have faith that God exists or that there is another dimension to life? Do you even just think about the possibility that there might be? If so, you may have already received a spiritual message. You may not be sure, however, for messages aren't magic. They won't often impose themselves on you or miraculously transform your life. They will, however, help you become more of the person that your beliefs, whatever they are, inspire you to want to become. Decoding messages will help you understand the spiritual experiences that give rise to your beliefs whether you are Christian, Jewish, Muslim, Buddhist, or none of the above, just as correctly interpreting the consequences of your actions in everyday life help you act better in the future regardless of whether you are American, Asian, African, or European. And decoding messages in everyday life doesn't take much extra time because there really is no new practice to do. You will be analyzing events in your own everyday life to discover the spiritual elements in them. In fact, decoding messages will save you time and energy because it will help you get a greater return for the efforts.

So how do you start?

First, read this book and let the many different examples you'll find sensitize you to the wide range of messages you can receive so that you can identify more of them in your life. Then get familiar with the Web site decodeyourmessages.com. On it, you'll find other experiences submitted by readers that supplement the examples given here. They'll help you see how other people of other temperaments, traditions, and life circumstances decode *their* messages. You'll be able to see how others answer the questions I offer for reflection in each chapter. There are even places for you to post your questions or sign up to receive alerts of new experiences as they are added in the categories that are most interesting to you.

Use the exercises at the end of each chapter to reflect on the aspect of messages that chapter highlights. As you learn to analyze your spiritual messages and understand the interactions between the material and spiritual dimension that give rise to them, you'll start to identify the areas of your own life in which you can most readily recognize the guidance of messages and discover the benefits of paying closer attention to them. By combining the wisdom of your own tradition and the valuable discoveries of modern psychology that I'll explain along the way, you'll learn how to attract the spiritual feedback that will set you going in the right direction.

ॐ ॐ ॐ

Keys to Chapter 1

- Spirituality today is in much the same state that psychology was in at the end of the nineteenth century. Before then, no one had succeeded in studying the mind scientifically, despite the remarkable success of scientific study in other fields.
- We all receive feedback from the nonphysical, or spiritual, dimension, and we can learn to recognize and decipher it using the tools of modern psychology and common sense.

- By interpreting this feedback from life's deeper dimensions—by decoding the spiritual messages that come in response to your everyday actions—you will be able to understand better the fundamental experiences on which your beliefs rest and connect more deeply with the spiritual in everyday life.
- To decode messages, you need to make two assumptions: that you have a soul and that spiritual events are connected by cause and effect. As you gather your own evidence, you will find ample proof to confirm that messages are not accidental, coincidental, or disconnected from other events in your life, but manifestations of a larger system that is constantly interacting with the material dimension.
- Messages are highly individualized. To benefit from their feedback, you need to take into account things like your culture, times, life circumstances, and individual character.
- Once you are convinced that spiritual messages are comments on what's happening in your life, you will be able to learn more about them by carefully planning actions that, like experiments, draw their help and guidance into areas that are of concern to you.

ॐ   ॐ   ॐ

For Your Reflection

To undertake any new endeavor, it's good to have a clear idea of your starting point. Before you begin to delve more deeply into the world of spiritual messages, take some time to reflect on these questions:

1. How has your upbringing influenced the way you think about spirituality today, and how have your own experi-

ences modified the beliefs you were brought up in? Have you had experiences that made spirituality real and relevant to you? To what extent do your spiritual beliefs influence how you act and think in your everyday life?

2. Identify experiences in your life and the lives of people you know that have made you interested in spirituality and keep you interested in it today.

3. Go to decodeyourmessages.com to review a sampling of experiences that made others interested in spirituality.

4. Take out a sheet of paper or turn to a blank page in a notebook and entitle it "The Opening of My Dialogue." If you prefer, you can go to decodeyourmessages.com to download these points for reflection to your computer or set up your own private notebook on the site. Try to express in one summary paragraph the basis for your interest in spirituality. Then continue on and write in as much detail as you'd like about the evidence that supports your conclusions.

We often think that we understand things very well until we try to write them down. I make this suggestion based on how much writing this book helped me clarify and commit to my own ideas. It helped me use the plainest possible language and the fewest possible specialized theoretical terms to describe my experiences and explain my conclusions. If something in you rebels at the thought of writing, pause to integrate your own thoughts in a way that does work for you, and try to use that method consistently at the end of each chapter so that by the end of the book, you will have a clearer understanding of your own beliefs based on your own experiences.

5. Go to decodeyourmessages.com, if you like, to add the experiences that have led you to believe there is a spiritual dimension to life.

CHAPTER 2

Recognizing
Spiritual Feedback

It's one thing to be interested in spirituality and aware of a spiritual dimension. But what makes us so sure that that dimension can actively influence our lives in significant ways? For most of us, it is because we have been in situations where things turned out far better than expected and something in us has attributed the result to a higher power. This leads us to the central questions of this book: What makes an experience, thought, emotion, action, or event spiritual, and what can we gain by labeling it as such?

The messages that we will look at in this chapter have both these elements: They help people in ways that are materially beneficial and at the same time guide their spiritual development. Messages seem to understand human nature very well; they recognize that if they are to catch our attention and hold it for very long, they will have to be relevant to our material concerns. So, even though the spiritual and material dimensions are often thought of as opposites, messages encourage us to think that we can learn a good deal by understanding how the vital material life that they seem to help us cultivate might be the very best place for us to grow spiritually as well. To help clarify what I mean, let's examine a couple of experiences that highlight the beneficial material effects messages can have.

An Invisible Hand

C.J., a forty-year-old Iranian-born doctor who is now living in London,* told me a story that shows how the spiritual dimension intervenes in some people's lives in near-miraculous ways. C.J. was raised in a spiritually minded family and would have loved to stay in Iran. Because of the political situation there, however, he decided at the age of seventeen to leave the increasingly oppressive conditions behind and join his father, who was already living outside the country. Since no one who was eligible to be drafted could leave Iran, C.J. had to do so covertly.

C.J. found someone who was taking small groups of people, for a good price, over the border. He traveled for several days by truck and then several more days by camel through almost desert-like terrain to Pakistan. As he made his way, he had many hair-raising brushes with the authorities in which he narrowly avoided arrest. He was sure that God was directly intervening to help him escape.

He finally found himself on board a flight to Spain, one of the last countries willing to accept Iranians without visas. The plane was filled with Iranians who were happy and relieved that they had made it. What they didn't know was that Spain had just that very day changed its policy and agreed to send back to Iran anyone who arrived without a visa. Just as the travelers were going through immigration, Spanish troops stormed into the airport and quarantined them.

"Everybody was crying," C.J. told me. "It was pretty scary.

* The names of the people as well as some of the identifying information and details of their experiences have been changed to protect the privacy of those involved.

Even though all these things were happening, I felt in my heart that God had been with me this whole time. I thought, He's going to do something again, and I am probably going to get out of this. I was sitting in the airport for two or three hours. All of a sudden, I got this intuition that I had to do something right now. So I got up, feeling that God was with me. There was a big staircase that led from the second level of the airport to the first. It had about twenty steps, six or seven yards wide. A good fifteen or twenty guards were watching the steps. Anyone who went within five yards of that first step was yelled at to stay back.

"But I followed my intuition anyway, saying to myself, I'm going to go toward the stairs and see what happens. I left my bag and my coat, and in just a T-shirt, I walked toward the staircase. A guy I had become friendly with on the flight asked, 'What are you doing?' I replied, 'I'm just going toward the soldiers and down that staircase.' He said, 'Are you crazy?' And then I walked right past all of them. It was as if time had frozen.

"As I passed the soldiers, not one of them said anything to me. Once in a while, I would turn around to see if one of them had noticed me, but they were looking straight ahead or in another direction. I mean *all* of them. And then I motioned to my friend to come and he followed me, and we went past the guards without anyone saying a word."

C.J. and his friend still had to make it past the immigration desk. When they got there, four of the officials joked with C.J. for several minutes about being from Iran. Then they laughingly stamped the boys' passports. "We went to a youth hostel that cost ten dollars a night," C.J. said. "On the news, they were showing the story of the passengers who had been forced back to Pakistan. They said, 'All of them were sent back except two, but we don't know what happened to them.'"

At that moment in the airport before he walked by the guards, C.J. felt his whole life was hanging in the balance. If he had been forced to return to Iran, he would have spent time in prison. Life would have been very difficult after that. When he followed his intuition to head toward the stairs, he believed that God was inspiring him to do something completely irrational. It was such an unlikely scenario that when he actually did escape, he was certain that an invisible hand had helped him.

Of course, we cannot judge for sure whether spiritual forces caused that event or not. We only know that C.J.'s escape defies rational explanation. However, the experience was intended for C.J. and not for us. The impact of the message was on him, not us. We can only really accept his conclusion if we have felt the unexpected help of spiritual forces in our own life. If we have, we can add his dramatic experience to our own as another example of how the spiritual dimension helps us in times of need.

The only way to be certain that an inexplicably lucky turn of material events is indeed spiritual is to see if it also plays a significant role in our spiritual development. (I will turn to the question of how we gauge our spiritual development in the last section of the book once you've learned more about how spiritual messages work.) That was certainly the case for C.J. He had been raised in a spiritually oriented family, but at the time of this incident, he was becoming more interested in soccer and girls. For him, this incident contained an important message: Spirituality is real and relevant. Don't ignore it. The message was a reminder sent to make sure that he wouldn't forget about his spiritual beliefs as he grew up. C.J. went on to become a successful doctor, a caring father, and a deeply spiritual person. Without this experience, he is unsure where he would have ended up, either materially or spiritually.

C.J.'s experience, and others like his, made it very clear to me that even though I was approaching the spiritual dimension in a rational way, I couldn't reduce it to fit my current rational understanding of the world. Instead, I would have to expand my understanding of what was rational to encompass such events.

It made me realize that if the spiritual dimension chose to open a dialogue with me, as it did in chapter 1 through the fall of a leaf into my hand, then there had to be a reason, and I had to learn why.

The Relevance of Our Messages

C.J.'s dramatic experience altered the course of his life. After that, he could never doubt the power of the spiritual dimension or its relevance to his everyday concerns. Most messages, however, are much more subtle; the material and spiritual benefits are not so clearly linked. Yet, as Beth's story will show, on closer examination, we see that they can help us improve our lives and foster our spiritual development just as much as rare, miraculous experiences like C.J.'s do. It is primarily this more subtle kind of message that you'll be learning to decode in this book.

"Before I heard that it was my spiritual duty to work and to make a living," Beth told me, "I didn't feel like working. My husband supported us. Frankly, I didn't believe in myself. But when a trusted friend, who was almost like a spiritual adviser to me, said that it would be good for me, both psychologically and spiritually, to support myself, I started to look for a job. Since then, I have experienced miracles that confirmed for me that God is not only encouraging me in this direction but watching over me as well.

"When I started job hunting, I was going from door to door, just hoping to find a job. I really didn't have any skills. After a few weeks, by 'chance' I got an interview with the director of a big financial newspaper. Actually, what happened is that when I called, the secretary had just stepped out of the office and the director himself answered and gave me an appointment for the next day. He hired me on the spot. I have to add that I didn't know much about finance. For me, that was a sign of God's hand in what had happened."

Getting a better job than she expected was enough for Beth to believe that God was helping her. Her experience underscores an important point about how messages work—they rarely sweep into our lives and solve our problems as they did with C.J. More often, they help us by solving one problem (in this case, Beth's insecurity and difficulty applying herself to her *spiritual* life) by nudging us into a material situation (like Beth's job) where we are faced with challenges that force us to grow in ways that will help our spiritual development too. In her new job, for example, Beth would have to develop her writing skills, set realistic goals, and meet deadlines. She would have to learn to interact under pressure with all kinds of people in different situations while remaining true to her own values. Over time, she became more creative, industrious, focused, and independent. She learned to like work and felt far more alive than when she had been huddling comfortably at home. These same skills helped her apply herself better in her spiritual life as well.

I asked Beth what made her attribute her success to spiritual forces and not to the regular forces of the job market. She acknowledged that other women who had pushed themselves to go to work might have reaped material benefits that were even greater than hers. What convinced her that spiritual forces lay behind her success was the fact that things had gone much better than she had a right to expect. In addition, the event marked a turning point in her life from which her spiritual understanding had increased over the years. "I started to look at things from a more spiritual perspective," she explained, "meaning that in each event in my daily work life, I started to look for a lesson, a point of spiritual wisdom. As I did, I started to believe in myself. I was more courageous in front of others and less scared about the future. My faith in God allowed me to be serene and look at situations more objectively. For example, when I knew that my firm had to lay off some employees, I wasn't scared. I became unafraid of diseases or death for myself and even for my children. Also, since I was working on my own shortcomings, I became more indulgent of others and less demanding of them. My relationship with others got better as a result. It was all because of my greater faith in God."

What is important in a message, then, is not the size or even the nature of the material effect that signals the arrival of a message, but the deeper effect it has on our own thinking, which depends on other factors that we will identify as we go on. What ultimately confirmed Beth's experience as spiritual—and enables us to think of it that way—is not just her intuitive belief that it was so, but the way it marked the beginning of a new chapter in her life in which she developed both psychologically and spiritually.

Most of us need to improve in so many areas that it's hard to know where to start. That's another way in which messages help us. They point out to us the areas of our lives where we will benefit the most from working to develop a particular quality—whether patience, humility, courage, or perseverance—that a given situation brings to the fore. In Beth's case, the qualities most important to her spiritual growth were best developed in the workplace. It wasn't just that work was important for her material life, but that it gave her the best opportunity to cultivate the specific qualities that would help her spiritual development progress.

How Brain and Soul Work Together

To understand spiritual messages another way, we can represent schematically what a message is and how it works on us. We'll start by depicting the relationship between our consciousness, our brain, and our soul.

Although modern science has yet to determine the precise nature of consciousness, we do know that it exists and in some way seems to emanate from the brain, as represented in FIGURE 1. To function effectively in everyday life, each of us needs to organize the feelings, fantasies, thoughts, memories, and knowledge stored in our brain's synapses into a mental model of the world—"the world according to me." We use this model as a virtual reality in which to imagine the outcomes of the various options available to us and choose the one that gives us the greatest benefit. Whether we suc-

Our Brain's Mind

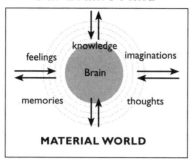

FIGURE I Our brain possesses a mind that organizes all of our feelings, fantasies, thoughts, memories, and knowledge into a coherent whole so that we can function well in everyday life.

ceed or fail at what we are doing, we can use the results to refine our understanding of how things work so that we can do better in future situations. When most situations turn out essentially as we had imagined, we can conclude that we know how things work.

From a spiritual perspective, we are more than a body. We are also an eternal soul, which survives the death of our body. Our soul, according to most religions, is conscious and intelligent.

Our soul has its own distinctive consciousness, its own "mind," which integrates all its feelings, fantasies, thoughts, memories, and knowledge into a coherent whole, as represented in FIGURE 2. This has been confirmed by studies of out-of-body experiences, near-death experiences, and reports of contacts with other souls. We know little for certain of how this soul functions when it is not housed in our body and connected to our brain.

Our brain's mind and our soul's mind perform similar functions. Our brain's mind analyzes everything from its distinctive material perspective, whereas our soul's mind analyzes everything from its distinctive spiritual perspective. Although the mind of the brain and the mind of the soul have different agendas, they integrate to form our thoughts and feelings about our everyday lives. What our brain contributes is most obvious in the drives and

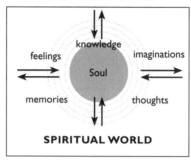

Our Soul's Mind

knowledge

feelings

Soul

imaginations

memories

thoughts

SPIRITUAL WORLD

FIGURE 2 Our soul possesses a mind as well that integrates all of our soul's feelings, fantasies, thoughts, memories, and knowledge into a coherent whole in relation to its goals.

desires we share with other animals, the drives that sustain individual life and preserve the species. Our soul's influence, on the other hand, is more visible in qualities that make us different from other primates, such as our more penetrating intellect, the voice of our conscience, and our attraction to spirituality.

FIGURE 3 represents our everyday consciousness, where most of the capacities of our soul are used by our brain to try to achieve its own material goals. We don't notice most of what is going on from our soul's perspective because we are completely preoccupied with meeting the challenges of everyday life. At times, when the input of our soul becomes strong enough, a spiritual inspiration will break through. FIGURE 4 shows what can happen when our soul is able to summon up the energy necessary to transmit the information to the brain in such a way that this information emerges into our consciousness as an inspiration. For us to recognize this information, however, our consciousness has to be sufficiently receptive to the advice being given. If it isn't, an inspiration may reach us but be ignored as irrelevant. To give an inspiration the attention it deserves, therefore, we need to be prepared to recognize and value its input. We can receive inspirations out of the blue, being grateful when they come our way, but we can gain far more by taking the next step: We can make our-

Our Bi-dimensional Mind Puts It All Together

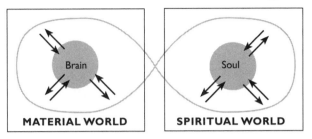

FIGURE 3 The brain and the soul are interconnected and in constant interaction with each other and their respective realities. We are most often so preoccupied with meeting the challenges of everyday life, however, that our brain automatically integrates our soul's inputs without our becoming aware of their origin.

A Spiritual Inspiration Makes Us Aware of Our Soul

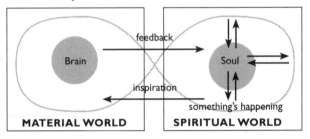

FIGURE 4 In a spiritual inspiration, our soul becomes aware that something is happening in the spiritual dimension that is relevant to us and passes it on to our brain. If the inspiration is strong enough, we act on it.

selves more receptive to these inspirations by creating conditions that encourage our soul's comments on our daily life—a subject that we will return to frequently throughout the course of the book.

A spiritual message, as represented in FIGURE 5, is an inspiration coupled with a real external event that has itself been influenced by spiritual forces. It not only helps us in our immediate situation, but also teaches us how the material and spiritual dimensions interact. By carefully studying these moments of correspondence, we can gradually become familiar with the wider range of influences that our soul has on our thoughts and feelings.

How Spiritual Forces Act in Our Lives

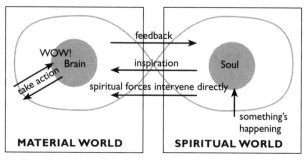

FIGURE 5 A spiritual message is an inspiration coupled with a real external event that has itself been influenced by spiritual forces. It not only helps us in our immediate situation but also teaches us how the material and spiritual dimensions interact. By carefully studying these moments of correspondence, we can become familiar with the wider range of influences that our soul has on our thoughts, feelings, and actions.

With this schematic in mind, we can see the elements of a spiritual message in Beth's example. First, Beth received an inspiration to look for a job. Second, she responded by looking for a job, thus creating the right material circumstances for a message. Third, she experienced an unexpected external event (getting the interview quickly and a better job than she had a right to expect). Fourth, she felt strongly that this confirmed for her that spiritual forces had arranged the whole situation.

Beth's story underscores something that I have found to be true: The more we understand that our messages are aimed at both helping our material life *and* stimulating our spiritual development in a balanced way, the more we can take advantage of our soul's input into our everyday thoughts, feelings, memories, and reactions. Both our brain and our soul benefit from the integration of the others' resources, as depicted in FIGURE 6, so that we can enjoy life more in the physical plane and develop our soul at the same time. What could be better?

Trying to express how messages work in this way starts us asking

Integration of Brain and Soul

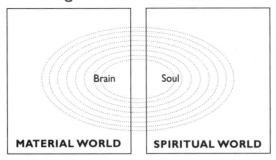

FIGURE 6 The better we understand our spiritual messages, the better we are able to integrate the wisdom of our brain and our soul and to come up with solutions to the problems of everyday life that promote our spiritual development.

questions. For example, why wasn't Beth led to do something nobler, such as working in a soup kitchen, instead of the mundane tasks of office work? Why didn't spiritual forces arrange for C.J. to get on an earlier plane or delay the order another few hours until after he had left the airport, if their goal was to help him escape? Why did those same forces arrange for that leaf to fall into my hand after I read Jung's essay on synchronicity, instead of a more spiritually oriented book, if they wanted to awaken me to the spiritual dimension?

People have always asked such questions, but now I believe that we are finally in a good position to answer them. By getting excited about similar questions, particularly in your own life, and believing that it is possible to find answers by approaching them rationally, you will open your mind so that you can understand and benefit more than ever from the feedback of the spiritual dimension.

A New Archetype of the Journey

Spirituality today is going through its own kind of evolution. That's because we are more rational than people who lived a century or more ago. Our intellects are more inquisitive about what causes things to happen and better informed about ways to investigate those causes. Our more highly developed analytical skills offer the hope that we can discern a deeper level of spiritual guidance than people in the past could. By using these skills to detect and decode the individualized spiritual feedback we receive in our daily lives, we can come to understand for ourselves what the great spiritual figures in all traditions have been trying to show us through the ages: how to connect to the source of such messages, whether you call it the spiritual dimension, God, a higher power, or a universal source.

To help us develop a deeper understanding of what messages are trying to tell us, I have updated the archetypal image of our journey. I see our task today as less like that of a pilgrim on a long and perilous journey and more like that of a student going to a university to study an experimental science. We may be no smarter than the pilgrims of the past, but we have a much better idea of how to understand the invisible forces that cause our experiences than they did. Adopting the attitude of a student will help you be more alert to what your messages are trying to teach you.

How does this change our approach? Just think of what makes a good student. A good student in a university aspires to think for himself and integrates the basic information and approaches that he is taught to come up with his own way of thinking. He studies his course material and draws on his own abilities and knowledge in the hopes of graduating and going on to a fulfilling material life that will make his efforts worthwhile. During his time in the university, he will take certain courses and not others. He will learn information and skills similar to those that other students in his major acquire, and he will learn how to think about the issues in a similar way, but by the time he graduates, he will have developed his own mind and integrated all that he has learned according to his own personal priorities. He will be prepared to take advantage of certain opportunities and not others.

This same attitude will help us decode messages and grasp what they as a whole are trying to teach us. Although I believe that today we are in a better position to discern deeper guidance in our messages, be assured that this new archetype of the journey and this rational approach to spiritual life are in no way meant to discount the wisdom and traditions of the past that are meaningful to you. Decoding your spiritual messages will help you develop the mental tools to come to a deeper understanding of the wisdom at the heart of your own tradition.

ॐ   ॐ   ॐ

Messages help us to see that our material and spiritual lives are not separate from one another, but intertwined and interacting constantly. They encourage us to have a normal everyday life and use it as a foundation on which to develop spiritually. You can confirm this in your own experience by paying closer attention to the balance between the material and spiritual effects of your own messages. As you consider their advice and act in line with it, you will most often find that they nudge you in ways that are beneficial for both. Once we grasp how they help us with our problems, messages then become the ultimate self-help tool, offering a kind of "spiritual therapy" by which we can actualize our deeper potentials and build a more vital and satisfying life for ourselves.

ॐ   ॐ   ॐ

Keys to Chapter 2

- A spiritual message is an inspiration coupled with a real external event that has been influenced by spiritual forces. It provides both help and guidance.

- The best spiritual messages to start decoding are the ones that come when things go materially better than you have a right to expect. They are a good place to start answering the central questions of this book: What makes an experience, a thought, emotion, action, or event spiritual, and what is the value of labeling it as such?

- At times messages help us solve crises, and at other times they show us how to develop the underdeveloped parts of ourselves to improve the overall quality of our lives. You can reason backward to discover why your message might have wanted to help you in the particular way it did or to push you to improve one particular characteristic rather than another.

- To make spiritual sense of messages, you need to assume that you are more than a body; you are also an eternal soul. Messages are the result of the effects of the spiritual dimension on you. Since the "minds" of our brain and our soul have different agendas and because the demands of material life are often very pressing, their inputs are integrated in such a way that you can't easily distinguish the input of your soul without the help of your messages.

- Although the spiritual dimension is constantly interacting with the material dimension, a spiritual inspiration will only break through into your awareness when your soul's input into your thoughts and feelings becomes strong enough to stand out from the background of your everyday thoughts and feelings because of the effects of a message.

- To decode what messages tell you about life in today's world, you will need to think of yourself not as a pilgrim, but as a student.

సౌ సౌ సౌ

For Your Reflection

The more aware we are of how messages help us work with material situations to further our spiritual development, the better use we can make of them. Pause for a few moments to think about the balance between the material and spiritual in your own life.

1. With C.J.'s and Beth's experiences of receiving outside help in mind, try to find examples in your own life of situations where things turned out better than you expected they would. Consider them good candidates for being messages, even though you may have attributed them to good luck at the time.

2. Try to identify the effects these experiences had on your thoughts, feelings, or actions, both at the time and subsequently, that might support the hypothesis that they were indeed spiritual messages.

3. Go to decodeyourmessages.com to review a sampling of other people's experiences of receiving spiritual help. This will help you tune your awareness to the way messages might impact your own life.

4. Take out a sheet of paper or turn to a blank page in your notebook and entitle it "The Effects of My Messages." You can also go to decodeyourmessages.com to download these points for reflection or log into your online notebook. In one summary paragraph, identify one or two experiences you see as potential messages and state why you think they might have been messages. Try to be as concise as possible and use everyday language that someone who does not share your beliefs would understand. If you can't find any examples in your own life that you're comfortable designating as possible spiritual messages, write about an experience of a close friend or about one of the examples in this chapter. Once you've written that

paragraph, continue on writing as much as you would like about any other thoughts you have on spiritual help. Try to anchor your conclusions in *experiences* rather than theories so that you can deepen your understanding of your experiences as you continue reading subsequent chapters.

5. Go to decodeyourmessages.com to add any experiences that you believe might help others grasp the benefits of being attentive to the spiritual messages in their lives.

CHAPTER 3

Making Meaningful Connections

Once we recognize a potential spiritual message, how can we figure out what it is trying to tell us? In the beginning, it seems near-impossible, because there is such a wide range of meanings we might give it and we don't know how to choose among them. It's similar to the kind of uncertainty that we face in all important situations where we lack the experience to know what to do. So we need to do just what we do in everyday life: Do our best, move forward with caution, and learn from our experience.

We start by basing our conclusions on the experiences of others. When I began decoding messages, I already knew what spiritual experts had to say about spirituality. I had been a religion major in college. Now I wanted to know how people like me chose a belief system to apply and validated their choice. I talked to everyone I met about my experiences and asked them about theirs. I especially loved hearing people's stories about how they first became interested in spirituality and how it influenced their lives. These stories warmed my heart in some inexplicable way and fanned my desire to understand them better. Each story was personal and unique. Each perfectly matched the individual's character and life circumstances. I listened to these touching stories with the ear of a trained psychiatrist trying to sense the underlying dynamic, common to all of us, that might be behind them. One thing I knew for certain—something different was at work from the psychological forces that I was by now so well acquainted with. If I could understand these effects, I might be able to understand my own experiences better.

When we start decoding messages, we draw upon all we have learned from others in order to come up with an interpretation of our experience that makes the best sense to us. To know whether our analysis is correct or not, we need to act in the direction that we think our messages suggest and observe the results. When we get it right, things will quite likely go better than we anticipated, thanks to a little extra push from our messages that enables us to follow through on what they have suggested. This extra push is usually easy to recognize, for after receiving a message, we can usually do things that we have wanted to do before to improve ourselves but have not been able to do.

A message's help is more than just the motivational boost of being certain that we are doing what needs to be done. It actually makes it easier to do what we are doing, as if someone else were helping us. When we act in the direction that a message suggests and see the beneficial results of doing so, only then can we truly say that we have decoded our message, for only then will we appreciate the value of what it was teaching us.

To help sensitize you to the impact of messages, I have chosen three stories of very different spiritual awakenings. Such awakenings are a good place to start analyzing the spiritual effects of other people's experiences because they are so clear-cut, causing a striking turn in the course of a person's life as he or she goes from little or no interest in spirituality to a strong interest. The more aware you are of the effects messages can have, the better you'll be able to recognize their effects in a wider range of situations in your own life.

Rachel's awakening came when her world had been turned upside down. Rachel came from a Jewish family that had strong spiritual beliefs. She had left all that behind when she was in her late teens. Then, when she was forty-six, she began to have experiences that she believed were divinely orchestrated. "They seem to come at times of despair or confusion," she said. "Some of my first experiences and awareness had a connection with numbers, maybe because I needed something tangible that had meaning to me.

"The event that had the greatest effect on me involved the number 313. My son, Peter, was killed on 3-13-93. So, naturally, every time I see that combination, I can't help but think of him—and now of God, too. There were four or five things that happened with this same number in relation to Peter. One was that the number 3:13 was clearly visible as the time on a clock in one of the last photographs taken of him several weeks before his death.

"But by far the most powerful incident happened on the first anniversary of Peter's death. I was anticipating it with dread, not knowing how I would get through it, and I desperately needed help. That Saturday morning at 8 a.m.—almost the same time my doorbell had rung a year earlier with the news of his death—my bell rang again. A friend who was staying with me answered the door for me. A conservatively dressed man handed him a booklet. When I looked at it, all I saw was one line: 'There are new heavens and a new earth that we are awaiting according to God's promise and in these righteousness is to dwell (2 Peter 3:13).' My son is Peter number two (his father is also named Peter), and the numbers matched the date of his death. To me, this was a message—a hello telling me that my son was fine. No one could tell me that

God wasn't trying to comfort me and to help me move on through that day and all the days that would follow."

This experience seemed too uncanny to be a coincidence. In Rachel's opinion, it had been choreographed just for her at the exact moment she needed it. It convinced her that her son still existed—that his tragedy wasn't really a tragedy but a part of his journey that wasn't over yet. He was doing fine. The spirituality that she had been taught as a child was once again relevant to her and gave her life a deeper meaning.

Rachel's message, like hundreds of other messages that I've studied, contains four characteristic elements—elements that suddenly came together in a meaningful way:

- **A material situation** (the anniversary of her son's death)
- **A heightened psychological state** (her deep despair and her desire for answers)
- **An unexpected external event** (the knock at the door on the first anniversary of her son's death and the delivery of a brochure that had Peter's name with the numbers 3 and 13)
- **An inspiration** (that this combination of circumstances was a message designed to help her move on)

Once she received it, many positive things began to happen. She still missed her son tremendously and thought about him every day, but she was less depressed. Her relationships improved as she tried to be more compassionate and helpful to others because this is what she believed a spiritual person should do. She did better at work. In short, she started living, and life gradually took on meaning once again. All of this was made possible by the little extra push that she got from acting in line with what her message seemed to be suggesting she do and trying one more time to move on with her life.

The Meaning That Is Meant for Us

Rachel's explanation of her experience is unlikely to prove the existence of a spiritual dimension to anyone but her, yet it can add to our own understanding of our own spiritual experiences. To learn something specific from her experience, however, we need to understand the nature of both Rachel's and our own experience so that we know how to combine them. By identifying her experience as spiritual and as a sign that her son still exists in another form and was well, Rachel was making what psychology would call a *meaningful* connection. It was for her a fact, self-evident only to her and those who shared her conviction.

A meaningful connection is different from a factual connection, which is mainly descriptive. Proving whether a factual connection is correct or not requires only a grasp of the definition of the words involved and the proper physical senses to verify it. The sky is blue, the pamphlet was delivered on the anniversary of her son's death, and the pamphlet contained 2 Peter 3:13. These are factual connections. Someone else observing the sky or the pamphlet would see just what Rachel did, observing the same simple facts. But the spiritual aspect of Rachael's experience was clearly not descriptive. It was a meaningful connection.

Meaningful connections are not purely subjective; they are formed by applying a certain system of meanings to our experience, whether that system belongs to our society, a subgroup of our society, or a religious or spiritual tradition. They are formed by acting in relation to that system of meanings in a way that also reflects our own preferences and values. By living as part of a society, we gain a tremendous advantage: We can share in its material benefits so that we can live more comfortably than cavemen. By making our choices based on a given system of meanings, we can share in the society's spiritual benefits as well so that we can live better than spiritual cavemen who prefer to do everything on their own. Once we choose a system, we need to master its fundamentals by seeing if we can get similar results to those that others get in simple situations of everyday life.

So what can we learn from someone else's experience, and how? To learn from Rachel's, we need to grasp how her experience helped her come to terms with the spiritual meaning in her situation in a way that helps us come to terms better with the spiritual meaning in our own life. We're acting on the assumption that we have a common spiritual nature that is expressing itself in different ways. Our goal is to define this common spiritual nature so that we can develop our own individual nature to its fullest.

We already know that the meanings that we give to things take into account our material nature, life circumstances, experience, goals, and preferences. So to learn from other people's spiritual experiences, we need to be able to consider how their material nature, life circumstances, experience, goals, and preferences influence their decisions. If you adjust for these material differences to the same extent that you do in everyday interactions, then you won't be stopped by the fact that Rachel's message was oriented to *her* background, *her* relationship with her son, *her* understanding of death, *her* proclivity for numbers, and *her* need for reassurance. You won't be stopped because you aren't Jewish, or a mother who lost a child, or even a woman. You will see Rachel as a soul becoming more aware of the spiritual dimension in a time of hardship because of a spiritual message that she received.

You can then put yourself in her shoes and imagine what it might be like for you to receive a message that would help you come to a similar realization or make a comparable change in your life. You might imagine, for example, an experience in *your* life that might open *you* to receiving a message. It wouldn't have to be the loss of a child or even any profound shock, if you haven't had such an experience. It might be that you had lost touch with the spiritual dimension of life that you deeply believed in and needed something to awaken you to it again. The better you can abstract from the particulars of Rachel's situation to other particulars that are relevant to you but correctly capture the essence of her experience, the more you can potentially learn from that experience.

The real key to decoding a message—whether it be your own or someone else's—is not just making an intellectually meaningful connection but acting on your analysis of the situation, discovering a benefit in doing so, and fully appreciating the value of this benefit. Only then do you truly understand what that message had in mind. Other people's conclusions about their messages become useful to you when you examine the actions that their messages encouraged them to take to solve their problems and learn something that *you* can do to more effectively solve your own problems. When you then come up with your own plan of action for getting similar benefits in your own life without having to wait for your own message to point it out to you, it's just as if you had received a message yourself. When you improve your life in a way comparable to Rachel's, you understand both her experience and your own—and the larger system of spiritual meanings you're working within—in a more useful way.

Once we realize that we have a soul, we realize that everyone else must have one too, so we look at their experiences differently. Once we experience our own struggle to decode our own messages, we are able to learn more from others' struggles to decode their messages. We then become a part of a larger community of people of all cultures and traditions who are guided by messages in ways that suit our life circumstances. We don't have to give up our own belief system to connect to the source of our messages any more than we have to give up our culture to be a part of a global community.

Attracting the Help We Need

At first, it seems as if messages come out of the blue and it is hard to believe that we can figure out what they might be trying to say.

Yet, as we continue to pay closer attention to our own and others' messages, we discover that there are some things that we can do to attract a message and know with greater certainty what it is suggesting that we do. First and foremost, we can make our best effort to solve whatever problems are troubling us on our own and then look for the help of a message to confirm or correct our approach, instead of looking to it to tell us what to do in the first place. The bottom line is, don't sit around waiting for a message to tell you what to do. Use your own head and do what you can do on your own. In this way, you will be able to tell what messages are adding to the effort you're already making and your progress in decoding them will be much faster.

Let's see how Greta, a fifty-three-year-old writer, made a good effort to find answers to her own questions about the meaning of life in such a way that her messages could give her far more detailed guidance. "One day, I went to a bookstore with the intention of buying spiritual books—something by Teilhard de Chardin, *The Tibetan Book of the Dead*, et cetera," Greta explained to me as she looked back at the events more than ten years ago that had begun her spiritual journey. "I had no interest in God at the time, but I felt that there had to be more to life. Every time I opened one of these books, after the third page, it would fall from my hands. I couldn't go on. I was looking for answers to questions like 'Who am I?' and 'Why am I here?' But I somehow knew that I wouldn't find them in that particular book. I didn't know why. With each book I picked up, I felt a rush of hope and then I lost interest almost immediately.

"I started to feel as if a huge, bright metallic wall was growing from the floor to the sky. I couldn't see where it ended. Behind that wall, I could hear and feel people. I couldn't reach them, but I knew it was urgent for me to go there. I knew that the real meaning of life was there—in another, invisible dimension of life. But how could I get there?

"This feeling continued to grow in me. Some months later, a long-time friend, Daniele, sent me a manuscript of a book that a friend of hers had just written. I was going to visit Daniele and had to take two planes to get where she lived, and so I decided to read this manuscript on the way. It was summer. The weather was beautiful, but as soon as I started to read, a violent storm erupted. Each word, each line in that book was answering the questions that had been plaguing me about the meaning of life. The storm within me was even stronger than the one outside. I kept asking myself, Who am I?

"Reading that manuscript changed the course of my life. But it took a long time. Even after I was completely convinced that there was a spiritual dimension to my life and I knew that this manuscript was describing in detail what I needed to do, I wanted to get away from what it was pointing out—that I had to be less self-centered. It seemed too hard for me. I thought I would have to change my habits, my behavior, the way I was seeing things, and I thought that it was impossible to do so at age forty."

Greta's experience had all of the elements of a message:

- **A material situation** (reading many books but still searching for the answers she needed)
- **A heightened psychological state** (the midlife turmoil in which she felt lost)
- **An unexpected external effect** (the violent storm happening while she read that particular book)
- **An inspiration** (the certainty that this book was giving her the answers to her questions)

In the grip of a midlife crisis at the time she received the message, Greta was reexamining the meaning she had given to everything. She wanted to know whether there was any deeper purpose to her life or not. It wasn't just an intellectual quest; she had an inner longing for spiritual meaning that she wanted to satisfy if at all possible. So she did what we all do today when we don't understand something. She read and thought as deeply as she could about it. She did her best to come up with the right meaning for her life on her own. Messages then helped her reject certain books and be inspired by another, the one she was reading at the time of the storm. The book could tell her in no uncertain terms specifically what she needed to do in order to connect with the spiritual dimension—something a message couldn't do on its own. Her efforts to find the meaning in life by reading books that others regarded highly made it possible for her message to give more precise guidance than Rachel's message gave her earlier in this chapter or my message gave me in chapter 1. Greta's was more like the experience of St. Augustine, who had immersed himself in his studies of the meaning of life so that his message could help him see more precisely what his next step needed to be.

Greta continued the dialogue by acting in accordance with the ethical principles outlined in the manuscript, and she received other messages that reassured her that she was going in the right direction. For example, whenever she tried to be more considerate of others, everything worked out better than she expected. Whenever she fell back on her old, more self-centered way of doing things, problems arose and "accidents" happened—a fender-bender, problems with her publisher, a traffic jam. This positive and negative feedback became part of a stream of subtle messages that helped her stay on course. They confirmed that her efforts really did have spiritual value. Little by little, as her understanding of her messages grew, Greta found more and more spiritual meaning in everyday activities.

Looking back several years later, Greta confirmed that this moment had been a turning point for her life. The message and the book it pointed her toward helped her to see that she had been so caught up in the rat race that her values had become reversed. Fame and money—instead of being the means for her material security and material fulfillment—had become the goal. She had been too self-centered and hadn't been treating the people around her very well. She had lost a sense of the meaning of life.

For me, Greta's experience underscores the fact that the better the effort we make, the greater the specificity of the message that we get in response, and the more consistent our efforts, the better the dialogue that we establish. But each of us will learn something different by putting ourselves in Greta's shoes. If you already have spiritual beliefs, you might find a new appreciation for your own moments of inspiration, when you understand a point in what you are reading more deeply and start to view these moments as subtle messages that push you to act on your insight. You might see from Greta's experience how important ethical behavior is to messages and become determined to act more ethically. Or you might see that it takes a lot of work to change yourself and feel encouraged to persevere longer in your own efforts. If you act on your conclusion, whatever it is, and get positive results that help you just as Greta's efforts to act on her message's advice helped her, then you will have learned something more about decoding someone else's message.

Generalizing from What We Learn

We often don't recognize the true meaning of a message until many years later, as in my experience with the leaf. That's because, just like events in our material life, certain messages start processes in motion whose ultimate meaning only becomes apparent long afterward—like your first chance meeting with the person you will later marry. So as you learn to detect and decode messages in your own life, you might try working backward by identifying events that could have helped you arrive at an important spiritual realization.

Ann had been going through rough times when something happened that altered the course of her life. But when spiritual forces first nudged her in a direction that led to a profound awakening, she had no sense that the event was spiritual at all. "I had started to think about moving out of the Berkshires in Massachusetts, where my husband had died, and into Manhattan," Ann told me. "But I had just bought a brand-new car and had a big dog that I loved. Because it's not easy to deal with either in New York City, these two factors kept me from moving. One night, when I was driving home from a friend's house in a nearby town and thinking about what to do with my life, I turned on the defroster in the car. Suddenly smoke started pouring in. Within thirty seconds, the dashboard was shooting sparks into the cab of the car.

"I barely had enough time to pull the car over and drag my dog out of it before it blew up. I am not exaggerating; it blew up as though there was a bomb in it. I sat on the side of the road watching the flames consume what was left of my car, wondering what I had done to deserve this one. Now I realize that that event was exactly what I needed—it was a good thing. It's what catalyzed me to make up my mind to move to Manhattan, which turned out to be the best thing for me."

At the time, the explosion of her car looked like the farthest possible thing from a blessing. It wasn't an "aha" moment, and Ann didn't see anything positive about it at all. It just seemed like another piece of bad luck. Yet spiritual forces had begun working beneath the surface to open her mind and her life to new possibilities. It's as if this experience created a crack in her old way of viewing life and this crack had to grow wider before she could see the spiritual dimension peeping through.

At first, you might be hesitant to make the kind of meaningful connections in retrospect that Ann did. You might feel that it's just too easy to make up any kind of story you want when you look back at an event. But if drawing such conclusions feels a little strange at first, realize that you do it all the time in everyday life, probably without even noticing it. What happens when you go from being a child to an adolescent or an adolescent to an adult? What happens if you get a divorce or retire? Life looks completely different and you see the events in your past from a completely different perspective. You are forced to reorganize your understanding of yourself to bring your views into line with your current realities so that you can successfully meet the new challenges you face.

Once you believe in the existence of a spiritual dimension, you realize that it was always there, and you have little difficulty going back to change your perspective to reflect what you now know. Looking back on her experience, Ann now believes that she couldn't recognize the spiritual element in her car exploding because she was too angry with God for all the "bad luck" she was having. Only after she moved to New York, found a better job, came into closer contact with friends and family who were interested in spirituality, and finally became interested in it herself did she realize the significant impact that her car blowing up had had on the course of her life. Only when she recognized this as a spiritual effect did she "get" the message that had started a new phase of her life with an unexpected bang.

We can learn other things from our messages by trying to recognize, as Ann did, a pattern in how messages communicate with us. When Ann looks back on the event now, she isn't upset that her car blew up or that it took years for her to realize why. It makes sense to her that she would get such treatment, because she has found that her spiritual messages are perfectly suited to her strong-willed character. To get her moving in the right direction, spiritual forces have often had to whack her with a stick rather than offer gentle encouragement. She's gotten this rough treatment so often that she takes such moments as signs of God's tough love and caring. She has seen her life improve from such treatment, and she is happy that God does not let her go too far astray. It helps her feel that she has her own personal relationship to the source of her messages.

Reading Ann's conclusion, you might wonder, how do your messages take *your* character into account in how they communicate with you? However you answer that question, all you need to do is act on your conclusion and see whether the results prove your interpretation useful. Each time you do this, you will get better at both decoding your own messages and learning from those of others.

Messages awaken us to the existence of a spiritual dimension. They inspire, guide, educate, and illuminate us. They start us thinking that life has a deeper meaning and there may be more to life than material existence. To explain what it might be, we turn to one or another belief system. Most of these systems encourage us to think that we are more than bodies and that we have souls that continue on their journey after our bodies die. They encourage us to believe that there is a purpose to life on Earth. As each religious and spiritual tradition has a different version of what needs to be done to fulfill that purpose and what the benefits of our efforts are, the best way to get started in establishing our own connection with the source of our messages is by developing the ethical qualities that are praised by *all* religions and using the guidance of our messages to help us know the best way to do so. We'll move on to the importance of developing ethical qualities under the guidance of messages shortly, in Part II.

If there is one thing that is distinctive about the approach in this book, it is a commitment to starting with the simplest experiences on which our beliefs are based and *systematically* decoding the meanings of the feedback that validates our beliefs. With such a commitment in mind, we will carefully examine in the next section what makes a thought, feeling, or action spiritual so that we can make certain that the spiritual meanings we give to our messages and ethical actions alike are not just psychological, but truly spiritual by nature.

࿐   ࿐   ࿐

Keys to Chapter 3

- We can draw valuable conclusions about how the spiritual world operates by studying how and when messages enter the scene, how they affect each of us differently, and what their ultimate impact on our lives is.

- We decode messages by making meaningful connections. Making a meaningful connection is different from making a factual connection, which is mainly descriptive. A meaningful connection may begin with a basis in commonly held beliefs, but it is enriched by your own experiences and unique way of thinking so that it helps you achieve your goals in a given area more effectively.
- When you analyze another person's spiritual message in order to learn from it, you will have to make an adjustment that makes his or her experience relevant to *you*— just as you have to do in everyday life to learn from another person's everyday experience.
- You can judge whether the meaning that you give to a spiritual experience—your own or someone else's— is functionally correct or not by the results that you get when you act on that meaning.
- The better your efforts in trying to solve a problem or overcome a challenging situation, the more effectively a message can guide you.

స్ స్ స్

For Your Reflection

To benefit from this book, you will need to do what you do in everyday life: find a meaningful relationship between the examples that you read here and your own experience. To get started, you might reflect on these questions:

1. How well do you learn from other people's experience in your material affairs? Think of something that you have

learned from other people in your everyday material life. What is it? How did the other person's experience help you to do better in a situation in your own life? How similar to you and your life circumstances do another person and his life circumstances have to be in order for you to learn something useful from him?

2. How well do you learn from other people's spiritual experiences? Can you learn from others who have beliefs different from your own? Did you learn anything of spiritual value from Rachel's, Ann's, and Greta's experiences, and if so, what? If not, why not? What do you hope to learn from my experiences and my analyses of other people's experiences in this book?

3. Go to decodeyourmessages.com to review a sampling of the kinds of meaningful connections that other people have made as they decoded their messages and what they learned from Rachel's, Ann's, and Greta's stories.

4. Take out a sheet of paper or turn to a blank page in your notebook and entitle it "Meaningful Connections in My Life." You can also go to decodeyourmessages.com to download these points for reflection to your computer or log into your online notebook. Write a brief paragraph that summarizes how your beliefs and experience combine to give meaning to your messages and those of others. Then write in as much detail as you'd like about the evidence in your own experience that shows that your interpretations are correct.

5. Go to decodeyourmessages.com, if you like, to add an example of how you ascribe spiritual meaning to your messages and how you think it might help others get more out of theirs.

PART II

Engaging the Spiritual Dimension in Everyday Life

CHAPTER 4

Tuning In
to Your Messages

Messages alter our perception of life so that we catch the spiritual dimension in action. In the moment of clarity when our messages first arrive, spirituality is no longer something vague and abstract. It is obvious and self-evident. It is real and relevant. It's as if a veil has been lifted or a candle lit in a dark place. We see a deeper meaning in what is happening and feel motivated to act in better ways. And while it may be hard to describe what makes this different from purely psychological moments of lucidity or "peak experiences," our previous idea of who we were now seems limited and superficial. We are acutely aware that we are not just material beings in a material world but also spiritual beings who are in that moment in touch with a spiritual dimension. We feel whole.

In those moments, we are in what I call a *state of spiritual attention*. And even though our new awareness fades all too quickly, we retain and treasure a vivid impression of what it's like to be in touch with the deepest levels of ourselves and to experience the world around us from a larger spiritual perspective. That impression becomes a touchstone or reference point we use to recognize other spiritual effects that are less forceful than the message but just as valuable.

Nancy's first real experience of the spiritual dimension had a typical effect on her, one that filled her with a desire to stay in tune with the source of this experience. "When I was young, spirituality was an amorphous undefined area of my life. Then I had a profound experience that clued me in to the tender kindness of God in my heart," she told me, with her face suddenly aglow. "When I was seventeen and traveling in England, I went hiking. It was pouring rain, and I reached a part of the trail that made me pause. I was struck with a strong inner feeling that God was truly watching me and encouraging me to come closer to him. This was the first time in my life I had had this feeling, and I was overcome by intense joy and pain at the same time."

Nancy sensed a sacred presence that made her feel alive in a way that she had never been before. She was certain now that there was a deeper purpose in life. To fulfill it, she needed to understand what had just happened to her. Not sure how to go about that, she went to college as planned that fall; soon she began studying the world's religions with a passion, hoping to find an answer. In the summers, she traveled to other countries in search of wise people outside the American culture whose simpler lives seemed more in line with the powerful but simple vision of life that she had experienced. When she found these wise people, to her surprise they all repeated the same thing: God is everywhere. Look within and follow the path in your own life and your own culture rather than turning your back on the life into which you were born. Honor the wisdom of the past but live in the present.

This was an important lesson for Nancy. She had thought that she might best solidify her relationship with the source of her messages and embrace the powerful sense of spiritual meaning that she had felt in that moment by living more simply, even leaving the country if necessary. Now she realized that this was not the path she was meant to take. She understood that she shouldn't radically change her life to get in tune with the guidance of her messages, even though it was hard for her to imagine what a spiritual life would be like if she just continued to live a normal material life.

Nonetheless, at times when she felt closest to the source of her messages and longed to disconnect from her materialistic society in order to feel even closer, these wise people's words rang in her mind and helped her to stay in her normal life. Something in her confirmed that they were right. Her attention shifted. From seeking that feeling of closeness through an altered state of consciousness, she pushed herself to seek a new kind of clarity in her thinking through which she could see how to live everyday life in a more spiritual way. This became for her the proof of a state of spiritual attention: that she could see the spiritual implications of choices she faced in everyday life.

Nancy's experience of being touched by a spiritual presence was like receiving a huge dose of spiritual energy that transformed her vision of herself and her life. She felt energized to make spirituality a central part of her life and did her best to stay tuned into this energy with its natural ebbs and flows. Over time, she learned to stay connected to a more subtle but more constant stream of spiritual energy in her normal state of consciousness that would keep her thoughts, feelings, and actions in better alignment with her messages' guidance while allowing her to remain attentive to the material business at hand. Now, more than fifteen years later, Nancy is a successful doctor who has a different idea of spiritual attention—to remain oriented toward her spiritual goal while being fully engaged in her everyday life.

Diagnosing Spiritual ADD

Despite her frequent successes in connecting to spiritual guidance, it remains a struggle for Nancy to stay consistently attentive to the spiritual elements in her life, as it does for most of us. We have trouble just paying attention to our prayers or meditation, much less keeping our minds focused on the more difficult task of acting in the ways a message might suggest, for we are all too easily distracted by the more tangible demands and rewards of everyday life.

Why do we have such trouble paying attention to our spiritual life when we have such moving encounters with it? You might say that most of us are the spiritual equivalents of children with attention deficit disorder (ADD). We have very short attention spans. We can't consistently apply ourselves to the lessons that our messages give us.

What are children with ADD like? They can't stay focused on things that aren't of high emotional value to them. They have a hard time concentrating on routine mental tasks like schoolwork, but they can stay involved for hours on end with computer games or TV. They have difficulty organizing and following through on tasks, understanding what others are trying to say or do, and going through proper procedures to get what they want. They have more school problems, home problems, relationship problems, and substance abuse problems than children without ADD because they have trouble keeping their attention in tune with what society considers important. They get so used to people thinking that they are lazy and criticizing them for not living up to their potential that they withdraw more and more into their own world and pay less and less attention to the guidance of teachers and parents. And because every routine thing they do requires far more effort than it does for others, as they grow up they continue to have great difficulty coping with the more complex mental demands of modern life. This is all because of a small inability—to sustain attention to things that are important but not emotionally stimulating.

As with children with ADD, most of us are easily distracted by material concerns. Even when we can stay focused on our spiritual life, most of us need some degree of emotional excitement to motivate us. When we lose the feelings of excitement, love, or peace of mind, we lose our focus too. Thoughts of future rewards for our current efforts aren't tangible enough to motivate us to do the more routine chores of spiritual life, like developing ethical qualities, any more than the thoughts of eventually getting a good job motivate a child with ADD to do his homework.

For most of us, our lack of spiritual attention and follow-through is demoralizing. We might even call ourselves lazy and think we had no spiritual potential if we didn't understand the nature of our problem and how we can learn to compensate for it. This problem exists because we have a bi-dimensional nature. We have strong material drives that want material satisfaction, and struggling with these drives in order to bring our thoughts, feelings, and actions into line with our messages is one of the major means by which we develop spiritually. Each message is like a piece of homework that we need to complete in order to understand the greater possibilities of thinking in line with them in everyday life. To benefit from what our messages are trying to teach us, we need to not just understand what they might be saying, but act on their guidance, just as children with ADD have to actually do their homework in order to benefit from going to school.

As we go on, I will frequently use today's understanding of how things work—as I've just done with ADD—as a basis for analogies to help us understand our spiritual experiences. I do this for the same reason that I encourage you to describe your spiritual experiences in everyday language. Past formulations of spiritual truths were naturally shaped by people's understanding of themselves and the world around them at that time. This made the truths vibrant and relevant to those people's lives. Since we now understand more about how the world around us works, we need to systematically update our formulations of our spiritual understanding so that they are compatible with our way of thinking today.

Analogies allow us to use what we know to grasp things that we don't yet understand. Science uses analogies this way all the time.

If we use our best scientific understanding of what goes on in the material dimension as the basis of analogies that illuminate our soul's interactions with the spiritual dimension, then spirituality will no longer seem to be in conflict with science or ideas such as evolution. The natural order that exists in the world will become our foundation for spiritual understanding.

Getting Swept Off Our Feet by Love

Spiritual ADD manifests both in our difficulty paying attention to the spiritual elements in everyday life and in our tendency to pay excessive attention to one element of spiritual life that fascinates us and ignore our messages' other lessons. We might want to, for example, pay attention *only* to spiritual experiences that generate states of ecstasy and love, like the one Nancy described at the beginning of the chapter. This is a common mistake, for many spiritual figures have emphasized the path of love and most of us need that feeling of love to motivate us to pay attention to our spiritual life.

My emotional and enthusiastic friend Haley explained to me how she learned that it was a big mistake for her to focus so intensively on love that she forgot about everything else. "I had a very strong feeling of God's presence; I saw him in everything," she told me. "I was studying a spiritual book very intensely. Every chance I got, I was reading and rereading it. It was a complicated book, so I had to think carefully about each word. After a couple of months of reading it, I felt totally different. I began seeing a lesson in everything—not just when I was reading the book.

"For a period of two months, I was high in the sky. I felt as if there were another hand organizing my life. Everything was going very smoothly, but I was not there. It was not uncomfortable; it's just that 'I' wasn't there. It was as if somebody else was setting the table, cooking, and taking care of my family. It was not me."

Haley's experience was so much like those that mystics in the past had described that she felt certain she was on course. She was seeing the spiritual element in all of life. "I felt God in everything—in a human being, a tree, a shadow, the wood," she explained excitedly. "He was telling me the reason for the creation of each thing I saw. It was like a short movie. If I saw a piece of wood, I saw a short movie in my mind about why this wood was created."

Despite Haley's rapture, she began to feel that something was not right. "Even at night, my mind was still functioning, processing all the information I was getting. It was like inputting too much data into a computer at once so that the data is still being processed for a long time afterward. So one night around midnight I heard a voice saying, 'Explosion!' It woke me up. That's when I knew I couldn't take it any longer. I had to stop myself from getting swept away by love. I felt so full of the love of God that I could have lost my marbles after awhile. I was accessing knowledge that I was not ready for. My capacity was just not that big."

When Haley started to come back to herself, she could see that she had been neglecting important aspects of her life. She had a daughter who needed her, but she had felt so high that it was hard to get meals together for her child, much less be there to help her with homework and daily difficulties. Later, Haley also found out that she had been on the verge of losing her job without realizing it. She was so full of love that nothing else happening around her mattered; everything seemed perfect to her eyes. She had thought that she would achieve her goal simply by surrendering to love. Now she knew that this wasn't right for her.

After she received that midnight message, Haley realized something similar to what Nancy had discovered at the beginning of the chapter—that staying in tune with spiritual energy didn't mean forgetting about everyday life, and that if she was to stay engaged in everyday life *and* pay attention to her spiritual development, she would have to find a better way of doing this. As she examined her experiences more carefully, looking for something she had missed that might have clued her into her mistake earlier, she could see that she had swept aside her vague feelings of guilt and discomfort about not being there for her child and not doing the work she was being paid to do as well as she had before. She had pushed them aside as if they were a small price to pay for being closer to God. Through this experience, she overcame a stereotype that she had held about spiritual experience—that it was all about love—and directed her attention toward decoding the lessons that her messages were delivering, rather than being enraptured by the joy of being in touch with the spiritual dimension.

Once she got the point, it made complete sense, because it's exactly the same thing that we all have to learn in everyday life. We might be tempted at times to devote ourselves completely to our love life, but if we do, everything suffers, even our love life. Just as we need to apply ourselves to all aspects of material life in a balanced way to have the best possible life, so we need to do the same in our spiritual life.

Although Haley's experience of love is more extreme than most of ours, it underscores an issue many of us encounter as a symptom of our spiritual ADD. Even when we can get ourselves to focus on our spiritual lives, we tend to pay more attention to the elements that have immediate emotional appeal and overlook the other aspects of spiritual life that require more disciplined work. A good way to double-check ourselves, as we can see in Haley's experience, is to keep our material life in balance and use our messages to understand the spiritual value of living a normal everyday life.

Refocusing on What Matters

The spiritual dimension is a vast and complex place, and we can connect to it in many different ways. Not only can we focus solely on the effects on our emotions, as Haley did, but we can also get involved with other beings. This is the equivalent of getting so caught up with a group of friends that we don't pay attention to school, work, or family responsibilities. We get distracted from the balanced system of feedback that our messages give us. It can be interesting and rewarding, and it may help us grow in certain ways, but it doesn't very often lead to the same balanced development and overall success we'd enjoy if we put our efforts into the lessons that come from messages. It becomes thus another manifestation of what I'm calling *spiritual ADD*—not paying regular and consistent attention to the elements in everyday life that our messages point out.

As an example of this, I'll tell you about a mistake of my own by which it became clear to me that not all communications with the spiritual dimension are a part of the system of guidance that comes from the source of our messages. When you tune in, I learned, it's possible to be misled.

My early messages started me thinking about a spiritual dimension. From my college studies of the world's religions, I thought that the best way of understanding it would be to connect with it myself and learn about how things worked directly from the different souls I would encounter. I had practiced different forms of meditation in the past and was already studying hypnosis to be more effective in my psychiatric practice; now I began to wonder if I could use the time that I had set aside for exploring self-hypnosis to get in touch with the spiritual levels of my unconscious.

Several months after my first few spiritual messages, I was about an hour into one of these self-hypnosis sessions when, with my eyes closed, I saw a huge eye looking back at me out of the inner blackness. This eye was like no other mental image I had ever seen. It looked like the eye of a real person suspended in space. As I relaxed into the image, the eye slowly took its place in the face of a wise man who smiled at me, a smile like no other I had ever experienced. It created an explosion within me. I beamed back with such an intense smile of my own that my face hurt. I was ecstatic. I had never felt so completely happy before in my life.

Having studied hypnosis extensively, I knew that people in trance often hallucinate, seeing things that are not really there. I thought I had finally gotten deeply enough into trance to have that happen to me. If I hadn't received several messages during the preceding months, I would have used the image as many other hypnotherapists do—as an inner advisor (a product of my own imagination) that could help me get in touch with the wisdom of my own unconscious. It would never have dawned on me that there was anything more to it than that, no matter how real the image seemed. But because of my experience with the leaf in the Botanical Garden that I related in chapter 1 and the several other surprising synchronicities that came soon after, it seemed possible to me that whatever had been behind those messages was now creating the image of a wise man to answer my questions about the nature of reality. This became my working hypothesis.

The image came with an infusion of tremendous energy that altered my perception of life so much that it no longer felt like my perception. It was as if I was looking through the wise man's eyes. Life seemed very simple. I saw the universe in perspective, with myself one of billions of human beings, an insignificant but meaningful part of a far larger whole. As with Nancy's and Haley's encounters, it was 100 percent intense emotion, a 10++ on my own scale of 1 to 10 that I like to use to characterize my experiences to myself.

Though this "wise man" never spoke to me, after a few visualizations I established more specific communication with him through the hypnotic technique of automatic writing. I would write my question, and he would take control of my hand to write the answer. For the next four years, I sat down and communicated with him once or twice a month, much the way I might write to or converse with a wise, elderly friend about his perspective on life. My idea of spiritual attention shifted slightly, from being the peak emotional experience I'd had at first to being the state of mind that allowed the spiritual dimension (or the deepest level of my unconscious; I still wasn't sure) to break through and take control of my hand to write an answer.

I had hoped that this entity would teach me how to attain the states of bliss that I had experienced when I first encountered him. He explained, however, that such experiences were like drugs; they would make me feel good but would not promote spiritual progress. His job was to help me learn how to value other aspects of spiritual life—the fundamentals. Spiritual attention to him was paying attention to everyday life in line with the spiritual values common to all religions. It had little to do with disconnecting from the material world or feeling intense emotion. Getting caught up in communicating with other souls might be spiritual but it was the spirituality of someone with spiritual ADD, for it meant I was not paying attention to my spiritual life in the balanced way that was needed for my development.

His words didn't suddenly stop me from doing what I was doing, any more than a parent's advice could instantly change the behavior of a child with ADD. I remained intent on getting him to prove that he was real and to introduce me to other spirits with whom I could communicate. I wanted to find one who would help me the way I wanted to be helped. He wrote back that he wouldn't tell me any information about his earthly life that I could verify—where he had lived and who he had been—because that would go against what he was trying to teach me. He certainly wouldn't introduce me to other spirits. I was stuck with him. His goal was to help me figure out that he was real without relying on the childlike proofs I wanted or even the altered states of consciousness that I was so fond of, for in the long run such proofs would be an obstacle to my overall development. I kept nudging, but he wouldn't budge.

There was a certain logic in his position, as he pointed out. It was the same process that people needed to go through to believe in a higher power. If this higher power wanted people to know that it existed, it could easily reveal itself in such a way that everyone would believe in it. If it chose not to, it was for a reason. If I were to hope to understand the purpose of life and connect to this higher power in any meaningful way, I had to learn how to recognize the spiritual effects in things while remaining attentive to my everyday life. I could not expect the spiritual dimension to make an exception when it came to me. The wise man told me that he would do his part and help me if I tried my best to do mine.

As for other souls, he made it very clear to me that I shouldn't be in touch with them. He explained that there were all kinds of souls I might meet, including some who would purposefully mislead me. They might say all the right things at first to gain my trust and then gradually lead me in the wrong direction over a period of years without my even knowing it. They might give advice that made me think that they were the source of messages. Relying on what a random soul might tell me would be just as bad as if I were to walk down Wall Street and hire the first person I met as a financial advisor because he claimed he was knowledgeable. What my spirit guide was saying made rational sense and fit with many other people's experiences I had read, though it seemed rather bizarre that he was trying to teach me the importance of not trusting or even contacting an entity like him.

Even when it came to what was important in material life, he was full of surprises. I had expected him to downplay the importance of material life and tell me to volunteer in a soup kitchen or to help the poor more. To my surprise, he wrote back that I should continue my regular life (working in an inner-city mental health clinic, as I was doing) and be more considerate of others whom I naturally encountered in my activities.

Over the four years we were in contact, he patiently repeated that in pursuing spiritual understanding, I should never do anything that was harmful to my material life or contrary to good common sense. I'm rather hardheaded, but after four years of consulting him, his advice sank in. I finally reached a point where I accepted that he was "real" and not the product of my own unconscious. It wasn't because of anything in particular that happened. It just emerged out of our ongoing relationship. I was like the child with ADD whose parents and teachers put in so much patient work in the hopes that one day he would see the value of doing his homework for himself. Then, one day, he does. The same was true for me: I suddenly appreciated the value of what the guide had been telling me. It just became clear to me that I had to pay more attention to the spiritual dimension in everyday life if I wanted to fulfill my purpose for being on Earth—a conclusion similar to those Nancy and Haley reached by different routes. Mine had just been more circuitous.

The week after I accepted that he was real, my spirit guide told me I no longer needed to be in touch with him. He had finished teaching me what he had come to teach me. When I asked why we couldn't continue, he wrote back: "Your pride is too great. Contact with me makes you feel special." He went on to explain that now that I actually believed he was real, I could get down to real work, and his relationship with me would only distract me from what I needed to do. He wasn't abandoning me because I had failed, but, on the contrary, because I had finally understood what he was there to teach me. Instead of just talking with him about what was going on in my life, I was now ready to do what I needed to do to change myself. I had to follow the system of spiritual development under the guidance of my messages.

This spirit guide had been a special tutor for me who helped me get over my fixation on states of intense spiritual emotion and contact with other souls, the bells and whistles of spiritual phenomena. I now think that communicating with a spirit is like talking with someone who is one or two grades ahead of you in school. You can be impressed by what he knows and his offer of friendship, but you can't judge how well his knowledge will help you develop your own potential to your best advantage. You are far better off paying attention to what the teacher says, in the form of your messages, which tell you what you need to learn at your level right now to advance in the best possible way.

This is a good place to emphasize one of the most important things that I learned through my contact with this spirit. Not every inspiration or communication with the spiritual dimension that we get is from the source of messages. We do better to connect instead with the school set up for our spiritual education—the natural system of messages in everyday life. My spirit guide helped me correct certain misunderstandings that I had about the spiritual dimension, but having done so, he put me back in the regular class, where I could have started much earlier if not for the time I spent contacting him.

There's another reason why our system of messages serves us better than spirit guides. When I compared notes with other people who had had contact with spirits, it was difficult to learn much from them because each of our experiences was so highly personal. But by tuning into messages from the higher power that I call the source of our messages, we can learn more from the experiences of others, because we are all tuned into this same source of guidance. It's like comparing notes with classmates who are in the same grade: We can learn from each other because our lessons are a part of the same plan.

ॐ　ॐ　ॐ

When we first start receiving messages, we are excited by everything that is spiritual but find ourselves more drawn to the way they energize us and inspire us than to do the grunt work that is needed to improve ourselves and our lives. We each have a certain preconception of what it means to pay attention to the spiritual dimension, and we can easily get so caught up in aspects of spirituality that fit our preconceptions that we become distracted from our messages. That's because we have a form of spiritual ADD. As we become more and more familiar with messages and develop the basic skills that they teach us, however, we discover that rather than helping us cultivate altered states of consciousness, states of ecstatic love, or communication with other souls, their main goal is to help us figure out how to use everyday life for our spiritual development. Once we realize this, we can apply ourselves with greater enthusiasm to the lessons that come in the natural course of our own life.

It is difficult to overcome our spiritual ADD and to pay attention to the spiritual lessons that our messages point out to us. Yet, if we systematically examine the effects of our messages on our thoughts, feelings, and actions in relation to everyday life, we will be in a better position to decode their meaning more fully and use their energizing effects to accomplish the objectives they point us toward.

ॐ   ॐ   ॐ

Keys to Chapter 4

- Messages change the way we view our everyday life. Even though this awareness gradually fades, you can retain a vivid impression of what it's like to be tuned in to the source of your messages. You will have a taste of a state that I call *spiritual attention,* where you experience yourself and the world around you from a larger spiritual perspective.

- It's hard to remain attentive to the spiritual dimension of life. Most of us are the spiritual equivalents of children with attention deficit disorder (ADD)—we have very short attention spans and get easily distracted by the challenges and excitement of everyday life.

- Past formulations of spiritual truths were naturally shaped by people's understanding of themselves and the world around them at that time. If we systematically update the foundation on which our spiritual understanding is based by forming analogies that reflect today's understanding of how things work in the material world, we will be able to integrate spirituality more fully into our approach to everyday life.

- In a common form of spiritual ADD, we are drawn to the powerful emotional states that messages arouse in us and can easily lose interest in the everyday manifestations of the spiritual. It's easy to get focused on these exhilarating moments and ignore the help and guidance that messages can give you in everyday life.

- Spiritual ADD can manifest in many different ways, leading us to focus excessively on some aspect of spirituality other than our messages. It's possible, for example, to get caught up in communicating directly with other souls, as some mystics did in the past, and in the process get diverted from doing the fundamental and practical things we need to do for our spiritual development that our messages are pointing out.

ॐ　ॐ　ॐ

For Your Reflection

It's time again to reflect on what you've read in this chapter and crystallize your thoughts about what it is important to pay attention to in spiritual life and why.

1. What are the main effects of spiritual messages on you? How do they influence your thoughts, feelings, and actions in general? Do they encourage you to pay attention to everyday life or to withdraw from it? What element in spiritual life do you consider the most important? Are devotional acts more or less important than the way in which you live your everyday life?

2. Do you have trouble remembering your spiritual priorities in the heat of everyday life? Do you have spiritual ADD? To support your assessment, review what you thought, felt, and did in the last twenty-four hours to see how well you stayed in line with your beliefs and your messages.

3. Go to decodeyourmessages.com to see how other people describe their experiences of spiritual attention and how they have influenced their everyday life.

4. Take out a sheet of paper or turn to a blank page in your notebook and entitle it "How I Tune In to My Messages." You can also download these points for reflection to your computer or log into your online notebook. Write a summary paragraph on what you consider important to pay attention to in your spiritual life and how well you do so. Imagine that you are explaining your ideas to someone with quite different beliefs from your own so that you put it as simply as possible. Try to avoid using special religious or spiritual terminology; instead, use everyday language and analogies to today's understanding of how the world works. Once you've expressed your conclusions, continue on and write in as much detail as you'd like about the experiences that support your conclusions.

5. Go to decodeyourmessages.com to add the experiences on which you base your own view of the relative importance of messages in your own life to your spiritual development.

CHAPTER 5

Expanding Your Spiritual Awareness

Messages suggest that the material and spiritual dimensions are two parts of a larger whole. They encourage us to use our everyday life as the means for our spiritual development. Everyday life thus turns into a classroom as they teach us how to take into account the spiritual dimension of each and every choice that we face.

As we saw in the last chapter, it's difficult to learn to appreciate the value of material life for our spiritual development. It's easier to keep the two separate and think that spirituality, instead of being connected to everyday life, is all about love or about communicating with spirits. Yet our messages keep redirecting our attention toward everyday life. To understand how we can be in better tune with their guidance, it's a good idea to have in mind what it really means to pay attention to something.

Paying attention to something means focusing our consciousness on a particular thought, feeling, or object, instead of any number of other possible thoughts, feelings, or objects, and thereby increasing its power in our mind. It feels like a simple process that functions instinctively and can be developed, much as a muscle is, by exercise, but neuropsychological research has found that attention is actually the product of three major interrelated sub-functions—*alerting, orienting,* and *executive control*—that is developed through a process of education. Each of these three functions is a product of a different brain pathway and integrates with the others in a fraction of a second so that we are conscious only of the final result. An understanding of how our attention works will provide the basis for another analogy that will help us develop greater spiritual attention. The more systematically we draw such analogies with our current understanding of our mental processes, the better integrated our material and spiritual approaches to everyday life will be.

Our alerting attention acts as a filter that selects what we should be conscious of. It creates our stream of consciousness, a coherent moving picture of what's going on around us and inside us. It is not like a camera, however, for it includes what is relevant to us based on our past experience and excludes what we have found irrelevant. Our alerting attention creates a picture of the world as it's relevant to us and what we are doing, the world according to us. It provides us with a context in which to live.

Our orienting attention takes this stream of consciousness, evaluates it, and assigns the appropriate mental and emotional meanings to the various elements, still without any involvement of our conscious mind. It focuses our attention on the most important elements and assigns things like the appropriate emotional state in which to deal with that situation—arousal, fear, comfort, and so forth.

Our executive function primes us to act in one specific way or another in that particular situation to which we are now well oriented. It too is based on our past experience and doesn't need our conscious participation. If everything moves along as expected based on past experience, there is no need to think about what to do. We will just do it naturally, in a way that feels instinctive. If there is a doubt about what to pay attention to or what to do, our executive functions can pass the issue to our conscious mind for more careful analysis.

How does this help us understand our spiritual attention? When someone has no belief in a spiritual dimension, she automatically filters out messages. If a message breaks through, she deems it irrelevant or comes up with an alternative explanation for it. When someone accepts through faith that there is a spiritual dimension, she changes the value that she gives to different things so that she does pay more attention to certain aspects of life that her belief system values, but she doesn't understand why this is important to do, so she can't generalize from her experience. When someone has a preconception about what it means to pay attention to the spiritual dimension—such as having a detached frame of mind— she filters everything according to that understanding and orients to things based on that belief.

Once we realize the nature of attention, we look for an educational approach to develop it. What does that mean? Just as our attention functions better in everyday life the better we understand the situation we are in, and just as I became a doctor by going to medical school and learning what to pay closest attention to in my patients' complaints, so we improve our spiritual attention through an educational approach, under the guidance of our messages. Messages help us learn what to be alert to, oriented to, and ready to respond to. However, to do this, we need to decode them and see the value of their meaning for us. As so many of our messages occur in relation to everyday life and encourage actions with material benefit, we can deduce different ways that we can adjust our attention in everyday life to become more receptive to the effects of our messages. In this chapter, we will see how slight adjustments in our common sense, our sense of self, and our knowledge of how the world works will help us become more alert, oriented, and ready to respond to a fuller range of our messages' effects.

The Value of Common Sense

Messages most often push us to act in line with common sense, so it is reasonable to try to act with common sense on our own and look for further corrections from our messages. Although some religious and spiritual beliefs would seem to exhort us to set aside common sense in favor of our faith, messages generally encourage the opposite. As we decode more of our own and others' messages, it becomes clearer that normal everyday life is a very good place to learn about the spiritual dimension. It certainly has enough challenges in it that bring our weak points to the fore.

Most discoveries in medicine and psychology derive from a simple observation. It's easier to see how a given system functions by studying what can happen when it malfunctions than by watching when everything is working smoothly. To show you the value of common sense, let's look at an example where it failed.

Marinka was a thirty-two-year-old housewife who had a very strong belief in God. She had grown up in a small, traditional village in Germany, and because she needed to work to help her family, she hadn't finished high school. She had married and moved to the city in search of a better life for her children. "We bought a house and lived in it for about four years," she told me, looking away and sounding embarrassed about what she was going to tell me. "Then through a series of events, we found out that the document used by the person who sold us the house was forged. The real owner was now claiming his home. I didn't know what to do. I was devastated. All I could think of was to ask for God's help. I prayed and prayed that God would make the owner change his mind, but that didn't happen."

Marinka pleaded from the bottom of her heart for what she wanted, but when God seemed not to hear, it triggered a period of negativity lasting several years, until she finally understood what her message was trying to tell her. "When I had first asked for God's help, I expected him to do what I thought he should do," she said. "But in time, I saw that he did what was best for me. Losing the house caused a major turn in my life's direction. My husband and I moved to a new city, where life became much happier for both of us."

This experience completely changed Marinka's perspective on life. She had been raised in a small village. She had often received messages that helped her out in times of need; it was common sense for her to believe this, for others in her village thought the same way. As a result, they all felt quite close to God. But when Marinka moved to the city, she found society corrupt and overly materialistic. She remained aloof from "the ways of the world." She even saw her naïveté in everyday life as a sign of how spiritual she was. So she never developed the kind of common sense that would work in her new environment. She was convinced that God would take care of her as he always had. After her experience with the house, though, she realized that God wanted her to be more responsible for herself and to learn the kind of common sense that worked in city life.

So, Marinka set out to learn how to handle her own affairs better and be clearer about what she had a right to expect from God and what she didn't. She seized the means available to her. She read the local newspapers and magazines that she had formerly shunned as too worldly. She turned to self-help books from the local bookstore to learn to evaluate the realities of situations more effectively and overcome her naïve attitude. She started discussing issues of everyday life with friends who had more common sense than she did. She was determined to become a part of society, as she now believed God wanted her to.

Marinka developed the kind of organized approach to life that common sense encourages so that she could function in the world of meanings that her society created. And as she did, she became aware of subtle feedback that seemed to encourage and guide her in her everyday affairs. When she took responsibility for her life, for example, things often went better than she expected. When she found herself clinging to her old expectations and thinking God should take care of the matter, something went slightly wrong. She might break a glass she was washing, for example, or encounter an unexpected expense.

Each step she took toward being more responsible for herself helped her feel more confident in situations where she had previously felt shaky, such as discussing her opinions with others or encouraging her children to play with others who didn't share their beliefs. Her attention was better attuned to the spiritual elements in a situation, for she was now looking for the spiritual within everyday experience instead of outside it. She was looking for it to be aligned with common sense rather than opposed to it. And God's presence seemed more integrated in her life than ever.

These changes in attitude brought Marinka into better alignment with the effects of her messages, because she no longer did what she wanted and expected God to wave a magic wand to make everything right. He was not her servant but her mentor. It wasn't very good common sense to think that she didn't have to make an effort on her own but could rely on God to do her work. Now she was trying to listen to what God wanted her to do rather than getting him to do what she wanted him to do.

This simple change in attitude marked the beginning of a new phase in her spiritual life. The world was no longer as confusing a place in which to live. So she became naturally more alert, oriented, and ready to respond to messages. From her new perspective, she could see that her old ideas about what it meant to rely on God had been limited, and she found that her new way felt more deeply satisfying. When she reread spiritual books, for example, she understood that they hadn't ever really meant for her to rely on God in the way that she had. She was living in reality instead of denying it. Her material and spiritual lives were working together.

Marinka's example demonstrates the kind of simple, concrete benefits that come from approaching our spiritual life with common sense. Gathering this kind of evidence in my own and others' experiences has convinced me that sound common sense is the most important factor—far more important than, say, our level of education—in decoding our messages and integrating what we learn into our everyday life. Having a theoretical understanding of ideas like ADD and the nature of our attention may be useful in extending our knowledge, but is not as important as having sound common sense, which provides a flexible but coherent frame of reference that allows us to make more systematic use of our messages in the unique circumstances of our own life. If we lack common sense, we may have strong faith, but if we can't decode the meaning of events in our material affairs, we are unlikely to be able to decode the meaning of messages beyond the most elementary level. If we have common sense *and* that same level of faith, however, it becomes far easier to be alert, oriented, and ready to respond to the important material and spiritual elements in each of the common situations that we face.

Rethinking Who We Are

A second factor that helps us orient to what's going on around us is our sense of self. Common sense organizes things according to a general understanding of how things work, whereas our sense of self provides our own more specific orientation to the possibilities available to us. We naturally think of ourselves as a body living in a material world. What matter to us are those things that are of material and psychological value. That's what we naturally pay attention to. We identify with a history that confirms the value of what we are doing and keeps us going in the direction we are going in. To take the best possible advantage of what our messages are telling us, we need to expand our sense of self to include the spiritual dimension. A good way of doing this is reformulating our sense of identity and our history so as to emphasize the importance of spirituality in our life.

To explain what I mean, I'll tell you how I started to reformulate my own life history as I began to decode messages. This also gives me an opportunity to tell you a little more about my own background so that you can understand how this rational approach to decoding messages emerges naturally from my life.

As I started to decode messages, I could feel how difficult it was to keep my attention on what they were trying to teach me. I began to feel a need to retell my life's story in a way that gave more weight to what my messages were saying. It's the same thing that we automatically do whenever we undergo an important change—becoming an adolescent, going to school, getting married, having children. We change our perspective on life and what is important to us. For example, when I decided to become a doctor, I looked back over my life and assigned more importance to those elements in my character that supported my decision and less importance to other areas that might have countered it. The new story fit well enough to go ahead. It wouldn't have worked, however, if I had tried to justify becoming a lawyer or a businessman or a physicist or a musician. Then this process of retelling my life would have made it clear to me that I was making a mistake. The real test came, of course, when I acted on this new hypothesis of who I wanted to be and saw the results. I became a psychiatrist, and it has enriched my life in ways that I continue to value today. I don't think about all of the other Pauls I could have become by making a different choice.

So, similarly, when I became interested in spirituality, I wanted to change my sense of who I am to be more in tune with what my messages had been suggesting: that I am a bi-dimensional being with both a body and a soul. I am here for a reason and this reason is the most important thing in my life, for I will continue as a soul when my body dies. To help me commit to this new vision of myself, I felt it was important to once again retell my life's story—which was currently the story of a psychiatrist who had had rather superstitious ideas about spirituality growing up—in a way that would help me be more alert, oriented, and ready to respond to the messages that I detected in my life today. What follows is the broad outline of this revision.

I was born into a family with traditional Christian beliefs and was very interested in religion. When I was a child, God and Jesus were the center of my world. They seemed even more important to me than my parents did. God was love. I felt loved and at peace in my small personal world. I was excited by everything having to do with religion. I remember at the age of nine rushing home from a Saturday morning catechism class. We had touched in passing on the question of how many angels could dance on the head of a pin. The answer was an infinite number, because angels weren't really material in the way a pin was. I couldn't wait to talk to my mother about this. I felt that I had understood something important about the spiritual dimension, and if I could grasp this as a child, how much more I would know as an adult. When I told her, she looked at me strangely, and I felt a little confused, but I still recall the fervor I felt for that distinction. That's the kind of kid I was.

Even as a child, I was a little too rational. Certain questions troubled me deeply. I had been raised in a fundamentalist Protestant church, the Dutch Reformed Church, with a belief that only a select few would be saved—those who believed in the ideas of that particular church had been predestined to go to heaven and the rest would suffer in hell for eternity. It seemed so unfair that others didn't even have the opportunity to hear about Jesus and his love that I decided to become a missionary. My father, a surgeon, wanted me to become a doctor instead and tried to convince me that that was the best way to get through to people. If I could help heal them physically, he said, they would listen to me. I wanted none of that. It seemed like cheating to me. I wanted people to be excited because of the truth within the idea, not because I could treat their physical problems.

When I attended Oberlin College, I took both science and religion courses for my first year and a half to keep open the option of going to medical school, just in case my father was right. But by the second term of my sophomore year, my heart won out and I gave up on science to devote myself to the study of religion. For me, it was the victory of faith over reason. As I continued on, however, I became increasingly unsettled by my college experience and the fact that many people with no belief in God seemed more ethical and honest than the religious people I had known growing up. What was even more confusing was that many of the people I met who belonged to other religions seemed more devout than those models of my youth.

As I studied the world's religions more closely, it became increasingly evident to me that all religions came from the same source and that the differences between them merely reflected the mentalities of the people who had lived in a particular time and place. It was a simple idea, yet deeply troubling for me personally. What did it mean for *my* beliefs and the way I lived *my* life? By my junior year, my passion for religion was fading fast. I knew that I could never go back to the way that I used to think. I had to go on. I clung to the more academic understandings of religious experience, still hoping that I might become a religion professor and teach the world's religions in a university.

By my senior year, the rational understanding of the world that I was learning about in courses on philosophy, psychology, and literature seemed far more relevant to my questions about life than any set of religious beliefs that I found. I didn't exactly become an atheist or even an agnostic, but I decided that if there were a God, he was no longer relevant to my life. I was living proof that faith and reason don't mix. Now I was on the side of reason. I would have to continue living as if there were no God until I saw signs of his presence in my life.

In the next twenty years, I learned how everyday life worked from a materialist's perspective. I went on to medical school and became a psychiatrist. Going through medical school at Cornell and training in New York hospitals, I learned about life and death. After finishing my training in psychiatry, I went to work in the South Bronx with the poor of New York City because it seemed like the right thing to do. I learned how to think about myself and approach human problems based on the best available evidence. I helped people solve life's problems as best they could, nurture love in real relationships, and create a sense of personal meaning that could sustain them through difficult times. I learned how the head and the heart work together. I learned to appreciate differences between people, tolerate ambiguity, and accept the limitations of what I could do or know.

When the leaf landed in my hand in that garden in Rio, as I described in chapter 1, I had been practicing psychiatry for fifteen years and felt no need for a belief in God to make life meaningful. But that leaf was a sign that some part of me had been awaiting for more than twenty years. When it arrived, I knew that nonphysical forces—forces from another dimension that people had historically considered to be "spiritual"—actually did exist. The leaf was a challenge: Make sense of this if you can! Having no spiritual beliefs at the time, I could only turn to common sense and psychology to try to understand what was happening. I couldn't do as Saint Augustine, Rachel, Anna, or Greta had done and embrace spirituality in any form that I knew.

The course of my spiritual education has not been straightforward. Yet, when I look back, I see that everything has been organized around one central life lesson: how to think about the spiritual dimension. My childhood beliefs, the religious beliefs that I later rejected, and the twenty years of my life that I lived without a belief in a spiritual dimension are no longer time wasted to me, but experiences that established the conditions in which I could approach spiritual life in a rational way. They helped me to develop a detailed understanding of human nature that would be the basis for the analogies that helped me to understand spiritual experience.

Although it might seem that we automatically transform our sense of who we are as we gain experience, I have found it very useful to deliberately review my own history to make certain that elements in my sense of identity in this material world don't encourage attitudes and behaviors that filter out the effects of messages. Each of our stories will have a different center, drawing our attention to the main lessons our messages give us. Each of us gets different lessons from our messages, and each of us needs to establish a life story that is in line with these lessons, so that we are more alert, oriented, and ready to respond to the elements in our messages that are relevant to us and our journey.

An important part of our sense of identity is established by our relationship with others, and in spirituality, this element is found in how we conceive of our relationship to the source of our messages. For me, getting to know the source of our messages is like meeting a therapist or mentor whom a friend of mine knows and has told me about. What my friend has to say about the person is useful information, and from my friend's description, I might think I have a pretty good idea of who the person is. Yet once I actually spend time with that person, my relationship with him and the advice that I get will be very different from my friend's. I will probably describe him differently and interact with him differently than my friend would simply because we are different people. And it's only when I follow his advice and see the value of it for myself that I will see his wisdom and trust his opinions.

Likewise, when we first become aware of messages, the descriptions that others provide, including the prophets and saints, give us a sense of what the messages' source is like. We may think we can have a relationship with it that's similar to theirs. But in fact their experiences can give us only a starting point from which we can form our own relationship with the source of our messages. We establish this relationship by acting on our messages and discovering their value. Then we learn to attune our attention to messages properly in a way that is personally relevant to us.

Searching for Clues

In addition to acting with good common sense and updating our sense of identity to center on our spiritual quest, we can become more sensitive to messages by pushing ourselves to see the spiritual perspective in whatever happens in classroom Earth, using analogies with our current understanding of everyday life.

Our classroom is our body and our environment. As infinitesimally small parts of a tiny ecosystem in a vast universe, our bodies and all of their functions arose to help us survive and flourish in our ecosystem. Our body signals us when things go too far out of balance—if we don't get enough food to eat, water to drink, or air to breathe—so that we can use our higher intelligence to come up with the most effective strategy to correct the temporary imbalance. Our minds scan our environment—our relationships with others, our possessions, our jobs—to make certain that we are functioning well in everyday life.

By drawing an analogy here and thinking of our soul as an infinitesimally small part of a spiritual ecosystem that is governed by its own set of rules, we can start to ask many interesting questions. If our soul is a part of an ecosystem, what kind of spiritual matter and spiritual energy define our soul's discrete existence and its interactions with everything else? Does our soul have a structure made up of different parts performing different functions? What distinctive properties might a human soul possess? Does it need to go through an orderly and sequential development, or is it fully developed at our birth? What kind of energy does it need to function?

What is its source of its nutrition and how does it digest it? How does our soul think, feel, and remember? Can our soul be sick, and if so, what are the signs and symptoms of different illnesses?

We can systematically use the analogies that come from this kind of thinking to sort our experiences into categories so that we know what is important to pay attention to from a spiritual perspective. All of us are deeply influenced by the discoveries of science. Regardless of your level of scientific knowledge, what you know can become the basis of your spiritual understanding. If you are a scientist yourself, you will do better being very precise and detailed. If you are not, you will do better using the level of understanding that helps you in your everyday life as the basis for your knowledge of how things work. If you run into an area that you don't understand, you can always look up more information if you need to make a better analogy to understand what is going on spiritually.

As in medicine, we learn more about how our soul works by studying what happens when something seems to go wrong than in trying to figure out what makes it work right. To give you a clearer idea of what I mean, let's look at the example of Venus, a savvy businesswoman, who came up with the kind of analogy I've just described and used it to powerful effect.

"Recently, I was in a difficult situation at work," Venus explained. "By the end of last week, it was very intense and my coworkers were becoming increasingly aggressive with me. It was really difficult. I knew that there was something that I had to do from a spiritual perspective to change the situation, but I didn't know what it was. I couldn't stop the negativity from over-whelming me. I felt spiritually drained from the anger welling up in me, the way I would from a virus. I had just gotten over a cold, so the feeling was fresh in my mind and made me wonder if there was a parallel. Perhaps my *spiritual* immune system had failed so that I was overwhelmed by negative, angry thoughts. If so, I would have to learn to create antibodies to fight off this negativity making me sick inside. I have to take control of my negative thoughts and actions. That's what God would want me to do, I said to myself."

It was clear that her soul's influence was now very weak, so weak that she thought it was probably sick. The negative thoughts and emotions had taken her over just as certainly as the virus causing the cold had recently taken over her body's cells. The effects were just as concrete and substantial as those of a viral illness. Her inability to control them was just like the failure of her immune system to effectively deactivate and eliminate the virus. It was real.

Venus had strong faith and pushed herself to think that there had to be a lesson in her difficulty. Like a modern-day spiritual scientist, she wanted to find the answer, even if it meant groping in the dark. She wanted to keep expanding the analogy that she had made in order to find as specific a solution to her problem as possible. "As I was thinking about my situation, I asked God to help me find the way to make this spiritual antibody," Venus said, knowing that an antibody is what our immune system manufactures to launch a counterattack against a virus. "To keep myself calm, I started cleaning and came across some notes in my desk from a lecture I had attended a year or so before. I picked them up and began to read them. One point leapt out at me immediately: Even if someone is hurting you, you should still wish them well. You should push yourself to think that either you deserved the treatment you were getting or you didn't. If you didn't deserve it, then God would take care of it. Why not wish these people I was fighting with well? I thought. At least this would transform me into a more positive person."

This became the clue to creating the antibody that Venus had been looking for. She had to neutralize the negative thoughts (the virus) by wishing the person well (making an antibody) instead of ill. Her positive thought would neutralize her angry, negative thoughts so that her normal way of thinking would return. The better she could do it, the better immunized she would be against an attack of similar negative thoughts in the future. Thinking in this way made what she was doing far more tangible and more important than thinking in purely psychological terms. She didn't want to be spiritually sick, and she wanted a concrete solution.

The next day, she took this new approach, saying to herself: What if I just try to find a way to bring something positive into this situation? How could I help this person or make him feel more comfortable? She realized that she had a choice. "I could be negative and defensive, or I could force myself to try to help each person," she said. "So that day, I forced myself to stay positive and to really help the people who annoyed me. Almost immediately, the situation was transformed. The people I had been so upset with are not even around me anymore! It turned out that I didn't have to work with them on that project any longer, and so I didn't see much of them. When I did happen to see them, I was much more positive, and they became positive toward me too. Everything is finished. It's all because I looked for the signs, put them together, and then thought about my intention and worked to improve the situation by acting in a way that I thought would make God more satisfied with me."

Initially, when I heard stories like Venus's, I wondered why she went through such a roundabout process to arrive at such a simple solution. Why didn't the source of her messages simply arrange for her to see the notes from the lecture on the first day she got annoyed with her coworkers instead of making her jump through so many hoops before she saw them? What did it want her to learn? Why couldn't she just realize from the beginning the importance of fighting off her anger and even wishing good for the person with whom she was angry? This seemed elementary. Drawing comparisons with the immune system didn't seem to add much to her solution.

Although Venus's laborious approach may not have changed what she finally did in that particular situation, it did change how seriously she took the incident and how she took responsibility for it. It also changed what she learned from it, for she was using analogies with the material world to organize her spiritual experiences in a systematic way. For example, this wasn't the only time she felt spiritually weak; it was one of many incidents. As in medicine, weakness can be caused by many different conditions. So, by carefully analyzing each of the times when she felt weak spiritually—by considering the different signs, symptoms, and treatments of each spiritual "illness" in relation to the systems of the body and the things that could go wrong with them—she would be able to distinguish different reasons why her soul might lose its customary power to assert itself.

We can see how, if this approach holds, it might help us sort, order, and categorize a wide range of dysfunctions in other people's spiritual lives in a way that adds to our own accumulated experience: from immaturity, as in Marinka's case, to developmental issues like spiritual ADD, and from transient malfunctions like Venus's to a more cancerous one I'll describe in the next chapter, in which a woman posed as a guru to take financial advantage of others. With experience, we can get to know if our soul is getting sick, if it is simply hungry and in need of its food, malnourished and in need of a spiritual "vitamin," or even poisoned and in need of aggressive detoxification.

By systematically using an analogy with the material world in general and medicine in particular to order, sort, and group our experiences into categories, we can hope to understand not just our own but each others' experiences better so that we can come up with more effective remedies for spiritual problems such as ADD that will be useful to people of all cultures and traditions. We will then understand better what to be alert, oriented, and ready to respond to in the future.

ॐ   ॐ   ॐ

This world is a classroom in which we learn. By taking an educational approach and upgrading our common sense, our sense of identity, and our knowledge of the world in a systematic way to take into account the implications of the lessons our messages are teaching us, we can become increasingly receptive to a wider range of messages and make faster progress. As we do, the material world and material knowledge cease to be obstacles to our religious faith and become the basis for analogies on which we build a more detailed understanding of the spiritual dimension.

This shift in attitude that comes as we gather evidence confirming the value of these adjustments enables us to be more attentive to spiritual feedback in our everyday experience that we might otherwise overlook. It puts us in a good position to learn from everything we do and gather enough information from our own and others' experiences to take on the next challenge, that of identifying more clearly what makes our thoughts, feelings, and actions reach beyond their material effects to engage the spiritual dimension.

꒳ ꒳ ꒳

Keys to Chapter 5

- Neuropsychological research has found that attention is made up of three interrelated sub-functions—alerting, orienting, and executive control. To refine your spiritual attention, you need to carefully educate yourself as to the spiritual value of the choices you make in everyday life under the watchful guidance of your messages.

- Although religious and spiritual beliefs often seem to exhort us to set aside common sense in order to assert our faith, messages generally encourage us to act in line with common sense. Sound common sense is far more important in decoding messages than your level of material education.

- To help you be more alert, oriented, and ready to respond to the elements in your messages that are most relevant to you, you can update your own personal story to give a central role to the lessons that your messages are teaching you and form your own idea of what your relationship with the source of your messages is like.
- By thinking of the soul as an infinitesimally small part of a spiritual ecosystem that is governed by its own set of rules, you can start to ask many interesting questions, draw analogies between the spiritual and the material world, and discover new ways to sort your spiritual experiences into more meaningful categories that will allow you to think more deeply and critically about the spiritual elements in your life.

ॐ   ॐ   ॐ

For Your Reflection

The challenge in this chapter is to clarify your basic strategy for getting your attention to be more alert, oriented, and ready to respond to the spiritual elements in everyday life.

1. My model of spiritual attention is based on the effects of spiritual messages in my everyday life and my understanding of neuropsychology. It encourages me to develop an educational strategy for the development of spiritual attention. Do you have a different definition of attention? Do you have a different strategy than the educational approach that I propose to improve spiritual attention? What experiences of your own verify the usefulness of your model?

2. I think that the better our common sense is in everyday life, the easier it becomes to focus on the spiritual benefits of our messages. Do you agree? How sound is your common sense in everyday life? Have you made the most of the opportunities available to you and realized your potential in your everyday life? Do you use common sense in your spiritual life by trying to think in line with the time-honored wisdom common to most spiritual traditions? Find several specific examples of what happens when you don't follow good spiritual common sense. If you lack common sense in any area of your life, consider carefully the advantages of developing it.

3. Go to decodeyourmessages.com to review other people's answers to these questions and the evidence on which they base their answers.

4. Take out a sheet of paper or turn to a blank page in your notebook and entitle it "How I Expand My Awareness." You can also go to decodeyourmessages.com to download these points for reflection or log into your online notebook. Write a brief paragraph that concisely summarizes what you do to be better prepared to hear what your messages might want to say. Frame your answer in as universal a way as possible, and identify the analogies with material life that underlie your approach, so that it will convey your conclusions to people with other belief systems. Then continue on and write as much detail as you'd like about the experiences that support your conclusions.

5. Go to decodeyourmessages.com to share the experiences related to spiritual attention that you believe might be useful to others.

CHAPTER 6

Entering the World
of Spiritual Intentions

M essages prove to us that the spiritual dimension is real and
relevant. But once we have glimpsed that reality and experienced its effects, how can we get it to be the center of our life and a
part of each decision that we make? As we saw in chapter 4, focusing on intense emotions or on exotic inner adventures to reveal a
secret shortcut can distract us from the work that needs doing in
classroom Earth. In chapter 5, we explored how we can refine our
attention to be generally more receptive to our messages. In this
chapter, I'll help you appreciate the central role spiritual intentions
play in consolidating your grasp of messages' lessons. In the next
two chapters, you'll see how you can act on this knowledge by
setting up a program of self-improvement that will help you bring
your thoughts, feelings, and actions more in line with the perspective of your messages.

To understand how important spiritual intentions are, first
you'll need to shift your attention away from the world of actions

and words to the world of ideas and values, for to act in a meaningful way—whether psychologically or spiritually—in a given situation, we need to have carefully prepared to do so beforehand. Of particular importance is a specific kind of thought—an intention. What is an intention? An intention is a commitment to act in a certain way under specific circumstances for a specific purpose. When we act on an intention and see the value in doing so, it becomes an integrated part of the executive functions of our attention, not just shaping our immediate response to a situation but determining what we are alert and oriented to as well.

There are three different kinds of intentions: *basic, meaningful,* and *spiritual.* Carlos Moya, a Spanish philosopher, wrote a book entitled *A Philosophy of Action* (Polity Press, Oxford, 1990) that helped me grasp the distinction between basic intentions and meaningful intentions. A monkey, for example, can perform a simple, deliberate action like raising an arm at an auction if it is conditioned to do so in response to a certain cue, but it isn't making a bid. It doesn't understand the meaning of this action. It can put its arm out of a car window as it's been taught to do in response to a different cue, but it isn't really signaling a turn. It doesn't understand the conventions of driving, and we certainly wouldn't want to set it free on the road. A monkey can form a lifelong bond with a partner and, as a result, treat its mate differently from every other monkey, but it can't plan to get married in six months. It can make simple plans and play tricks on other monkeys, but it doesn't have the brainpower to understand well enough what's going on in the minds of others so that it can make commitments and form intentions in the same meaningful way we do in our everyday life.

Although a monkey's actions aren't purely reflexive or instinctive, they are limited by the nature of its thinking. It can form only basic intentions that manifest as basic actions. To act the way it does in the above situations, it has to be prepared by training with appropriate rewards. Its real goal is the reward its trainer gives it for the action—a very basic reward of food, for example—and not the greater rewards that we seek by adhering to the set of conventions of our society.

To form a meaningful intention, we need to be able to take into account a whole system of meanings that govern how things work in our society. Children, adolescents, and some mentally challenged adults, for example, may understand quite a lot about how things work but still be unable to form the kind of meaningful intentions that are required to operate freely in the world of adults. We don't let a child sign a contract to buy a house because his commitment can't be considered meaningful (even if he has the money in a bank account under his name and wants that house) since we don't believe that he can protect his own interests adequately. Even if he can grasp certain elements of what's going on in situations (and sometimes vehemently argue that he *can* make a meaningful commitment), he doesn't yet grasp how things work as a whole well enough to participate in the more complex systems of conventions that govern our modern society.

This world of thoughts, meanings, and intentions creates a kind of virtual reality that we need to be able to function in if we are to live a normal life in our society. Reality in this world is the comprehensive set of rules that govern how things work in our society. To participate in this reality, we form a corresponding comprehensive set of intentions that commits us to acting in particular ways in relation to society's rules (even if we choose to knowingly defy them) in the hopes of enjoying a certain share of the benefits that the society offers.

Intentions are complex mental functions. We begin by forming a basic plan of how we want to act in a specific situation to accomplish a given goal. We then attach an appropriate emotional state so that we react the way we would like in that situation. Since nothing ever happens exactly as planned, our intention needs to be connected to our intelligence so that we can modify our plan based on the exact circumstances at the time we act on it.

Our attention and intentions need to work together very closely. Each time we form a firm commitment, it modifies what we are alert, oriented, and primed to do in the situation covered by that intention. Each time we act on that intention, we use the results to refine both our attention and intention further so that we are more attentive to the determining elements in the situation the next time and better prepared to act on our evaluation of those elements. If we are correct, our common sense gets better.

Our intentions are the smallest unit of our character and our common sense. When we act on an individual intention repeatedly in consistent ways, it becomes a part of our customary way of doing things—our character—and determines how we think about things—our common sense. As Professor Moya points out, our self is the sum total of our intentions. Our intentions are what *we* add to the circumstances of our life—things like our genes, instincts, upbringing, and environment—and thus they best define who we really are. They are the things we freely commit to doing, without any coercion. They determine what we pay attention to and what we choose to do. Psychology itself might be seen as a way of recognizing and correcting faulty intentions so that we can achieve our goals more effectively. By getting to know our intentions, we can change the way we think and act in an incremental way that is within our grasp to do.

Adding On Our Spiritual Intention

With this understanding of how important both basic and more meaningful material intentions are in coordinating every aspect of our everyday life, we can now turn to our spiritual intentions. Spiritual intentions are the specific *material* acts that we commit to doing under specific circumstances to realize a *spiritual* purpose. All progress in our spiritual development depends on our ability to form spiritual intentions and act on them.

The best way to learn how to form a spiritual intention is by committing to act in line with the recommendation of most religious and spiritual traditions to be ethical. You can then observe the results that you get and consider how they are different from what you would have seen if you had done the same action without a spiritual intention.

I only started realizing the importance of spiritual intentions after I was caught off guard in the subway in the incident I described in chapter 1. I had planned to give ten dollars to the first person who asked for money. But when a drunk urinating in the subway station demanded money from me, I just couldn't do it. Since giving money to the needy was obviously a good deed, I realized that something had to have been wrong with *the way* I had done it. The experience thus helped me form my first real spiritual intention, as I resolved to learn what kind of intention the source of my messages wanted me to act with. This was a serious intention in itself, for I acted on it and it has gradually led me to a better understanding of the central role of intentions in our spiritual life.

Spiritual intentions commit us to acting in specific ways in *material* situations for a *spiritual* purpose, so the better we formulate the basic and meaningful intentions on which our spiritual intention has to be built, the easier it will be for us to observe what our spiritual intention adds and thereby know how to refine it. It is useful to think, therefore, that the vast majority of our spiritual intentions need to work coherently with and build on the system of basic and meaningful intentions that govern our material choices and contribute to the forming of our common sense.

A typical example of the kind of results that come from acting with a sound spiritual intention in everyday life can be seen in the experience of Beth in chapter 2. Beth committed to going out and getting a job for mainly spiritual reasons. Without the spiritual motivation, she would not have done it. She took the exact steps that anyone with the same material goal would take in order to be successful, but she added on her spiritual intention. She was doing it because she believed that it was beneficial for her spiritual development not to be completely dependent on anyone other than God. Her financial dependence on her husband was undermining her own sense of personal competence, a quality that she knew she needed for not only her material well-being but her spiritual development as well. Her intention was a good one, and acting on it helped her become more effective in both identifying and taking into account the spiritual elements in her everyday choices.

Staying Grounded in Everyday Life

One mistake that people commonly make is that of confusing an intention with a wish. Although it's important to want to be more spiritual, sincerely and from the bottom of our hearts, it's not enough. An intention is only as reliable as the knowledge and experience on which it is based.

Jane's painful experience will underscore how important it is to know what goes into formulating a spiritual intention. Jane is a sincere and honest woman. In her twenties, she felt a powerful spiritual hunger. "At a point in my life where everything seemed meaningless," Jane told me, "I met a woman, a kind of guru, through a chance encounter with a friend I had known many years before. I was feeling desperate and believed that this chance encounter was the answer to my prayers. Everybody close to this woman adored her and accepted what she was telling them. I, too, wanted someone to adore and felt that I needed someone to tell me what to do. She would tell us: 'You have to live here. You have to work there. You have to give all your money to this spiritual cause and live with such and such a person.' Her directions were very specific. She said the underlying goal of this guidance was to help us work on detachment from money or anything material. To accept not having good clothes or a good job was hard for me, but I went along with it.

"We would just sit and meditate to put our minds at peace. At first, I felt uncomfortable sitting on the floor for hours and doing this. Since everybody around me was saying that you have to do this and it is good to do it, I thought that this was the price that all true believers should be ready to pay. I felt I had to do this so that my old self would die and my new self could awaken.

"In fact, one day, I concluded that continuing to live the way I was and trying to meditate for hours was like committing deliberate suicide. For me, it was nearly the same as real suicide because I was starting to think that I would completely lose my identity. I persisted, though. I tried to go as far as I could. I knew that spiritual progress required sacrifice, so I was determined to continue and to pass this frontier. I had no contact with the world or with any of my old friends. Even my parents didn't know what I was doing because I called them so rarely. Nobody knew what I was doing.

"I gave all my money to the leader and had nothing to live on, but I still had an apartment. When they found out that I owned it, they came to me and wanted me to sell it and give them the money. At around the same time, the would-be guru lost her mind and went into a mental hospital. I understood then that I had made a mistake. I realized they wanted my money and they wanted power over me. Only then did I see that I had to leave."

Forming a good spiritual intention involves knowing what both the material and the spiritual elements contribute to a situation. Jane wanted to develop spiritually so badly that she was willing to give up everything and endure great hardship. Yet she didn't know what to do, so she hoped that her sincerity and willingness to sacrifice everything would guarantee that God would help and guide her. For her, meeting this guru at a time of great spiritual longing was the answer to her prayers—a spiritual message—especially since other people confirmed how wonderful this guru was. She didn't notice anything wrong for a long time because many of the things she was told to do—such as to meditate and detach from material pleasure—were in line with her expectations. It took several long and difficult years in this cult for Jane to learn that she had made a mistake. Her sincerity had not been enough.

It's not that there is anything wrong with meditation or with following the advice of a more experienced person. However, as we have seen in several examples already, messages encourage us to be as responsible for our own choices as possible and *then* see the results as coming from the source of our messages. We are therefore better off mastering the fundamentals of spiritual attention and intentions in smaller actions, like helping others, before making such a big leap of faith.

Jane would have done better to use her common sense to evaluate her guru with the same rigor she would have used to decide which job to take or which car to buy. Her sincerity, however, did have some value. It helped her correct her error when she realized that she had made one. Jane returned to her spiritual roots—in her case, to Catholicism—and gradually learned to decode the spiritual messages in her everyday life. She is doing well today and thinks of her experience as a painful but important lesson that opened her eyes.

One of my mantras goes like this: If Jane can make this mistake, what equivalent mistake would I make? I have to repeat it fairly often, because it is easy to see the mistakes of others and feel in some way superior. Most of us are unlikely to make the exact same mistake that Jane did, but it's not hard to imagine that our spiritual beliefs might in some way lead us to step outside the norms of the society we live in and surrender our common sense. I know that I have a tendency in this direction. So to set a secure base for my intentions and to lessen the chance of making the kind of error that Jane made, I add my spiritual intention to a sound material intention by looking to

- society to provide laws, customs, and social order,
- medicine to help me keep my body healthy,

- science and technology to make my life ever more comfortable and interesting,
- psychology to solve everyday problems, create emotional balance, and fulfill my potential,
- the entertainment industry to amuse me, and
- spiritual experts to help me make my every action consistent with my spiritual purpose.

By approaching situations in this way, we take away the confusion between the material aspects of our intention and the spiritual aspects. The more we focus on improving our attention and intentions, the more we see how hard it is to not treat the material elements as if they were the spiritual elements. For example, most spiritual traditions will say that it isn't the material size of what we do, but the quality of our attention and intentions, that is important. Compare a very rich person giving a billion dollars to help millions of people to a poor person who gives the same percentage of his savings, perhaps $100, to help one needy relative: The billion dollars certainly has greater material value, but we can't know which has greater spiritual value. Since the amount of money given in both cases is proportional, all else being equal, both acts are likely to reflect similar intentions to help others and express similar qualities of character in the givers' different circumstances. Because we can get so tied up in trying to make the most heroic material efforts to the neglect of the spiritual elements, we do far better separating them as I have suggested here.

We find another precedent for making this kind of distinction between material and spiritual elements in the separation of church and state. In society, these two spheres of life have different goals, so when they remain separate, both work better. Having sincere and strong faith does not excuse us from adhering to the laws and customs that govern material life. This is why I recommend adding the strictly spiritual elements of your intention onto a sound material intention, particularly when you are first learning how to form a spiritual intention. You'll end up with choices that reflect good spiritual common sense.

Shifting the Balance

If having a sound material plan is the first thing we need to do to form a spiritual intention, then the second is to make our goal as spiritual as possible. It can be hard in the beginning to know what makes an intention spiritual, but it's fairly easy to see what makes it material. So, by decreasing the part of our intention that serves purely material goals and doing actions that most spiritual traditions generally deem good, we shift the balance of our intention toward the spiritual.

One of the most useful rules of thumb I have found is that the more we seek the approval of others, the weaker our spiritual intention is. In the past, in order to keep from acting for others' approval, some spiritually oriented people took extreme measures, such as living in complete isolation in caves. While that may have been appropriate in the past, messages today do not seem to recommend this kind of extreme action very often. They teach us instead the benefit of living a regular life *and* at the same time significantly reducing how much we look to others for approval. There are countless ways to decrease our reliance on the approval of others while doing simple acts encouraged by all religions. Everyday life thus offers us many opportunities to learn how to improve the quality of our spiritual intentions.

My wife, Susan, had a breakthrough in this area when a message helped her understand the importance of not seeking to please other people in a simple, everyday situation. Susan and I have been married for twenty years, and if there is one word that describes what I love in her, it's her sweetness. One day, she decided to watch out for a small opportunity to help other people by acting in a way she thought God would want her to act. A few hours after she made that decision, she was sitting on a crowded Manhattan bus when a woman got on who appeared to be very pregnant. My wife remembered her intention to help others. "You shouldn't have to stand up when you're pregnant," she said sweetly, offering the woman her seat. The woman stared at my wife, infuriated. She was not pregnant—just overweight. At the top of her voice, as the crowded bus lurched from stop to stop, she stood over Susan and berated her for her insensitivity to "fat people."

Completely embarrassed, Susan hurried off the bus a few stops later, where I was waiting for her. When she told me her story, I laughed. (Things like this can be funny when they're not happening to you.) I reminded her of the spiritual principle that says the universe throws obstacles in our way to test our sincerity—to see if we are acting to satisfy God or if we are acting to impress other people and get their attention, gratitude, and praise. If we are truly acting with a spiritual intention and the action itself is a good one, we should and will continue to act on that intention, no matter what happens. If instead we are acting for self-centered reasons, we are more likely to get annoyed and not finish what we intended to do.

Susan then recalled a story from a friend of ours who had endured something far worse than she (and the poor woman whom Susan mistakenly thought pregnant) had. Our friend had given money to a needy person and been stunned when he spat in her face. There are a lot of panhandlers in New York, and, just a few blocks later, someone else asked her for money. She forced herself to give him exactly what she had given the last person in order to assert that she was doing this small act of charity as a spiritual duty. In other words, our friend wasn't giving the money just to prove to herself what a good person she was or to enjoy the recipient's gratitude. She was giving money to the poor because she felt that it was a good deed and God would be pleased.

Our friend's story helped us remember that people are often ungrateful and insulting when we try to help them, but that is not what matters in the world of spiritual intentions. What matters is that we're doing it because we consider it right to do. That doesn't mean that we should absorb abuse, but in clearly delineated situations like this that seem to be tests of our intention, it's better to continue with our plan despite what has happened. (This is not a formula, however; in another situation, the better thing might be to find a policeman.)

Two hours later, with this story in our minds, we caught a bus going uptown. The bus was crowded and only Susan could sit. At the next stop, a woman with a very round belly got on the bus and stood near her. Susan and I looked at each other and grinned. The woman sure looked pregnant. Susan cringed a little, but stood to offer the woman her seat. This time, she was greeted with warm thanks.

In that moment, Susan saw the spiritual dimension at work. She felt a little burst of spiritual energy as the last piece of the message she was receiving fell into place. That burst of energy changed her perception of herself and the world around her. She described the shift like this: "The spiritual dimension was showing me which of my many weaknesses to work on—that of wanting other people's 'bravos' for being good."

Susan's message had delivered a lesson on intention that helped her see that she was in the habit of looking for other people's approval too much. Like all messages, it involved a material situation (the incident with the seemingly pregnant woman on a bus), a psychological state (her preparedness to offer her seat again to assert that her intention was to satisfy God), an unexpected external event (another chance to offer her seat to another woman who seemed to be pregnant), and an inner spiritual impact (the awareness that the universe had given her an opportunity to improve her intention and that she had done well).

It wasn't that Susan had formed a conscious intention to please other people. In her mind, she was offering the seat because she thought it was a spiritual duty to be more considerate of others.

Yet her character was so naturally oriented to being a good social animal and seeking the approval of others that it automatically colored her intention. She could see it in her reaction to the woman's berating her.

Our intentions will probably never be 100 percent spiritual. We are bi-dimensional beings invested in both our material and our spiritual well-being. For most of us, it is a part of our nature to seek the approval of one or another subgroup of society. It lends substance to our sense of identity. We need to be sensitive to the reactions of others while holding on to our values. We need to be aware that we can make mistakes, and we need to use others' reactions to trigger a reexamination of the evidence on which we've based our decisions. We can make significant progress in refining our intention by constantly trying to decrease the part of our motivation that comes from seeking approval and increase the part of our motivation that comes from doing what we see as being "right" for spiritual reasons.

A correct intention attracts spiritual energy that may not be strong enough to register as a message but affects you nonetheless. You'll know you have gotten the spiritual part of your intention right if you notice a subtle influx of spiritual energy making you more alert, oriented, or ready to respond to the spiritual elements in that situation. It will warm your heart and keep you motivated to act in line with the beliefs common to all religions, while at the same time providing information that will help you further refine your intention and reprogram the executive-control function of your attention to take into account what you've learned in the future.

Moving from Obeying to Understanding

Once we have set our intention on a sound material plan and tried to decrease the strength of our material motives for doing an action that our tradition deems good, what else can we do to make our action spiritual? We can bear in mind that each intention is spiritually meaningful only insofar as it is a part of a system of intentions that work together to bring us toward our spiritual goal. Our individual intentions set specific goals for specific actions, but our system of intentions contains a *core* intention that expresses the goal of all those individual intentions. On the material level, we might think of our core intention as to have a "satisfying" life, defined in the terms we alone can choose.

An interest in spirituality changes what most of us perceive a satisfying life to be. All my life, I had heard people say that the best intention is doing something "for God's satisfaction." Whenever I heard that idea, it revolted me. Not only was it so vague that it seemed to justify people doing whatever they wanted, but it seemed to imply that God had nothing better to do than to watch each of us doing our good little deeds and be satisfied with us, or to watch us being selfish and get upset. It made him into a rather unfortunate and pathetic figure in my mind.

This phrase kept bothering me until a few years ago. While I was working on a draft of this chapter, I had to go out of town. On the way to the airport, my mind was occupied with many thoughts about the journey—the taxi meter ticking away as we made our way through New York City traffic, my hoping to get a seat with extra leg room because I'm six-feet five-inches tall, and what I would do when my plane landed. These little worries went round and round in my mind without leading anywhere. They became boring after a few rounds because I couldn't really do anything about any of them at that moment. Trying to find something to do with my time that would better reflect my core intention—which had now boiled down to the level of "finish this book"—I began to think about what it really meant to "satisfy God" so that I could incorporate it into this chapter once I was comfortably seated on the plane.

After about five minutes of reflecting on the word *satisfy*, I suddenly had a breakthrough. I realized that I could think about "satisfying" God in the same way we use the word when we're talking about trying to meet the conditions for completing an assignment, a course, or a degree in school. As students, we *satisfy* our school's requirements for receiving a diploma. As spiritual students, we *satisfy* God's requirements by decoding and learning the lessons our messages deliver, completing the assignments in our own life, and developing the everyday virtues they encourage. When we are doing these things, we are "satisfying" whoever (or whatever) is behind our messages. Like a good teacher, this source knows what we need to learn next better than we do. If we don't accept and complete our assignments in the order given, we are no more likely to reach our goal than a university student who spends his time partying, taking only courses that interest him, or handing in only the assignments that he deems worthwhile to do.

As if to emphasize the significance of this new understanding, I suddenly realized that I didn't have my passport. I could see in my mind exactly where I had left it. We were only halfway to the airport, so we turned back. I easily retrieved the passport and made it to the airport on time, where I was given my extra-leg-room seat.

This little reframing of what it means to "satisfy" God shifted the emphasis in my intentions from *obeying* to *understanding*. Satisfying the requirements for spiritual advancement was more about forming meaningful spiritual intentions based on an understanding of what was required in the schoolroom of everyday life than it was about pleasing some lofty figure who lived in another domain far removed from my life. Of course, I couldn't understand the goal that I was moving toward in any meaningful terms, as I had been trying to do. I could, however, based on what I had already learned, have faith in the spiritual system that I was engaging in everyday life.

In this light, I can now consider seeking God's satisfaction to be my core intention, for it encompasses all of my other intentions. Yet this intention is made meaningful only by acting on it and doing assignments one at a time. As with our individual intentions, our core intention is unlikely to be 100 percent spiritual. Yet the more spiritual it becomes, the more we feel a greater stability and warmth inside of us, as if we are more firmly connected to the source of our messages and experiencing a more constant flow of spiritual energy that makes it easier to keep our spiritual priorities in mind.

ॐ ॐ ॐ

I cannot overemphasize how important intentions are—both psychologically and spiritually. They commit us to thinking, feeling, and acting in certain ways in particular situations for specific reasons. They are the most basic unit of our character and common sense. They express who we are. Once we appreciate the value of our individual intentions and are convinced that a sound spiritual intention is based on a sound material intention, we can make plans to improve ourselves both materially and spiritually, one intention at a time. As we get to know our intentions better, we will be able to decode the feedback of our messages better as well, for they always contain a comment on the nature of our intention.

To be sure that we are learning the fundamentals about forming spiritual intentions correctly, it's prudent to start with those intentions and actions that are praised by humanistic and religious traditions alike—being kinder, more compassionate, more courageous, or more perseverant. In the next two chapters, I will walk you through the details of how to form the kind of sound spiritual intentions that will help you more effectively engage the spiritual dimension in your everyday life.

ॐ ॐ ॐ

Keys to Chapter 6

- A spiritual intention is a commitment to act in a certain way under particular circumstances for a specific spiritual purpose.

- We live in a material world and our spiritual intentions need to take into account how things work here. To form the best spiritual intentions, it's wise to do the same thing that we do in separating church from state: look to material authorities for basic guidance as to what material actions to take while turning to spiritual authorities for guidance in how to transform them into spiritual actions.
- In forming a good spiritual intention, being sincerely willing to sacrifice everything for the sake of God isn't enough. You need to base your intentions on accurate knowledge of what is spiritually important.
- The more you seek other people's approval in whatever you do, the weaker your spiritual intention is likely to be.
- Many people talk about "satisfying God" as the measure of whether they are acting with a spiritual intention. As a student, you sought to satisfy your school's requirements to be able to call yourself qualified in your chosen field. As a spiritual student, you can similarly seek to "satisfy" God's requirements. Thinking this way will shift your purpose from obedience to understanding in everything you do.

ॐ   ॐ   ॐ

For Your Reflection

What makes something that you think, feel, or do spiritual? As you know by now, to me, more than the thought, feeling, or action itself, it's the intention that gave rise to it. To prepare yourself to improve the quality of your intentions (or whatever element *you* find most important in making something spiritual) in the next two chapters, think about the following points:

1. In making a sound spiritual intention, we commit to doing *material* actions under specific circumstances for a *spiritual* purpose. To see how well you form the material intentions on which your spiritual intentions are based, examine carefully how well you achieve your material goals. How well do you take advantage of the opportunities available to you? How satisfying are your relationships? How productive are you at work? How much do you enjoy your leisure time? All of these reflect your ability to plan and commit to goals.

2. What do you think makes an action spiritual? How would you evaluate the effectiveness of your spiritual intentions (or the factor you think is most important) in taking you closer to your spiritual goal? Have you had any messages that confirm or dispute the effectiveness of your spiritual intentions?

3. Go to decodeyourmessages.com to find out how important intentions are to others and what they believe makes their thoughts, feelings, and actions spiritual.

4. Take out a sheet of paper or turn to a blank page in your notebook and entitle it "My Spiritual Intentions." You can also download these points for reflection to your computer or log into your online notebook. Write a summary paragraph on the factors that you consider the most important in making a thought, feeling, or action spiritual. Then continue writing as much as you like about the experiences that helped you come to this understanding and the things that you have done to try to improve your intention.

5. Go to decodeyourmessages.com to add the messages and lessons you have received about your intentions to the ones in this chapter.

CHAPTER 7

Putting Theory
into Practice

Spiritual messages warm our hearts, increase our faith, and change our vision of life. In those moments of clarity, we feel more peaceful, benevolent, and optimistic, inspired to live in line with their wisdom. Yet because of our spiritual ADD, we all too easily forget those moments of inspiration and once again become so absorbed in our everyday affairs that we completely lose sight of the spiritual elements in what we are doing. We live, despite all of our convictions, very much as we would if there were no spiritual dimension to our life.

With a sound understanding of the theory of what makes something spiritual, it's time to start pushing ourselves more toward action. Theory without practice gets us nowhere, and practice not based on correct theory can do us more harm than good. So once you have a solid grasp of what your messages are encouraging you to do, it's time to act on what you have learned.

The most obvious way of getting yourself in gear is by *regularly* using a practice recommended by your own tradition, but rather than doing it as an act of devotion, approaching it as a kind of spiritual experiment that will prove the value of your belief. For example, you might regularly seek help with the problems you are facing through prayer. You can view whatever happens next as a response to your request, decode it as you would any other message, and add what you learn to your other experiences.

The goal in setting up an experiment is to systematically study how variations in your attention and your intentions influence the responses that you get. So a good place to start is by identifying the part of your attention and intentions that is psychological—oriented toward gaining a better material life in one form or another—and the part that is spiritual—oriented toward getting advice from the source of your messages *and* following it. As we are at all times both material and spiritual beings living in a world that is both material and spiritual, carefully constructed experiments that help us reliably identify these different elements in different situations can lead to the beginnings of spiritual self-knowledge.

Katherine prays by having an intimate conversation with the source of her messages about whatever she is planning to do. "I was going to visit my mom to help her move, and I had reserved a plane ticket," she told me. "I would be leaving on a Friday and had to be back by Tuesday. I had a spiritual intention in doing this. I was forcing myself to make this trip because I have a difficult relationship with my mother and I saw it as my duty to help her. As the time approached, though, I began to have a strong feeling not to go. But I had already told my mother that I was coming, and I thought it would break her heart if I didn't.

"I started to wonder if this feeling not to go was coming from God or from my own desire not to go, so I started talking to him aloud, as I often do. I said: 'You don't want me to go? I thought you would want me to go on this trip because it's such a good thing to do, particularly since I don't get along very well with my mom.' I knew from experience that I couldn't trust my feelings in situations where I really did not want to do something, so I decided to go ahead with my plans despite my feelings.

"I had to buy the ticket that I had booked on Thursday by five o'clock, but when five o'clock on Thursday came, I couldn't get through on the phone. I was wondering, Maybe you don't want me to do this, God? Then I said, 'This is it! You have to give me a sign whether I should go or not, because I still have these strong feelings not to go. Should I go? Do you want me to go or don't you? Keep on giving me signs.'

"Finally, at eight o'clock, I got through and the airline agent said, 'No problem.' I was confirming the flights when the agent said, 'We don't fly on Tuesdays, ma'am.' I told him that I had already booked the flight to leave on Friday and return on Tuesday. 'Maybe the return is with another airline,' I suggested. He just repeated, 'We don't fly on Tuesdays.'

"So that was it. I didn't buy the ticket. It's all because I had this contract with God and I had said, 'If you want me to go, help me to do it. If not, then block it.' Sometimes my signs are *very* clear."

Katherine had such conversations with God regularly. Instead of talking decisions over with herself in her own mind, she talked them over with God and believed that whatever happened next was a direct answer to her prayer, which she would decode like any other message. As a result, she received messages specifically targeted to her concern at a given time. Katherine's problem with her tickets was not very unusual, but because she had put so many matters in God's hands and gotten so many responses, she felt certain that this mess-up was an answer to her prayer, a spiritual message with an external manifestation (no ticket) and an inner impact (the feeling that she had received a definitive answer to her prayer). For her, it was a meaningful connection. It was just as clear as if she had heard a voice saying, "Don't go!"

For the experience to have any significant impact on her, however, Katherine would have to extract a lesson from it by figuring out the reason *why* she had come to one conclusion, to visit her mother, and the source of her messages had come to the opposite conclusion. If she could, then she would be able to reformulate her intentions for similar situations to give more weight to that aspect of things in the future. By acting on this intention again and seeing the results from that action, she would become ever more alert, oriented, and ready to engage the spiritual elements in future situations.

To try to get the clearest possible idea of where she had gone wrong, Katherine reviewed the material elements in her material decision to go. She had considered things like how much her mother actually needed her at a time when she had so many other pressing things to do and how much money it would cost to take the trip at a time when her funds were tight. If she had based her decision on these factors alone, she would have decided not to go.

Katherine, however, had been raised with the same spiritual dictum that many of us grew up with: "Honor thy father and thy mother." She had thought that acting on this principle was more important in this situation than the purely material factors she had been weighing. She concluded that her inability to make the flight probably meant that planning to honor her mother did not (in this particular case) outweigh the fact that she was acting against her own interests. She decided that her experience was encouraging her to form spiritual intentions that would make her pause to consider giving greater weight to a situation's material elements in the future.

Was there something else wrong with the quality of her intention, or was it just that she had not balanced the considerations correctly? She questioned herself carefully. Did she want to help her mother mainly to satisfy God or to gain her mother's love? Was she just doing it so that she could look good in her own eyes? Was she really ready to accept either course of action or was she looking for a way to wiggle out of something she didn't want to do? Had she really done her best to solve her situation on her own, or did she unfairly shift the ball into God's court?

She felt that the quality of the spiritual part of her intention had been good in these regards, but to make sure, she reviewed other feedback she had received. Based on her past experiences, she had developed a schema to interpret her feedback. If something had been more deeply wrong with her spiritual intention, there most likely would have been some hardship for her in the situation. She might have missed her flight and lost her money, or she might have made the trip and had a falling out with her mother. Since she received a lesson that corrected her decision and didn't entail any hardship but actually made things easier for her, it was more likely that the main point of the message had been that she hadn't given enough weight to her own material interests. She would be more alert to them in her future decisions.

After Katherine told me her story and her analysis of it, I asked her the question that's never far from my thoughts: "Why was she so sure that this incident was spiritual at all, something to be thought about so carefully, and not simply some fantasy she had imagined?" "It's because in this kind of transaction, there is always a signature," she answered. "In this case, my mom's reaction was proof that God didn't want me to go. My mom usually gets disappointed very easily, but when I called her and told her about my feeling and the confusion over the tickets, she said, 'Oh honey, I've sometimes had the same kind of feeling.' She was so understanding."

A *signature* is the confirmation that we have correctly interpreted a message. Each of us will recognize this signature in a different way because each of us has a different relationship with the source of our messages. It is up to us to learn to recognize the signature so that we have an additional basis on which to confirm that we have interpreted a message correctly. It requires us to develop our own relationship, and that's why we have to carefully analyze what happens to us on a regular basis through a regular practice in order to learn what that signature looks like in subtle instances such as this.

Another way of confirming our approach is by seeing the

overall benefits in consistently analyzing our experiences in this way. So, I asked Katherine whether this approach had made her more superstitious or improved her life in some recognizable way. "By thinking that God's in charge, I don't get angry and bent out of shape like I used to when something doesn't go the way I think it should, like not getting the tickets that I was sure I had reserved," she said. "Even though I don't always understand why things happen the way they do, if I just remember that God's in charge, I soon feel much more peaceful and secure."

The more clearly we see the differences that our spiritual perspective makes in the outcome of everyday events, the more inclined we will be to notice those factors and take them into account in the future. That's why it's important to think about your experiences and draw your best conclusions as to what you have learned from any given experience. If you do this, over time, your experiences will have a more meaningful effect on the way you act.

By approaching the spiritual practice of your choice as Katherine did her intimate conversation with God—in a systematic, experimental way—you can increase your understanding of the spiritual forces at work in your life and strengthen your intentions. Just as we develop our potentials and grow psychologically through our encounters with the material reality around us, so we develop our spiritual potentials and grow spiritually by gaining a greater understanding of our relationship with the source of our messages. All it takes is getting used to observing the feedback you get, asking *why* you get the results you do, and finding different ways to validate or disprove your conclusions so that you do better each time.

Setting a Practice

The most certain way of strengthening your spiritual character is by developing more of virtues that are praised by all religious and spiritual traditions—kindness, diligence, honesty, humility, and courage—but, as we've said, doing it with the mentality of a student determined to discover *why* it is valuable to cultivate these virtues. My practically minded friend Michael explained to me why he believes that small actions taken with a spiritual intention to be slightly more virtuous over extended periods of time are most beneficial. It's for much the same reason that scientists craft small experiments to prove their theories. When you want to be sure that you are actually developing spiritual attention and intentions, you want to do so in a careful and deliberate way, as it is often so difficult to discern our psychological motivations and results from our spiritual ones.

"I've come to see that if you have an intention to help others more and you say to yourself that you will *always* try to help other people, you will be doomed," Michael told me, "because it is not possible. You need to be specific and choose to do something that is actually possible for you to do to improve yourself. For example, if you want to be more honest, you should not think I'll never lie, but you should try not to lie in specific situations or at least not to lie to particular persons, such as your parents or partner."

That's the program Michael set himself to do—to make small, repeated efforts over time to act on his intention until it became a part of his character to be a little more honest in a particular situation. I asked Michael how he knew that he was making progress. "Before I started working on being more honest," he said, "if I lied, I would never think about what I had done again. But now, if I lie, the incident comes to my mind again and again. If I did something wrong before, it just didn't bother me, even when I thought about it again. But now very minor things keep coming to mind, and I ask myself whether I did the right thing or not. As a result, I've become more careful about my relations with other people." This is an example of the kind of realistic, incremental change that comes from acting with good, meaningful intentions. It represents a real change in character, not a superficial change.

I believe Michael's (or anyone's) conscience would have become more sensitive in this way even if he had been trying to be more honest for sincere psychological rather than spiritual reasons; however, by acting with a spiritual intention and approaching it as an experiment instead of an act of devotion, he came to understand more deeply spiritual matters that were not directly related to his efforts and see that they had in fact come from his efforts. That's because his efforts to be more honest had changed his character ever so slightly, and therefore he saw things slightly differently in a way that was consistent with other changes that he saw from other similar efforts.

He gave me the following example of the kind of effects that he noticed. "I like to read spiritual books like the Bible, the Koran, or Buddhist scriptures and build what I'm working on around what I read," he explained. "I knew that I was developing spiritually because I saw that when I reread a passage I had read six months earlier, I would understand something that I hadn't understood before. And I could see the same thing happening in my everyday life. I would face a certain situation and see it in one way. When I found myself in a similar situation six months later, I understood more clearly what it was trying to tell me about my own spiritual life. This was a sign for me that the small actions that I was undertaking to improve myself were actually leading me to develop spiritually."

Understanding results not from the kind of dispassionate analysis a computer might make, but from an analysis of a situation's relevance to us. As we develop our potential and our character improves in line with the time-honored wisdom common to all religions, we see things differently. The more important the trait we are intending to develop in our character, the greater its impact will be on us. In the same way that Michael's conscience improved in all areas through his efforts to be more honest, so his spiritual attention also improved across the board because he made these efforts with a spiritual intention. It's not magic, but the result of an improvement in one aspect of his character resulting in an overall change in his way of viewing life. It's the same kind of change others have reported.

Why such little steps? Because changing our habitual way of doing things is a difficult task. If we try to make too big a change in ourselves, it often leads to less real change in our character than we could achieve through small, persistent, well-chosen efforts that are in our power to make, as Michael did. Just as scientists conduct small reproducible experiments to prove larger and more interesting theories, so we ground our own understanding best in small actions done with a similar experimental mindset. Material logic leads us to aspire to great action to achieve our lofty goal of spiritual development. When you clearly see in your own life the positive results from making the kind of small effort that Michael made, you will understand why you don't have to make great changes in your behavior to develop spiritually.

Overcoming Resistance

We don't always get the kind of straightforward results that Michael and Katherine did from acting with a good spiritual intention. Sometimes we don't notice anything. Sometimes we may even arouse resistance, because we are programmed to resist change—even change that we think is beneficial to us. You'll see this any time you try to change your normal way of doing something, one of your habits. We'll consider later on, in chapter 10, the kind of resistance to change that is specific to our acting in line with our spiritual principles. Here, let's simply consider how to deal with the resistance to change that occurs whenever we set out to improve ourselves, whether for psychological or for spiritual reasons. As you learn more about the nature of your spiritual intention and what makes it different from a psychological intention, you will become increasingly adept at adapting the evidence-based strategies of psychology for dealing with resistance to your spiritual intentions.

So when you are not making the kind of progress you would like or have run into a brick wall that seems to block your path, don't be discouraged. It's time to draw upon the systematic approaches of psychology to deal with the resistance that's holding you back.

In this spirit, I'll briefly introduce you to (or, if you're familiar with it, remind you of) one of the hallmark techniques of psychology, cognitive-behavioral therapy (CBT). Cognitive-behavioral therapy is the best-researched model in psychotherapy and the basis of most self-help books. It offers a set of techniques that people use to solve all kinds of problems. It is less concerned with probing the origins of a problem and more concerned with correcting the dysfunctional thoughts and beliefs that stop us from acting in our own best interests. It pays particular attention to recognizing and correcting our misperceptions of the feedback of reality in certain situations. So, its approach becomes very useful in helping us correct any of the mistakes we might make in decoding the feedback of spiritual reality—our messages. In the pages ahead, I'll give you a brief sketch of how CBT approaches a problem. Then, in the rest of the chapter, I'll show you how you can use CBT's approach to overcome your own resistance to acting in line with your messages.

To understand a little more about CBT's basic methods, imagine a person who gets extremely anxious in ordinary social situations. The first step in treatment is helping a person who may feel (by the time he comes for help) that his situation is hopeless to realize that there is a name for his problem—*social phobia*—and a cure for his suffering—CBT. Since other people have overcome this problem by following the methods of CBT, there is no reason why he can't do so too.

The second step is to help the person to recognize that perhaps his anxiety blocks him from seeing the reality of what is really going on in social situations. He feels so anxious for no visible reason (like the other person pointing a gun at him) that he can only explain his extreme anxiety—and the feeling of stupidity that comes with it—by assuming that the other person thinks he is a complete jerk. Why else would he feel like such a jerk? He can't consider other possibilities, and everything he experiences confirms this false belief: No one seeks him out and talks to him. As he is anxious in all social settings, he soon believes that *everyone* sees him as a jerk *all* the time. The therapist encourages him to accept that perhaps he is overreacting to elements in his situation, pointing out that other people who were as anxious as he is found themselves to be wrong when they examined their beliefs more carefully.

To appreciate how a person's severe anxiety can combine with an erroneous belief to make him misinterpret the realities of his situation in an overly negative way, let's compare his reactions to those of someone else who doesn't have severe anxiety. Say our man with social anxiety goes to a party, sees an attractive woman, and summons up all of his courage to approach her: "Hi. It's a nice party, isn't it?" "Yes," she says, but looks away. He is so overwhelmed by anxiety and self-criticism that he slinks off into a corner, feeling humiliated in front of everyone. Someone without social anxiety, on the other hand, would pause, perhaps ask a few more questions, continue trying to engage the woman in a conversation, and maybe end up with a dinner date for the next week.

The different outcomes stem from the fact that the person with social anxiety has dysfunctional beliefs that cause him to misinterpret situations in line with his extreme anxiety. His belief is that he is a jerk and everyone can see it. His certainty of this stops him from being able to consider other possible interpretations for his reactions. It stops him from being able to seriously consider his friends' reassurances that he is not a jerk, an idiot, or unattractive, which just leave him feeling more self-pity than ever: Even his friends have to lie to him! He is a prisoner of his emotions and misperceptions. He feels so bad that he is willing to consider anything.

So he accepts the therapist's challenge to gather his own evidence to see whether he may be interpreting situations incorrectly.

In a third step, CBT helps him set up an experiment to gather his own evidence and examine the validity of his conclusions. He exposes himself to a situation in which he feels anxiety, but at a level that he can tolerate without running away immediately. Before entering that situation, he must be prepared to do something different that will test his belief, such as not walking away instantly but forcing himself to stay and ask the woman at the party where she was from or how she knows the host. He has practiced this with the therapist, or with friends or family members, working on making eye contact and smiling. If he has structured his plan right and had enough practice beforehand, it will work, as it has worked for everyone who will stick with the process long enough, because no one is as much of a jerk as a person with social anxiety believes himself to be.

This is just the bare-bones structure of CBT. If you want to know more about how it works, you can buy a self-help book that speaks to some tendency you have, such as anxiety, fear, depression, anger, communication problems, relationship problems, or work problems. It will help you define a systematic psychological method of uncovering and challenging the self-defeating beliefs that hold you back from fully realizing your potential in that area.

If some other psychological approach appeals to you more, you can use that as the basis for a self-improvement program that will help you get to know your resistance better and use the knowledge for your spiritual advancement. I find that CBT, which has the least theory and looks the most like common sense, is the easiest approach to adapt to our spiritual intentions. What is most important, from my point of view, is to apply an approach to self-improvement similar to the one you use in everyday life, much as I've suggested using analogies to your best understanding of how things work in the material world (such as attention deficit disorder or the immune system) to integrate your spiritual and material understanding. When you do, spirituality will fit more naturally into your approach to everyday life.

Toward a Spiritual Psychology

Spiritually, we too are prisoners of our own misperceptions. Much as we would like to change our way of thinking, we can only think inside the box of the material world. However, there is hope. If others like you have been able to overcome or effectively compensate for their spiritual ADD, why can't you?

By detecting and decoding some messages, you have already done most of the first two steps of CBT. You have realized that messages are there to give you the kind of feedback that you need to help and guide you. Now we'll look more closely at how to adapt the systematic approach of CBT to our program for spiritual self-improvement. The key to this approach is setting up your own experiments to observe more carefully what happens when you try to act with your best spiritual intention in ways that others, like Katherine and Michael, have found to promote spiritual development. If you get the kind of satisfying results that they did, all is well. You can just continue using common sense. If you don't get the kind of results you believe you should, the knowledge of CBT will help you identify and deal with the most common blocks that get in the way of positive results.

Linda, a fifty-two-year-old psychologist, is just as scientific as I am, and we have discussed her experiences together in some detail. She came up with a plan similar to Michael's following a motivating experience. I will use her story to show how to draw out into the open the thoughts that keep us from taking the spiritual dimension into account.

"My friend was very sick and I went to visit her," Linda explained. "Even in her state of pain from a serious illness, she was concerned about my comfort, asking her helper if I had a good bed and if she had made me my favorite cookies. When other guests arrived, she did not try to instruct them from her vast store of knowledge but was simply kind to them. Her actions were natural, not a show. When I asked her about this, she told me that being polite and kind is one of the pillars of spiritual life. She said that we shouldn't think that spirituality is all about high-sounding ideas."

Linda had heard this idea before, but on that day it had a strong impact on her. She took her friend's words as a sign that she needed to work on being more polite and considerate of others. And although she was already polite and considerate compared to the average person, she had a long way to go compared to her friend.

She knew that she needed a well-thought-out plan because, though she was inspired by her friend's example, it would be easy for her to "forget" her intention to be more polite and slide back into her old ways. She wasn't like Michael, who could keep working consistently on not lying. Her lack of follow-through often prevented her from making the progress she thought she should.

In accordance with the fundamentals of CBT, Linda created a systematic, common-sense plan that started with doing one very simple thing a day that she ordinarily wouldn't do, like getting coffee for someone at work who was busy or simply greeting a coworker she used to ignore. If she didn't get the chance to be more polite and considerate at work, she would try to create an opportunity in the street by holding open a door for someone or smiling on the elevator, since she didn't customarily do either of these things. If she didn't find an opportunity there, that evening she would call someone she would not normally call, just to see how that person was doing.

These things might be easy to do for a few days or a week. However, understanding the nature of change, Linda intended to do them daily for three months. Just thinking about that time frame started the inner rebellion that would ordinarily have stopped her. Her reaction made it very clear that her real problem was not that she wasn't polite enough, but that she had a too lackadaisical attitude toward spiritual life in general, as if she could not expect more from someone like herself. Now she wanted to challenge this belief and see if she could do better.

Prepared for resistance, Linda would now be on the lookout for the thoughts that might stop her from being more considerate of others. She would do her best to be more polite each day, but she would focus more of her attention on recognizing any thoughts that came to her mind that suggested she really didn't have to do what she had committed to doing. She shifted her focus from *her actions* to *her reasons for doing them* and thus to the quality of her spiritual intentions. As she did so, her task took on greater value. It was no longer about just being polite. She was using the situation to overcome the larger blocks that interfered with her doing anything for her spiritual development.

If you recall your own past efforts at self-improvement or simply listen to your thoughts as you carry out a plan now, it won't take long to find a whole list of reasons that come to mind why you don't have to carry out your plan today. Linda thought of these:

- "This isn't important. It's not really spiritual."
- "It's not going to make any difference."
- "I'm a little tired today. I don't have the time or the energy."
- "You are doing the best you can."
- "The other person doesn't really deserve it."

If Linda weren't prepared to reject these thoughts and consider others, they would gradually undermine her resolve and soon stop her in her tracks. However, she was prepared for them. When she considered carefully what the thoughts were saying, she could see that they weren't as true as they felt.

One of the most useful things I've learned as a psychiatrist is that when I give my clients common-sense advice, I can't really expect them to follow it in the beginning. If it were that easy, they wouldn't come to see me. I give that common-sense advice anyway, but I rivet my attention on what will stop them from acting on it. With this in mind, I advise you to do what I do when you devise your own program. Be prepared for the likelihood that even the simplest plan is unlikely to go as well as you hoped. Forewarned is forearmed. You will then be primed to identify the ways you let yourself off the hook and to challenge the excuses that come to mind more effectively. You won't be content with blanket statements like the excuse that your faith isn't strong enough or that you need to humbly accept your limits.

It's a skill that needs to be developed. In the beginning, you might recognize the real danger of these thoughts only after the fact, when you look back after they have stopped you from acting on your plan. With practice, however, you'll recognize the thoughts when they first come up and you'll remind yourself that it isn't enough to simply brush them off.

Identifying Errors That Hold Us Back

Once you turn back the attack of your erroneous beliefs, you may begin to wonder why they don't just go away. Why do those thoughts keep coming back if you have recognized and corrected their false logic any number of times? And why do they win most of the time? Where do they get their power?

Correcting our intentions so that we will actually think, feel, and act differently in the future isn't so easy. In brief, it's the power of our emotions and the way that they work that keeps these errors going. CBT shows us that our erroneous beliefs persist whenever we have a pattern of emotional thinking akin to that of a person with social anxiety that prevents our erroneous beliefs from being easily corrected by the feedback of reality. Emotions play an important role in our life, of course; they help us respond in appropriate ways in the common situations we face so that we don't have to stop to consider what to do every time. They provide the energy that powers much of what we do, and this is just the way it should be when things go well. When things don't go well, however, we want to be able to figure out why and make corrections. To do so, we need to be able to suspend our automatic way of thinking and examine the evidence. Only when we have done this enough times to actually change our deeply embedded emotional reactions will our beliefs change.

CBT advises us that to identify errors in our thinking that support emotional logic and make us more resistant to correction, we need to adopt the attitude of a scientist and be as objective as possible. Below are several of the most important of the errors in logic that keep us reacting to situations from an emotional perspective and prevent us from accepting the real truth of a situation. They all work together to keep us thinking that things should be the way we think they should be, not the way they are.

- **All-or-nothing thinking (also called black-and-white and either/or thinking)**—At its most extreme, this way of thinking views anything that falls short of our standard of perfection as a *total* failure. In our spiritual life, for example, the more we think in terms of heaven or hell, saved or damned, spiritual or material, and virtue or vice, the more we overlook the nuances in situations and see only things that prove our beliefs correct. The more we use all-or-nothing thinking, the more difficult it becomes to gather the kind of evidence we need to decode the feedback of our messages in the complex situations of everyday life. We find we are just using spiritual messages to prove the existence of the spiritual dimension, and thus validate our own belief, without considering anything else that a message might be trying to tell us. This error is common in an area where we have little experience to draw on, like decoding messages, and tends to decrease with experience.

- **Catastrophic thinking**—All-or-nothing thinking easily combines with catastrophic thinking so that anything short of perfection becomes a catastrophe. Every little failure turns into a disaster; we lose hope and think that we can't *ever* expect to make *any* progress. The messages that we decode only seem to confirm that we are hopeless, for otherwise they would give us the transforming help we need or solve our problems as they did C.J.'s in chapter 1. Overwhelmed, we stop really trying.

- **Using "should" or "must" statements**—Emotional logic can easily lead us to have overly rigid or perfectionist expectations of how things *have to be* in a given situation in order to be acceptable. We believe something so strongly that everything *should be* or *must be* in line with that belief. Since we can't see the spiritual dimension clearly enough to correct our misperception, we keep trying to impose our ideas of how it should be on what is happening and don't even notice any feedback that contradicts our belief. We become intolerant of other people who think differently from how we know it must be. We feel either great superiority when we look at others or great guilt when we look at ourselves. Both stop us from making real efforts.

- **Selective attention and memory**—The more strongly we hold a belief, the more we see the world from that perspective. Everything we see and do only confirms our view of reality. We ignore or forget anything that doesn't fit our view of things. Most of us are so caught up in our material life that the spiritual elements seem, by comparison, not very relevant to everyday choices. We forget about the evidence we have gathered and what we have learned because we don't see its actual value. We lose our orientation, for we don't see any progress and always feel we are at square one.

All of these errors are driven and maintained by emotions. The more intense the emotion, the more it resists change. When all of these errors in logic (and others I haven't mentioned here) work together, they stop us from decoding any feedback that might cause us to question our beliefs, because our beliefs feel so right. The stronger our emotions become, the more we cling to our beliefs; we take the emotion as a sign of how strong our faith is and how committed to spirituality we are. We no longer need any other evidence than the strength of our emotional certainty. By considering the trouble these common errors in logic can get us into in everyday life, however, we can push ourselves to question our conclusions more carefully, particularly when we are not making the progress that we wish.

Disputing the Errors

Once we recognize that we don't change as quickly as we expect, we can start looking for these errors in our logic and challenge them—both the specific errors (the equivalent of feeling like a jerk) and the more general errors in emotional logic that we've just discussed. We want to do whatever we can to cool the emotions that drive these errors enough to see the objective truth in the situation.

Let's look at how understanding the harm of *selective attention and memory* helped Linda formulate a better strategy for combating her spiritual ADD. Linda had decoded enough messages to be convinced that the spiritual dimension was real and relevant to her life, yet she often forgot what she knew. So when she found herself losing interest in her plan, she reminded herself of the evidence that had led her to set up this program in the first place. Then she disputed any thought that devalued her action. She might argue, for example: This is what spirituality is all about. Remember what your friend said. Don't you want to be more like her? If it's so insignificant, then do it and don't complain so much. What's the big deal? I know the stakes. I won't let you stop me!

Linda recognized that she was vulnerable to other errors in logic, too. She had a tendency to *all-or-nothing thinking*—when she didn't see immediate results, she felt her efforts became meaningless—and to *catastrophic thinking*—when anyone was ungrateful or nasty to her, she would give up. So she prepared herself with a strategy that CBT suggests: to remind yourself that there's a difference between something *having* to be true and your *wanting* it to be true. Linda might start off with a standard analogy: "It would be nice if the sun shone brightly and warmly every day, wouldn't it? But does the sun have to shine for me to be happy? If it does, I have made my life and happiness unnecessarily contingent on outer circumstances." She could then add in the problem she was confronting—someone being ungrateful. "Just as I don't let bad weather ruin my day, why should I let the impoliteness of others, which is also out of my control, do so?"

Linda thought that it would certainly be preferable if other people got her coffee or smiled at her and called her on the phone, but she was prepared to accept that they didn't *have to* do those things in order for her to act as kindly as her role model would have in that situation. It wasn't a catastrophe if others didn't behave in a respectful way. She was prepared to be more polite, no matter what, as long as people didn't take her courtesy as license to take advantage of her. By labeling the errors in her thinking, she calmed the emotional force driving her false logic, successfully disputed the thoughts, and stopped them from undermining her effort. As a result, she began to understand herself better as her character slowly evolved in a more ethical direction. It became easier to repeat this action in other situations, for she was developing a very intelligent form of willpower.

To underscore the spiritual part of her intention and undercut these errors in her logic even further, she would add on her spiritual reasons for acting in this way so that they became the motivating force in her action. "Why do other people have to be considerate of me in order for me to be considerate of them? I'm not doing this to win their approval, but because I want God to be satisfied with me. Certainly, it would be nice if they were more considerate or appreciative of me, but they don't have to be. I don't have to trust them or become their friends. I just have to be polite. How can that hurt me? If I'm not turned off by them, I'll really assert my true intention and follow through with my intention. What a great opportunity. I'm ready for whatever they do."

When Linda prepared her basic arguments to keep her thinking straight under fire, she had to make certain that they were convincing enough to counter the emotional force of her errors and get her back on track. When they didn't work, she learned something from the failure and tried to use it in her next project. She was practicing good psychology with just the right twist of spirituality.

Boosting Your Motivation

For emotional support, it will help you to remember that you are not alone in your struggle. If you are doing your best and carrying out the kind of plan Linda was with a spiritual intention, messages will come to support and encourage you to think and act in more spiritually functional ways. For example, Linda noticed that when she was more polite, her day went more smoothly. When she snubbed someone, she might spill coffee on herself or another person might be uncharacteristically rude to her. She took this as feedback reminding her of God's presence and the importance of what she was doing.

You can also use the kinds of methods that both common sense and CBT might suggest to motivate you to carry out your plans, with a spiritual intention, of course. You can, for example, read your favorite spiritual book or talk with others who are interested in spirituality about what you are doing. You might impose a small penalty on yourself when you slip, such as not watching TV the next night, not drinking soda the next day, or not allowing yourself to eat ice cream. You could also reward yourself for completing a month of your program by giving yourself something you like, perhaps buying a sweater you want or eating out at your favorite restaurant. Each of us has to find the method that makes it more desirable for us to perform the small acts we commit to doing than to give up.

When I first thought of using such tactics, I didn't like it at all. I didn't think it was right to give myself a material reward or punishment when what I was interested in was spiritual progress. However, I gradually learned that this was just another erroneous belief that would get in my way. You need to be smart about what you are doing to succeed, and that means using whatever works, with a spiritual intention, of course.

Regularity is very important in keeping your motivation up. To help you stick to the plans you make, CBT recommends that you record your results every day. Just sitting down for even a few minutes every night and thinking about what you've done that day to identify and combat irrational and self-defeating arguments will help you do better the next day. When you can't find any new examples, simply review what you have already discovered and renew your intention to continue. If you stop, don't beat yourself up. Just return to it as soon as you are able to and start all over again.

If too much consistency disturbs you, no problem. You can take a break; just make it a planned holiday so that you don't give up your program altogether. For example, you might act on your commitments for four or five days of the week and take the weekends off. To make sure that you'll actually start again after your time off and not lose sight of your plan, ask a friend to call you every Monday morning to make sure that you're back on track. To design a plan that is both flexible and determined, you need to have good common sense and know yourself well enough to anticipate your reactions and take them into account in your plans.

If you do stay on course and use evidence-based methods of psychology like the one I've outlined, you are certain to succeed. You will defeat those thoughts and the emotional logic that holds you to your customary ways of doing things. You will make faster progress by being more systematic, whether you are a man or a woman, black or white, liberal or conservative, illiterate or well educated, rich or poor, shy or assertive, Christian or Buddhist, religious or religion-phobic, evangelical or New Age. You just have to set your mind to using every available resource to get yourself to do things that you know to be good for you psychologically and that fit in with your best spiritual intention.

Each time you work on a program, you automatically refine both your attention and intentions so that you will do even better on the next one. You will not only become a little more polite (or honest, kind, compassionate, courageous, humble, or any other virtue you are working to improve) but be more content with life as well. You will have better concentration in your prayers and understand more deeply the concepts in spiritual books. With your material and spiritual lives better integrated, you won't be so stressed out by what others do. And with those signs of progress, you will be even more motivated to overcome your spiritual ADD by paying even closer attention to the feedback of your messages.

୬ ୬ ୬

If at first it took a large influx of spiritual energy to encourage us to try to become more spiritual, we can learn to use the more subtle but more consistent effects of spiritual energy that our spiritual intention connects us to by carefully constructing experiments and seeing for ourselves the beneficial effects of actions done with a spiritual intention. It may seem revolutionary to systematically use psychological methods to refine our interactions with the spiritual dimension. Yet it is really evolutionary—an expansion of past practices that helps us improve them.

People have made progress in so many other areas of human life by using an experimental approach. Why shouldn't we be able to adapt psychology's experimental approach to the requirements of spirituality to come up with a more objective and universal approach to our spiritual experience that can enrich our understanding of our own spiritual nature? The potential rewards are great, for if we can agree on an approach, we will be able to learn so much more from each other's experiences that our collective knowledge will start to grow exponentially, as it has in every other field, and our sense of spiritual connection will become even stronger.

ॐ　ॐ　ॐ

Keys to Chapter 7

- The most obvious way of drawing spiritual energy into your life is by *regularly* using a practice recommended by your own tradition, but instead of doing this as an act of devotion, approaching it as a kind of spiritual experiment that will prove the value of your belief.
- A good way of strengthening your spiritual character is by developing more of the virtues that are praised by all religious and spiritual traditions—like kindness, diligence, honesty, humility, and courage—but doing this with the mentality of a student in an experimental science determined to discover *why* it is valuable to cultivate these virtues.
- When you act with a good spiritual intention, you might arouse resistance because our character is by nature set up to resist change, even change that you think will be

beneficial. When you run into obstacles that block your progress (and we all do), you can use one of the evidence-based
techniques of psychology, cognitive-behavioral therapy
(CBT), to systematically analyze and correct the thoughts,
emotions, and beliefs that might otherwise stop you from
following through on your plans for self-improvement.

- Through small, insignificant-sounding actions, like being
consistently more polite, you can draw out into the open
the self-defeating beliefs that block your spiritual development so that you can dispute and refute them, drawing upon the well-researched methods of psychology to
help you.

- CBT points out that our erroneous beliefs persist when we
have a pattern of emotional thinking that prevents our self-
defeating beliefs from being corrected by the feedback of
reality. Several of the most important errors in logic that
lead to trouble are all-or-nothing thinking, catastrophic
thinking, using "should" or "must" statements, and selective memory and attention.

ॐ   ॐ   ॐ

For Your Reflection

Having seen several of the ways that you can gather evidence to
help you think, feel, and act more in line with your messages, it's
time to clarify your own strategy for spiritual self-improvement.

1. You learn a great deal about intentions by examining the
   way others make their plans. Review in your mind how
   Katherine and Michael improved themselves in ways that
   seem like good common sense. Did you learn anything

from them? Now think of the practices you have found most effective in improving yourself. What evidence do you have that they have strengthened your spiritual attention, intentions, and character?

2. Can you think of a small action (like Michael's trying not to lie in a particular situation or Linda's committing to being more polite) that would improve you in some way? Imagine yourself doing it for several months and outwitting the thoughts that might come up to undermine your efforts. If you imagine the scenario vividly enough, it will have almost the same effect on you as if you actually did it. If you feel ready to act, go ahead, but make certain to gather enough motivation to follow through and make a chart (or go to decodeyourmessages.com to download one) to record the results of your daily efforts.

3. Review how Linda dealt with the thoughts and feelings that would have stopped her from following through on her plan and what she learned about herself in the process. Think of plans that you have made and not followed through on. Based on what you have read in this chapter, try to define as clearly as you can the thoughts and feelings that stop you from following through on your plans and come up with counterarguments to dispute these excuses the next time they come to mind.

4. Go to decodeyourmessages.com to find out what others have done to strengthen their intentions and orient their character toward their spiritual goals.

5. Take out a sheet of paper or turn to a blank page in your notebook and entitle it "Putting Theory into Practice." You can also download these points for reflection to your computer or log into your online notebook. Write a summary paragraph about the kind of efforts that you believe are most essential for your progress and what evidence

you have that suggests that you are making progress. Then continue on and write as much detail as you'd like about your struggles to get to strengthen your spiritual side.

6. Go to decodeyourmessages.com to add the theories you try to act on and how you keep yourself at it.

CHAPTER 8

Setting the Foundation of Your Spiritual Character

According to most humanistic and spiritual traditions, we become fully ourselves only by embracing time-honored ethical values. By acting ethically with a spiritual intention, we strive to bring ourselves into line with the guidance of our messages. As we continue, we recognize more and more, in the conscience that pushes us to be virtuous and is satisfied by our efforts to act virtuously, the voice of our soul. So one of the best ways to learn to decode messages is by analyzing the ethical dimension of situations that we are in, acting on our conclusions, and looking for feedback that helps us see more clearly the spiritual value of acting in a particular way.

Marie, a thirty-five-year-old housewife, gave me a good example of how a message pushed her to be more ethical in a way that fostered her spiritual development as well. "For fifteen years, I had problems with my parents-in-law," she told me. "I wanted them to love me and approve of me, but I didn't really want them around.

I wanted my own parents to visit but not my husband's. I felt that my in-laws were always interfering in our lives. The pressure became so great that once I collapsed in the street and had to be taken to the hospital. I saw a psychiatrist, who put me on medications and encouraged me to express my anger. But none of this helped. Spiritually, I knew that the right thing to do was to force myself to at least be civil to my in-laws, but I couldn't bring myself to do even that. So I felt guilty."

Marie had read many magazine articles and books full of good advice about how to deal with unmanageable anger or troublesome in-laws, but she didn't see how they were relevant to her situation since, from her point of view, the presence of her in-laws was just unacceptable. She was sure that she was right and that God was on her side. She had fallen victim to the emotional logic we discussed in the last chapter. Her analysis of her situation was driven by her emotions rather than by an understanding of the ethical issues involved.

"As a last resort, I turned to God in a different way," she told me. "Of course, I had already asked for his help—to get my in-laws off my back or to make my anger go away—but this time it felt different. After yet another incident that left me feeling worse than ever, I was reduced to crying in my car in the middle of the city. I couldn't take it anymore and pleaded with God from the bottom of my heart to help me in whatever way *he* thought best. I really meant it. Suddenly, a great peace came upon me, and at last I had hope that things could change."

It wasn't until Marie finally hit bottom that a spiritual message got through and helped her see that she had been wrong. She saw that her in-laws had as much right to visit their son and their grandchildren as her own parents had to see her and her children. Her in-laws weren't the cause of the problem; she was. Once she accepted that she was the cause of the problem, finding a solution was relatively easy. She did what anyone might have done based on common sense, sound psychology, and ethical considerations. She forced herself to reach out to them.

"Several days later, I picked up the phone and invited my in-laws to visit us for a few weeks," Marie said. "My husband was shocked that I had done this. My mother-in-law was so touched that she sent me back a card saying how much she and my father-in-law loved me. Now, several years later, I can honestly say that I really love my parents-in-law, and that it is all because of God's help. I realized that the solution to all my misery was quite simple—I just had to apply the Golden Rule."

Shedding Our Illusions

Marie had felt so sure she was right that no other possibility could enter her mind. It's natural for us to believe that the more strongly we feel something to be true, the truer it must be. Yet this feeling of certainty is not a reliable gauge of whether we are acting correctly from either a material or a spiritual perspective, for we are usually too self-centered to take into account another's position. The purpose of ethics is to help us challenge the naturally self-centered ways that feel so right to us but all too often aren't.

Ethics help us generate alternative possibilities that have proven so useful that they have become the core of time-honored wisdom. The most universal way of generating alternative hypotheses is putting ourselves in the other person's shoes to see what he might be thinking and then applying the Golden Rule: to want for others what we want for ourselves and not to want for others what we do not want for ourselves. Once we have analyzed a situation this way, we form an intention to act in line with our conclusion. Groups of related intentions work together to build different characteristics or virtues in us, and these different characteristics work together to form our character. We thus develop a virtuous character one intention at a time and one characteristic at a time. The more our character develops in this direction, the easier it becomes to recognize the contributions of the soul.

The theory sounds simple. If you don't like to be disturbed by others, don't disturb others. If you don't want to be badmouthed, don't speak badly of others. If you don't want to be lied to, don't lie to others. This puts others on an equal footing with us so that we can more objectively evaluate the rights of the different parties involved in a given situation. I think you will agree, however, that following the Golden Rule is easier said than done, for it involves a change in our character, one intention at a time. If we want to act better in the situations of everyday life, we need to be *prepared* to act better by having formed specific intentions to do so.

Almost every time-honored philosophy advises us to build the foundation of our interactions with others in such a way that we automatically apply the Golden Rule. Our intention determines the result. If we do it to be good citizens so that society functions better for all our benefit, then we become better citizens. If we add the intention of a philosophy or psychology to foster other aspects of our nature and achieve our "higher" human potentials, then through our efforts we will gain this level of benefit as well. If we add our spiritual intention, then we develop ethical qualities in a way that also facilitates our spiritual growth and our ability to decode the deeper meanings of our messages. So by putting ourselves in another's shoes and applying the Golden Rule with a spiritual intention, we seek to accomplish all three—to be a good citizen, a noble human being, and a spiritual student—in a way that creates a fundamental harmony between our material and spiritual lives. We establish the foundation of a well-integrated bi-dimensional character.

As we saw in the last chapter, a spiritual intention is built on a solid material intention. Marie knew that if she wanted to change, she would have to make an effort, so she set up a practical program that would help her put herself in others' shoes. She started to read the newspaper and appreciate the merits of the arguments on both sides of an issue. She discussed her own opinion on the issues that she read about in the papers with friends and acquaintances. She read books on parenting and on relationships in order to improve her communication skills so that she could check out with other people what they were thinking and feeling. She made a habit of asking friends' advice about different everyday situations and carefully weighing the evidence to see which advice made the most sense.

As a result of her efforts, her characteristic way of thinking and acting changed. She now made fewer of the errors we defined in the last chapter—all-or-nothing thinking, "must" thinking, and catastrophic thinking. She made fewer mistakes of other kinds, such as imagining that she knew what others were thinking and overly personalizing events in a way that put her at the center of everything that happened. Now she began to stop herself, for she understood others' positions better and gave them the right to have their positions because she wanted the right to have hers. Things didn't have to be her way in order for her to be happy. She could compromise.

To fully integrate these changes into her way of being, Marie decided that for the next year she would deliberately analyze with a spiritual intention three situations a week in which she saw things differently from her husband. She would first imagine herself in his shoes and try to come up with several different explanations he might have. She would then apply the Golden Rule. Whenever there was a doubt as to whose position was more valid, she would give his position the benefit of the doubt rather than her own. This was ethics in action in everyday life. As she became more confident, she began to discuss the pros and cons of the different alternatives with her husband. When she got even more comfortable with it, she began to do the same thing with friends and then neighbors. Each relationship was different and required a different application of the Golden Rule.

Marie became a better citizen and a better human being. She felt a greater sense of dignity and integrity in what she did, for she was no longer so self-centered. Because her real motive was her spiritual development and she made these efforts with her best spiritual intention, she started to see that something had been just as wrong in her relationship with God as it had been in her relationships with other people. She hadn't really thought about what God's perspective might be because she thought she knew what was right and, therefore, that she knew what he thought. Thanks to the changes that she made, Marie could see that she had been thinking of God like a puppet that would do her bidding if she pleaded enough. Now she saw that she had to *first* do her best to solve problems, *then* ask for God's help, and finally be satisfied with whatever result she got.

We are unlikely to ever be in exactly the same situation as Marie. We can learn something, however, by putting ourselves in her shoes. We can then wonder how *we* might make a similar mistake in our own life by not giving other people the consideration they deserve. We can wonder how self-centered we are and look for the mistakes that causes us to make. We can also wonder about *our* relationship with the source of our messages and how well we are actually seeing its perspective on a situation. By putting ourselves in the shoes of others whose experiences we read or hear, we can arrive at a more universal understanding of how ethical principles and spiritual intentions form the very foundation of all spiritual practices so that we can develop the force of character to think, feel, and act in line with our own beliefs.

Getting Our Expectations Right

Years ago, when I was beginning to understand the basics of spiritual development, I would puzzle over the question: If spiritual messages are such a help in improving ourselves, why don't spiritually oriented people seem more mentally healthy, more intelligent, and more virtuous than those who receive no spiritual help and feel no connection with their souls? It seemed logical that if spiritual messages were as important as I was finding them to be, they would make spiritually oriented people into greater paragons of virtue and mental health by helping them correct their weaknesses. Yet when I looked at myself and others who were interested in spirituality, this didn't seem to be the case at all. We were all too human. It was a similar conclusion, in fact, to one I had come to years before in wondering why mental health providers didn't seem more outstandingly mentally healthy for all of our training in helping others solve their problems.

Like a good scientist, I reviewed hundreds of the many thousands of studies, as well as many overviews of studies, that had tried to do the same thing I was trying to do—identify concrete benefits of religious and spiritual beliefs. To cut to the bottom line, although many studies claimed to have found a whole range of clear benefits related to particular religious or spiritual beliefs— from better physical health to better psychological adjustment— others had not. Most of the positive results could be explained by the greater social support that religious people experienced through being members of communities that cautioned against harmful behaviors such as drug addiction and isolation. None seemed obviously related to the interesting effects of what I think of as spiritual energy.

Although I was initially disappointed by these results, I gradually realized that they were in keeping with my own observations of the effects spiritual messages had on me. Messages had a positive effect, but they made me only slightly better than I was before I had spiritual beliefs. They certainly didn't make me or others I knew stand out in a crowd as more virtuous. In fact, I probably had less desire now to do the more heroic and virtuous deeds that gain the notice of others. This helped me to understand that integrity of character is achieved not when we become paragons of virtue but when we do the best that we honestly can to try to be true to our values.

Messages help us put ourselves in other people's shoes and

apply ethical principles like the Golden Rule. By following their guidance, we develop levels of virtue sufficient to enable us to live more normal lives and align ourselves with the will of our messages. We become better than we were before, but not better than others. We will be much better able to decode messages if we adjust our expectations accordingly.

Learning Persistence and Perseverance

Realizing the limits of our efforts and how unlikely it is that we will become saints, should we just settle in and accept our all-too-human ways as the best we can do? No! Every ethical tradition encourages us to resist our tendencies to act against its principles, for if we don't actively struggle, we will go backward until we are acting quite unethically. You might say that the power of our intentions has certain inherent limits that will be different for each of us depending on our nature and our upbringing. We must accept these limits and make the best of our circumstances.

Shirley, a dentist who was raised in a spiritually oriented family, has an ongoing struggle with a weak point in her character that causes her to think, feel, and act in ways that are at odds with ethical principles. She has a good marriage, a successful practice, and lots of friends. She is generally quite ethical but has a tendency to be overly perfectionist and hypercritical of herself and others. Even though she's been struggling with a spiritual intention to correct this tendency for years, it's such a part of her character that it keeps popping out.

One Thursday at work, Shirley found herself right in the middle of one such instructive incident. "It was such a long day," she told me. "One of the other dentists in our office was a little slow, so he didn't have time to see his emergency patients that day. Instead, I had to see them, which really got me upset. I complained to a coworker, who told me, 'You know, he is not doing that on purpose. He is a little slow, and he just started.' I said, 'Oh, fine, but I don't know why *I* have to see his patients.' The next day, for some strange reason, I got really far behind, and not because my schedule was overloaded. At four o'clock, I still had three people waiting, so other dentists had to see two or three of my patients. When I saw what was happening, I knew that it was because I had been overly critical of that dentist the day before for the exact same reason."

Shirley had gotten feedback like this many times before, so she recognized its familiar signature and thus its source. It was a simple case of action-reaction. Shirley had criticized a colleague in an unjustifiably harsh way; the next day, she found herself in the same situation that she had criticized him for causing. Her message had once again made it clear how spiritually harmful it was for her to unjustly criticize others as if she were somehow better than they were. Shirley was painfully aware that she shouldn't be so critical or gossip with coworkers as she had done. She had made many efforts to correct this tendency, but she had to constantly fight against it because it was a part of her character.

After it was over and she felt calmer, she knew that she had acted wrongly. In her reactions, she could find many examples of the errors in logic described in the last chapter that made her response so exaggerated and difficult to correct. For example, when other people didn't live up to her standards and act as they *should*, it was black-and-white or *all-or-nothing* to her. They were wrong and to be condemned. Little things became *catastrophes* in her mind, and she seemed to have *selective attention to and memory of* the negative things others had done rather than the positive. All these things made it harder to stop her from getting carried away by her criticisms and thus made it even more important to stop them in their tracks.

This "failure" produced another struggle: to make certain that it didn't demoralize her and cause her to stop trying. To stay on course, Shirley needed a good understanding of the importance of her effort and a realistic expectation of the kind of results she might expect in a whole range of different circumstances, for from a spiritual perspective life in this classroom Earth is filled with lessons. Hardship is not a punishment, and failure to succeed in becoming more ethical is not spiritually important *in itself*. It may even bring greater rewards by forcing us to struggle against our weaknesses more. If you have trouble believing this, you can study the lives of the prophets and those commonly acknowledged to have been closest to God. Most of their lives were filled with challenges far greater than the ones most of us will ever face.

We all have weak points in our character. If one of our weaknesses is not so easily changed, we can learn to compensate for it in much the same way we would a physical handicap, so that it doesn't stop us from realizing our potentials as fully as possible. Shirley assessed her situation and concluded that she was doing the best she knew how to do. She was convinced that her message wasn't there to blame her, but to help her renew her intention to fight against this tendency by remembering the spiritual importance of doing so. It was tangible evidence to her that God hadn't given up on her, but agreed that she was doing the best she could. Perhaps one day she could do better, but not now. Now, through her struggles, she would have to be content developing other qualities such as perseverance, patience, and humility.

A good goal is the one set out in the opening of Reinhold Niebuhr's famous Serenity Prayer: "God grant me the serenity to accept the things I cannot change, courage to change the things I can, and wisdom to know the difference." It's up to each of us to make the best of the conditions of our own life move forward despite our many failings.

The more we do our best to live according to ethics with a spiritual intention and keep from being demoralized by our weaknesses, the clearer our conscience will become and the stronger our connection with the source of our messages will be. We will become kinder and more benevolent. Our relationships will work better. We will be more resilient to stress and feel more content with our lives even during hardships. We will find ourselves at home in a bi-dimensional world, both material and spiritual, where each dimension is enriched by the other.

Listening with Another Ear

How do we know that our efforts to be more ethical are resulting in significant changes in our spiritual understanding? One sign is that we become naturally more alert, oriented, and ready to respond to spiritual guidance. To explain what I mean, let me describe my own experience. Soon after my spirit guide left me, as I described in chapter 4, I found a discussion group that had been set up to help people of different belief systems make sense of their spiritual experiences. We found common ground in our efforts to be more ethical. We would discuss what we had done each week and come up with plans for what we might do better in the week ahead.

In the beginning, I was content with this level of sharing. My heart was warmed by hearing others' struggles and successes. After several years, I found that the group was no longer helping me very much, and yet I liked going to the meeting for the same reason that people have always liked to gather in worship or prayer. God seems to love groups, as there is more spiritual energy when a group gathers together for a spiritual purpose than when we work alone. So I changed my expectations. I no longer expected others to help me directly; instead, I hoped our mutual intention would attract greater spiritual energy that would help me receive inspiration to help me solve a problem that was on my mind, whether it was a difficulty at work, a little disagreement with my wife, or the nature of a spiritual intention.

I continued making the same kind of efforts to apply ethical principles during the week and coming to the group without any real expectation. Then, during one of the meetings, something magical happened. Someone was talking about a topic of interest to him, not of much interest to me, but what he was saying helped me see the spiritual perspective on a completely different issue I had been thinking about in my own life. It was as if I held a piece of a puzzle in my hand (my question) and then all at once I saw where it fit (the answer). It wasn't an esoteric answer or a deep insight; it was more like seeing that two plus two really did equal four, grasping an ethical aspect of the situation that I had lost sight of, like seeing that the root of the problem I was facing was in my pride or my jealousy. It was a subtle spiritual message with this unexpected visible material aspect: hearing an answer to my question from the mouth of someone who was talking about something else, an answer so specifically relevant to my problem that it convinced me I wasn't just making a connection on my own.

For years we push ourselves to be more ethical and more responsive to messages until one day we find ourselves one step more attuned to them. We then realize that all our efforts are now paying off. Although it feels like magic at the time, it is just like what might happen with a child with ADD whose parents and teachers had been trying for years to impress upon him the value of schoolwork. One day, when he feels good solving a problem that he hadn't been able to solve before, he suddenly gets it, and thereafter he starts making the extra effort that is required to do his homework on time. It is similar as well to what took place in my psychiatric training. After years of studying psychiatry, there came a time when I could recognize what was causing people's problems by just talking to them. Because of all my training and experience, it was suddenly self-evident. Maybe you've noticed a similar shift in some area of your life.

The more we work to improve ourselves with spiritual attention and intentions, the more we find that we don't have to passively wait for a message to get help and guidance. I soon discovered that if I were properly alert, oriented, and ready to respond, messages could guide me by using whatever was going on around me. I could even go to an entertaining movie and find an answer to the question I had been thinking about in what one of the characters in the movie was doing or saying. Similar inspirations, of course, happen to people with no spiritual beliefs; however, their inspirations are of a psychological nature. Mine were spiritual inspirations that helped me live a life that was more in tune with the effects of my messages.

Focusing Within

Since, in spirituality, it isn't the material size of an action but the quality of the effort that is important in shaping our character, we can find spiritual opportunities for self-improvement even at quiet points in our life when nothing important is pressing. We do this by focusing on our *thinking*. Thoughts are so important that I have heard and read reports from students with many different spiritual masters of how their teachers would correct their thoughts without their having spoken about them at all. Their masters had known what they were thinking and found it important enough to mention it to them.

Although at first I wished that I had a master who would correct my mistakes right then and there, I eventually found similar guidance from messages. Let me give you an example. If I was walking around my apartment lost in thought and hit my leg against a drawer that was sticking out of my desk, I used to just grumble, rub my leg, and carry on with my reverie. Now, I react differently. I stop and look for a potential spiritual meaning in that irksome event. I look to direct the emotion caused by the pain against any thoughts or feelings that I discover that are not in tune with my messages.

I imagine that the incident is a message to alert me to the

harmful effects of the thoughts I was thinking, and I have an intimate conversation with the source of my messages to try to discover what it wants me to know. If no meaning is self-evident, I consider the ethical weakness that I am working on at the time. Say I had been focusing on controlling negative thoughts about certain people that week, and at the time I hit my leg, I was having negative thoughts about someone. That would be easy. I would then take this unexpected bump as confirmation that my negative thoughts about others really do have negative consequences for me and resolve to work harder at controlling them. If I were focusing on my excessive pride that week and found that, at the time I hit my leg, I was mentally putting others down, then I would surmise that my collision with the drawer was showing me that excessive pride *was* at the root of my negative thoughts and resolve to work harder at overcoming it.

My bump thus becomes a blessing in disguise. It makes me pay more attention to what I am thinking or doing. My small pain allows me to confirm a principle common to most religions and humanistic philosophies alike—that it is better not to dwell on another's weak points or to make too much of myself even in the secret recesses of my own mind. It motivates me to fight against the everyday rationale that such thoughts are natural as long as I don't act on them. If we fight with small negative thoughts, we prevent them from getting bigger and predisposing us to act in ways that we wouldn't want to.

Each time you look for a spiritual element in what happens to you, you challenge the material logic that has an explanation for the event good enough that you don't have to look any farther. You generate alternative hypotheses and gather evidence as to the benefits and drawbacks of a given interpretation. A word of caution: You must be wary not to interpret little incidents as calls to important action. For instance, if you are worrying about a problem at work when you bang into the drawer, don't jump to the conclusion that it is a sign you should quit because your job is hurting you. However, you're always safe interpreting situations in ways that remind you to improve yourself in line with ethical principles.

Another caution is not to lose perspective and get so caught up with small things that you ignore more important things, as a student might give so much importance to brushing his teeth that he doesn't think he needs to go to class. However, the student also mustn't get so caught up in the big things that he stops brushing his teeth. By putting each thing in its place and staying focused on the ethical implications of everything that we do without becoming obsessed, we can establish a sense of integrity that runs through all the moments of our life.

If I happened to be having positive thoughts about others when I hit my leg, and if I couldn't see anything else that the bump might be trying to tell me, I would conclude that the bump wasn't a spiritual message at all, but that I was just being clumsy. The incident might remind me to be more mindful of what I'm doing and not so inattentive to my surroundings. It might remind me not to become superstitious. I might go on to wonder if perhaps I had been too out of touch with everyday realities or wasn't being very orderly because I had left the drawer open. I'd imagine the source of my messages smiling benignly at me and encouraging me to be less superstitious or more orderly.

What if you can't figure out *what* an incident is trying to tell you? I once heard a bit of wisdom that applies here: If something happens to you and you can't figure out which of your weaknesses it may be pointing out, choose one that is prominent in your mind. Use the situation as an excuse to work on that weakness. Don't lose an opportunity to work on yourself because you don't know precisely what the cause of a particular situation is. We can never go wrong by making efforts to be more generous, kind, humble, courageous, or understanding.

Ethics help us set the solid foundation of our spiritual character in a way that makes all further growth far easier. That's why it is a central part of Spirituality 101, the core curriculum of our spiritual education, in which we align ourselves with the wisdom of our messages. By creating a network of intentions that commit us to strive to develop ethical virtues in human proportions, we become automatically alert, oriented, and prepared to act in line with our messages. A deep and abiding peace rises in us as our own spiritual nature becomes more and more a part of our everyday life.

Once you've gathered enough evidence of the spiritual value of your intentions in trying to live by time-honored ethical values, you will be well prepared to apply a comprehensive set of spiritual principles and develop spiritual intelligence, the capacity to systematically take on the challenges in everyday life from a bi-dimensional perspective. We'll move on to these stages of your journey in Parts III and IV of this book.

☞   ☞   ☞

Keys to Chapter 8

- Ethics is a central part of Spirituality 101, the core curriculum of our spiritual education, in which you learn to align yourself with the wisdom of your messages and lay the foundation for your spiritual character.
- Ethics helps us generate alternative possibilities that challenge our naturally self-centered ways and help us act in line with time-honored wisdom. The most universally accepted way of generating these alternative hypotheses is putting yourself in the other person's shoes to see what

he might be thinking and then applying the Golden Rule: to want for others what you want for yourself and not to want for others what you do not want for yourself.

- You won't become a paragon of virtue by following messages' guidance, but you will become better than you were before. You'll develop sufficient virtue to enable you to decode deeper levels of your messages and to more clearly recognize the contributions of your soul to your thoughts, feelings, and actions.
- Some of our self-centered ways are part of our character and not so easily changed. You can learn to compensate for them much as you might for a physical handicap and develop other characteristics, like perseverance, patience, resilience, and humility, that are equally important for spiritual development.
- Messages push us to find a lesson in everything that happens to us, even things that might seem inconsequential from a material perspective. If you avoid doing small things that go against ethics, you are less likely to do larger things that go against ethics.
- If something happens to you and you can't figure out which of your weaknesses it may stem from, choose one that is prominent in your mind. Use the situation as an excuse to work on it. Don't lose the opportunity to work on yourself.

ॐ   ॐ   ॐ

For Your Reflection

The practice of ethics sets the best foundation for decoding spiritual messages and developing our spiritual character. These are a few questions to help you clarify the role that ethics plays in your spiritual life:

1. What role does ethical practice play in your spiritual life? Has a message ever helped you to see someone else's perspective or act in a more ethical way? Has a message ever helped you apply the Golden Rule? Choose a situation where you tried to apply the Golden Rule and see how well you balance your own rights with others in deciding what to do.

2. Examine several situations to see whether you are acting ethically to win others' approval, be a good citizen, and develop psychologically and spiritually. How can you tell the difference and what might you do to improve your spiritual intention in your ethical efforts?

3. Go to decodeyourmessages.com to find how others used ethical practices to learn to decode spiritual messages and set the foundation for their spiritual character.

4. Take out a sheet of paper or turn to a blank page in your notebook and entitle it "The Foundations of My Spiritual Character." You can also go to decodeyourmessages.com to download these points for reflection to your computer or log into your online notebook. Write a summary paragraph that describes your thoughts about what a strong spiritual character is and what the major strengths and weaknesses in your own spiritual character are (in areas like faith, perseverance, compassion, and so forth). Indicate how a stronger spiritual character aligns you with the effects of your messages. Then continue on and describe the experience on which your conclusions are based in as much detail as you would like.

5. Go to decodeyourmessages.com to add what helps you strengthen your spiritual character and decode deeper levels of meaning in your messages.

PART III

Cultivating Your
Spiritual Intelligence

CHAPTER 9

Connecting to the Power
in Principles

Everyday life is a virtual reality in which we learn to interact with the spiritual dimension. It is a classroom in which our daily challenges are the lessons that lead us to develop our spiritual intelligence so that we can balance our material and spiritual interests in a way that serves both. And, as in school, to make the most of our opportunities for growth, we need to use the wisdom that others have attained as a kind of ladder to help us advance. In school, ladders are the facts, findings, and methods in fields from algebra to zoology that education experts have packaged in a way that will take us from one level of understanding to the next. In the spiritual classroom of a vital everyday life, the best ladder is a set of solid principles that help us know how to act in the material world so as to gain the greatest spiritual benefit. By applying these principles in your own life, you can hope to make their wisdom your own.

Which set of principles you use is up to you. It can be based in the time-honored wisdom of any sacred text, such as the Torah, the Koran, the Gospels, or the Upanishads. Every spiritual tradition has authentic principles that have helped many people reach a deeper understanding of their own spiritual nature. They remind us of another dimension of life and tell us how to think, feel, and act in ways that actualize our spiritual potential. Each time we apply a principle from a set of principles, we form a spiritual intention and we get feedback on how well we have applied it that enables us to apply it even better in the future. As each principle is a part of a larger whole, there's a kind of synergy among them; each in some way helps us apply all the other principles in that system more effectively.

As our everyday life is largely material, spiritual principles help us know how to make choices in common everyday situations in ways that take into account the spiritual elements in a situation. Our job will be easier if we can find time-honored principles that have been pulled together and reformulated into a coherent system designed to stimulate our development in a balanced way by someone who lives in our time and has faced the same kinds of problems we face. If in your own tradition there isn't a collection of such principles formulated in simple sentences, then take the spiritual book that you use as a resource for living your everyday life and abstract principles from it yourself. Start with those principles that you consider common to most approaches, so that you'll have a starting point that doesn't simply reflect an idea that appeals to you at present.

As my own source of basic principles, I've chosen *100 Maxims of Guidance* (Robert Laffont, France, 2000) by the twentieth-century Persian judge and spiritual philosopher Ostad Elahi. They have helped me solidify my grasp of the fundamentals of spirituality in much the same way that the principles of psychology have helped me understand the fundamentals of material life. As I believe that all religions come from the same source and am wary of those who think that theirs is the only way, I was drawn by Ostad Elahi's universal intent, expressed in the following two principles: "Those who faithfully study and practice the authentic principles of their religion shall reach the Truth" and "When you consider all saints and prophets as legitimate and no longer differentiate between religions, you have reached the stage of true mysticism."

I use the principles of Ostad Elahi throughout this section to illustrate what I have learned from the experiences that I relate. In some cases, the people involved were aware of Ostad Elahi's principles; in others, they weren't. I have substituted his principles in my analysis in ways that I believe honor both what each person thought about his or her experience and what I found relevant in their experiences, although the latter is certainly the more important to me. In order for us to benefit from thinking about other people's experiences in any practical way, it is essential for us to put ourselves in the others' shoes and integrate their experiences into our own frame of reference. In that spirit, I suggest that you analyze the experiences in this book by doing the same, using principles from *your* system and comparing your conclusions to mine.

Clarifying Our Attitude Toward Everyday Life

Where do we start? As a psychiatrist, I've learned that our understanding of a situation depends in large part on the context in which we view it. So a good place to start is by making certain that our principles help us see the value of approaching spirituality in everyday life. To show you the importance of having principles that are meant to be applied in the normal lives most of us live, let's look at the unfortunate experience of Ernest, an intense young man with strong spiritual desires. Remember Jane from chapter 5, who had sincere intentions but ended up ignoring common sense and following a self-proclaimed guru? In Ernest's similar story, you'll see how principles help us be very sure of the value of everyday life.

"I set out on my spiritual journey with all the enthusiasm and energy of a twenty-year-old," Ernest told me. "I was thirsty for answers to questions I just couldn't stop asking myself. Who am I? What's the meaning of my life? What am I here for? I searched everywhere for these answers, but nothing seemed to quench my thirst for meaning. I certainly couldn't find answers in my religion, Catholicism, which I found altogether dull, hollow, and just impossible to believe in. By that, I don't mean that I didn't believe in Christ. On the contrary, I had a real, strong faith, but I just couldn't reconcile this faith with the institution.

"I met some people barely older than I was who talked about such things as past lives, communication with another dimension, and out-of-body experiences. To me, it was like a breath of fresh air: no dogmas, no meaningless rituals, and no more endless and boring sermons."

Ernest loved God, but he had developed an allergy to institutionalized religion, in fact, to every traditional system of thinking. He was excited just to be in the company of others who were not hampered by tradition, but drawn to spiritism and paranormal phenomena. "I began attending spiritual gatherings during which we would focus our attention on spiritual energy," Ernest continued. "I must admit I wasn't a great receptor, since I could barely feel anything. But other people did, and that was good enough for me. Over time, I began to slowly see myself drifting further and further away from people who were preoccupied with their everyday lives. At the same time, I drifted away from my own material responsibilities as well."

Ernest took as an authority the community of like-minded people in which he now found himself, and he gave special authority to those who claimed to have the unique powers that he lacked. Their beliefs filled in for his own lack of experience. He stopped going to school and set aside his family and friends to live in a commune, isolating himself completely from society's ways. As with Jane, he was following someone whose charismatic appeal

drew him in, a leader who talked with passion about the corrupt-
ness of material society and the importance of paranormal powers.

Ernest had started with a genuine thirst for spirituality. It was
so strong that nothing else in life interested him. He thought that
he was following a good example in turning away from a corrupt
world to devote himself to God as the disciples of Christ and other
spiritual figures had done. It felt so right that it didn't even dawn on
him that he might be directing his spiritual drives the wrong way.

Having given up on society, Ernest next gave up on ethics. After
a few years of living in his commune, he started doing things he
never would have imagined doing before. For example, he sometimes stole food from the local supermarket before going to his
room to study the Bible. He justified his action by thinking how
corrupt society was. The farther he went in this direction, the
harder it became for him to see his mistakes and correct himself.
As he put it, "You cannot believe how strong you feel when, in
the name of God, you think you are right against the rest of the
world."

Eventually, Ernest figured out that the group's leader was using
spiritual-sounding words to solidify his power over the others
and to make them into his adoring subjects. Ernest finally left
the group, realizing that the fault was his and not God's. He had
learned a good, if hard, lesson about the false beliefs that had gradually led him into difficulty, and he continued on his path in a far
more cautious way.

How can we learn something useful from Ernest's story? The
best way is to analyze it by choosing principles that underscore the
fundamental error that you think got Ernest (and Jane in chapter
5) into trouble. For me, it is found in three of Ostad Elahi's closely
interrelated principles:

- "To be useful to society is a universal duty."
- "What are piety, altruism, and love of God but to do our
  utmost to benefit society?"

- "Attending to one's social etiquette and conduct is a prerequisite for the education of the soul."

Each has a slightly different slant, but all point to the structure of society as the natural context in which we grow spiritually. That structure has built-in protections that prevent us from going to extremes.

Many of the most basic principles seem like good common sense, nothing we need to think about more deeply. We discover a principle's deeper wisdom, however, not by thinking about it in the abstract but by applying its seeming common sense in our own life. If we examine each word in a principle and try to understand why the author of our set of principles chose to highlight this one in this particular way, the principle becomes a reference point around which we sort and organize our experiences. We might think, for example: What does it mean for us to be useful or to do our utmost in our family and in our neighborhood? What society are we talking about, and what if we don't agree with its values? What is social etiquette, and why is it important? Why are there three principles that are so similar? What is the different intent of each? How do they interconnect to create a synergy? Each of us will ask different questions and come up with different answers. By asking our questions and answering them as best we can, we gradually make the wisdom of those principles our own, yet in a way that is relevant to the circumstances of our own life.

Most of us are unlikely to make the same mistake that Ernest did. We can, however, learn from his experience by seeing what it would mean if we made a mistake similar to his—not going into a cult, specifically, but ignoring principles that encourage us to live a useful life in our society. For example, I can see how the many things I object to in my society, with its overly materialistic bent, might make me think that I was above it somehow. The three principles I've mentioned encourage me to acknowledge the debt that I owe to society for giving me the stable structure in which

I live—electricity, roads, law, and so forth. They encourage me to contribute to that society instead of withdrawing from it. They remind me how important this order is for developing spiritual intelligence. Thinking in this way alters the meaning that I give to different situations, how I pay attention to things, and how I intend to respond to common situations in everyday life.

Strengthening Our Inner Muscles

Let's turn to another example and see how principles encourage us to confront our weak points within the kind of everyday life we've discussed. Florence had a propensity to isolate herself for reasons quite different from Ernest's and Jane's. She was extremely shy. She often looked down as we spoke, as if embarrassed to tell a story that I thought she should be proud of. "I was always a person who was lazy and afraid of almost everyone and everything," she told me. "I had never really applied myself to either my relationships or my schoolwork. I was also very sensitive and felt that nobody understood me. This sensitivity made me turn to spirituality. I was happy for several years, but I gradually realized that if I continued being lazy, I wouldn't make any progress in my spiritual life either. It was a sad moment when this suddenly became self-evident to me as I saw how others seemed to be progressing faster than I did. I had been using spirituality to justify my laziness by downplaying the importance of material life. Now I felt that I had to improve myself if I wanted to make spiritual progress."

Previously, Florence had thought that spiritual actions were things like going to church, reading spiritual books, or talking about spiritual subjects. She now decided that it would be even better for her spiritually if she went back to school and became a teacher. She had read Ostad Elahi's maxims, and she was struck by one of them: "Among the various branches of knowledge, those that are beneficial to society also have a positive spiritual effect."

Florence discovered one of her dysfunctional beliefs—that spirituality had little to do with everyday life—as the principle made this error crystal clear.

It's not that Florence's previous focus on principles that emphasized the importance of faith was wrong; working on her faith had motivated her to take this next developmental step. When she did, she found that going to school with a spiritual intention helped her develop better habits than she had ever had. It's in line with another principle: "Being organized, active, and diligent not only leads to success in our daily material lives, but also contributes significantly to our spiritual development." Indeed, many of the qualities that lead to success in the material world contribute to our spiritual development. However, basing her efforts in a spiritual principle helped Florence be more certain that her efforts to improve her everyday habits were truly valuable to her spiritually and create another reference point by which to bring other aspects of her life into a more spiritual perspective.

"Now I have finished my degree, I am teaching, and I'm a mother," Florence says. "I still struggle against my inertia, but I don't have the time to sit around much anymore. I'm more content with my life and don't feel afraid of everything like I used to. I am sure this change is because of God's help in my life, which made each of these efforts possible."

Once Florence enrolled in school, she had no need to set up a program of change such as we explored in chapter 7; a program was effectively set for her by the demands of her course of study. Finishing school made up the material part of her intention. Her efforts became spiritual when she added her spiritual intention and acted with the principles in mind that encouraged her to be organized, diligent, and responsible. As she did, she developed a sense of her own dignity that became a reliable touchstone for her in deciding what to do; it became beneath her dignity to give in to her laziness. It no longer felt right to use excuses, such as lacking energy or wanting to watch TV, for not doing her work on time.

Instead, she felt encouraged to do her homework, say her prayers, and read spiritual books regularly. She was now in touch with a growing desire to improve herself.

For another way to see how Florence's material life was influencing her spiritual development, think of the film *The Karate Kid*. In that story, a boy who wants to learn karate is told where to find the best teacher. But when he gets there, he doesn't do the exercises that he expected to do, the exciting kicks and punches he has seen everyone else practicing. Instead, he is told to wash windows, paint, and do other mundane things, always in certain specific ways. The teacher knows that by doing these movements, the boy will strengthen all the right muscles in his body and build the "real" karate skills he so desires on a level he doesn't even perceive. When he finally has to fight with his opponent, with only a few additional instructions, he wins.

Forging Intelligent Connections

Principles give us reference points that enable us to think about our spiritual experiences in a systematic way. The more we apply them in our daily life, the more we will begin to think in line with the overarching vision of those principles. Systems of principles help us take advantage of the way our brains work. The brain forms billions of connections, or synapses, that are constantly being updated based on new experience. Certain synapses are broken down that aren't being used or that lead to wrong conclusions, while new ones are formed based on better understanding of our experiences. The human brain is so much more effective than that of other animals because it is structured in ways that allow us to take in large amounts of information, discover patterns, and define principles that guide future decisions. By providing our brains with a sound set of reference points that have been proven to work together by others before us, we gain a tremendous advantage.

Newly adopted principles are in many ways like the brain cells of an embryo. They are filled with potential that is dictated by the plan encoded in them, which determines what we will become. One brain cell or one principle functioning in isolation from the others can't do very much, but when it is linked to others, it can organize the functioning and development of a whole complex being. So each principle can't get us very far on its own, but when correctly interconnected with other principles, it powers a whole way of thinking, feeling, and acting that makes us who we are.

What I want to make clear by this analogy is that although it may sound miraculous that we can develop true spiritual intelligence just by applying a set of basic spiritual principles in different situations, in doing so we are taking advantage of how our brains work to speed up learning. We're also using the wisdom of the person who put our system of principles together so that we don't have to go through the same effort that he or she did to construct an effective system of thought.

By learning sound principles that have been distilled from others' experience, we gain a tremendous advantage over anyone who insists on learning everything himself. To use a different analogy, it's like finding the right software to install on a computer. Once you install it and learn how to use it, you can take advantage of all the work that programmers have done for you without having to even understand why some of the operations you do are important or what connections are being made at a level you can't see.

Honoring the Spirit of the Law

The application of principles in Ernest's and Florence's situations seems straightforward because they were looking back on what went on in their lives over a period of years. It's far more difficult to know how principles apply when we are in the middle of a situation. Yet one thing is for sure—if we are to gain the wisdom of a set of principles, we can't apply them just in retrospect. We need to apply them in the heat of everyday life and have messages either correct us or confirm that we have applied them correctly. Although you won't always get the kind of unmistakable feedback that a judge I know received, if you keep at it, you'll learn how to decode the more subtle feedback that is always there.

One day, this judge decided that he'd been putting material comfort ahead of his spiritual principles. He wanted to give more attention to his spiritual values and less to his material comfort. He was likely basing his decision on the common idea that the pleasures of this world are ephemeral and that, to live a spiritual life, we should seek instead things that are lasting. He felt a noble intention to put his belief into practice.

The judge was zealous about his beliefs but had not yet mastered the fundamentals of his principles by implementing the kind of ethical program I outlined in the last chapter. He hadn't learned to process the various responses he got while trying to act on the Golden Rule in simple and straightforward situations. Thus, he threw himself into his project in a single-minded way that left him vulnerable to missing important details, for he was prepared to do only one thing: assert his devotion to God by applying his principles in the most unbending way possible to make up for having been lax.

Soon after, he found himself in a situation that tested his intention. He had just used most of his life savings to set up a health club in a building that he had owned and lived in for many years. When everything was finished, the inspectors came around as part of the permit process. "When they started asking, 'Who lives in this building?' I gave completely honest answers," the judge told me. "Then they casually informed me that the zoning laws prohibited mixing business and residential units in the same building, even though no one paid any attention to this technicality anymore, as anyone could see by looking up and down the street. The regulations were fifty years old, and people had bent the law more and more as the neighborhood had changed.

"The inspectors suggested that I say—just as others in the neighborhood had—that the units in the building that my family was living in were actually lofts used for business purposes, not residences. After all, the club was a family business. They weren't trying to get a bribe, just be helpful. But I saw this as a test of my commitment. I didn't want to lie or even bend the truth, so I insisted on the whole truth and nothing but the truth."

The judge believed that, from a spiritual perspective, he could never go wrong by being completely truthful. As the Golden Rule suggests, if you don't want to be lied to, you should not lie. Because the judge wanted to put his spiritual priorities first and he had just formed the clear intention to do so, he decided that this was a test for him and that he should be 100 percent honest regardless of the material cost to him. To justify the harm this might do to his life, he could even invoke other principles that seemed to underscore the spiritual value of overlooking things of material importance. Ostad Elahi puts this very common spiritual attitude in the following way: "To gain inner peace, one should not fear such things as loss of employment, poverty, death. . . ."

The judge felt certain of his decision at the time, yet after the perplexed inspectors left, he began to doubt himself. He felt, uncomfortably, that he had been too rigid, although he couldn't put into words how telling the truth in that situation could have been wrong. Hadn't spiritual people since the beginning of time sacrificed their material interests to get closer to God? Wasn't he doing this to put his beliefs into practice?

A little confused by his own doubts, the judge consulted several trusted friends who had more experience in applying spiritual principles than he did. Much to the judge's surprise, his friends first asked him, as an expert on the law, how he would have analyzed this situation if he hadn't seen it as a spiritual test. If I had been there, I would have asked the same question.

Clearly, the judge would have come to a different decision if he had not applied his principles so literally, and that would have been a better way to use them. In his courtroom, he always put the spirit of the law above the letter. Throughout his judicial career, he had made sure that his rulings were not based on a rigid, dogmatic interpretation of the law, and he believed that this was true wisdom. When he became interested in spirituality and wanted to learn to think according to its principles, however, he set aside his more highly developed ways of thinking and adhered rigidly to the letter of a higher law. His experience with the inspectors brought his dysfunctional belief to the fore, where he could see it and examine it. He saw that he had made his decision impulsively because he had no grounds, no precedents, on which to base decisions in the spiritual realm. Taking the whole picture into consideration, he decided that he had probably made a mistake.

Fortunately for him, the story was not over. A couple of days after the inspection, he got a call from a classmate he hadn't seen since law school. The man said he wanted to come by. "When my colleague arrived," the judge told me, "he said, 'I'm in charge of the legal department of the mayor's office, and with what you've written on your application, you've destroyed yourself. It's ridiculous, because that law was no longer relevant to what was going on in the neighborhood and had been ignored for years. However, the law is the law. So, I have brought a new set of blank forms. Let's fill them out together in such a way that you can get your permit.'" The judge filled out the forms, got the permit, and opened his business, which became quite successful.

His colleague's arrival was a message. It confirmed for him that he should not apply his principles in such a black-and-white way, but in the more discerning way in which he had learned to apply laws in his courtroom. He had made a natural mistake of emotional logic such as I pointed out in chapter 7, for we all tend to think in black and white when we have little experience in spirituality. We think that, because it's a "higher" law, it *should be* or *must be* applied more rigidly; we don't take into account the realities of a situation, because in spirituality it's *all or nothing*, right or wrong, and *catastrophic* if we are wrong. But we can correct our tendency in this direction if we carefully examine the results of using emotional logic in purely material affairs, and, of course, if we learn from others' mistakes.

The judge decided that there might come a time when he truly should not lie, even if it meant losing his life's savings, but he would be more cautious in making that decision. He would think about situations more carefully so that he could be honest but not a fool. All of this became clear to him because of the impact of spiritual energy in his message, which altered his attention and helped him see how he could act better. It helped him see that not attaching ultimate value to things of this world didn't mean setting aside common sense and that he needed to understand the deeper meaning of his beliefs.

We learn the most from someone else's experiences by seeing how his message helps him understand the implication of his principles better. We can then look to our own lives to see if our messages encourage us to honor the spirit of our principles and apply them in a discerning way or to apply them in a more rigid, black-and-white manner. This is very important for setting the emotional context in which to apply principles and decode messages. It is just as important as learning the material context of everyday life, as in the cases of Ernest and Florence. When we find evidence that we're being guided to be less dogmatic and more discerning, then we can use the judge's experience to help us be more certain of our own conclusions.

Keep It Real and Relevant

Principles help us solve problems better than common sense alone, for they give us grounds on which to examine intuitive conclusions more deliberately. They also provide a set of reference points that our messages can use to help us anchor our thinking in complex and demanding situations.

Let's look at how my friend Giorgio learned the value of principles in the dog-eat-dog world of the computer software industry. "After I became interested in spirituality, I thought that I had to be ethical above all and that I couldn't consider the politics of a situation," he said. "So for many years, I had the same problem in different companies, exactly as if my career track were on a damaged computer disk. When I encountered anything that seemed at all unethical, I would just walk out in disgust and find a new job. I felt above working with such people."

Giorgio made a mistake similar to the judge's for similar reasons. He had elevated spirituality to such a high level that it was no longer relevant to what was going on in his everyday life. As a result, he couldn't see how spiritual principles could be applied in his own real life or how he could work in that business and still be spiritual. He loved computers and he loved business. It was in his blood. Yet, even more than success in business, he wanted to develop spiritually. He didn't see any other choice than to leave a company when he encountered a problem.

"Then I found myself on this new job as part of the commercial department," Giorgio said. "I had a very good idea, and my immediate supervisor wanted to take it. He started presenting my idea to the big boss as if it were his own while trying to find grounds to fire me. All of my friends were telling me that I would lose. It was extraordinary. I had to do my own job—selling programs—and at the same time, I had to avoid the traps that he was laying for me. I even had to make traps so that he would fall in. I found it horrible but at the same time exciting."

Giorgio had been raised as a Christian and taught the value of sacrificing material advantage for a higher principle, much as I had been. He thought that he should turn the other cheek rather than fight for his own interests. All his life, his willingness to give up his material advantage had been the sign of true faith to him, so he didn't even consider any other possible interpretation.

However, Giorgio talked to several other friends who were

interested in spirituality as well as active in business. They thought that he should defend himself, not just quit. He had actually never considered this possibility before, but it opened his mind to alternative strategies. "At first, I couldn't see any spiritual benefit at all for me in continuing to work in this corrupt world," he told me. "Then one day I suddenly saw it differently. In fact, I went one step further and thought that not only might it be beneficial to defend myself—it was my *spiritual duty* to do so. It was like an inspiration that came out of nowhere. I knew that I couldn't just let myself be taken advantage of and I couldn't count on God to take care of it for me. At the beginning, I was shocked by this idea, for I had always felt that my religious beliefs encouraged me to take the higher ground and not get my hands dirty. But I was newly married and my wife was expecting a child, so I also felt forced by my responsibilities to at least try to defend myself rather than just walking out again."

With this new perspective, Giorgio had to strike a delicate balance. He knew that respecting the rights of others was an important ethical principle. He thought about the rights of the various "others" in his situation: the owner of the company, his immediate boss, his own family, and even society. If he gave in to his unethical boss without a real fight, he would be disregarding the rights of many others: If ethical people didn't protect themselves, they would all be run out of business and society would be run by the most ruthless. The situation was no longer a question with one clear answer, but a problem with many factors to be weighed. It was a very tangible and immediate, as well as complex, test that tied into all of his other attempts to apply the Golden Rule in other situations.

Giorgio's new analysis convinced him to approach the situation in another, more strategic way that was still in line with the best *business ethics* he knew. Everyone knew what kind of person his boss was; there just needed to be a little slip-up to make it clear that his actions weren't in the best interests of the company. So Giorgio devised a kind of trap that would make his boss's true nature apparent without him having to be the one to bring it to the director's attention. The correctness of his new strategy was confirmed for him by a turn of events that he took as a message. "I was really protected because of my spiritual intention," he told me. "It turned out that the director who had begun fighting against me to steal my idea and get me fired—he was the one who got fired. It was a miracle."

His surprising victory came with the inner impact of a message transforming his perception of the event and bringing the principles he had considered into a different balance than before. He could see from a spiritual perspective how everything worked together. He had set his business dealings in a business context and applied the same principles—of not fearing material loss, turning the other cheek, and defending his rights—differently than he might have in another context, and they had worked together better than if he tried to apply them in the same way everywhere. He was happy to see that he could become a lion in business and pursue his spiritual interest at the same time. His spiritual and material lives were integrated so that both benefited, for he no longer felt pulled apart by such situations—challenged and stressed, yes, but not pulled apart.

Since I had been raised like Giorgio to think that the essence of spirituality is to "love your enemy," it was difficult for me to imagine that a spiritual person could aggressively defend his interest against someone who was trying to take advantage of him. To help me relate to Giorgio's decision, I looked through the principles of Ostad Elahi and found several that encouraged me to think that being a wimp was no virtue and that standing up for myself could have a positive spiritual value—principles like "Allowing oneself to be swindled is to be unjust to those who are truly in need" and "Humility should be reserved for those who would interpret it as a gesture of politeness and magnanimity rather than one of fear or inferiority."

But in the challenging situations of everyday life there is another side to every decision you make. In this situation, for example, another principle of Ostad Elahi seems to counsel a different direction: "How noble it is to do good, be wronged in return, and yet forgive." I felt that both positions had to be taken into account, so I wrote them on an index card and read them several times a day while I was at work, where I was wrestling with some of the same issues Giorgio faced in his own setting. It helped me balance the politics of certain situations that I was in with the "higher" principles that I wished to apply. It increased my awareness of the need to be discerning and view each principle in light of the particulars. Although I might sometimes be too assertive of my rights and at other times not be assertive enough, by basing my decisions in principles I have developed a better sense of how these principles work together, and in this way Giorgio's experience has added to my own experiences.

꒓   ꒓   ꒓

Messages and principles work well together, and getting the two to combine gives us a tremendous advantage. Principles put into words the conclusions that messages lead to, while messages confirm whether or not we are applying principles correctly in particular situations. Both help us align better with the spiritual dimension and thus bring the influx of spiritual energy that we need to develop the kind of spiritual character and intelligence that will work in our everyday lives.

The more we make the wisdom of a given principle our own, the more we think, feel, and act like bi-dimensional beings at home in a world that is both material and spiritual.

꒓   ꒓   ꒓

Keys to Chapter 9

- Spiritual principles exist in every religious and spiritual tradition. If you search, you can find a system of principles that will help you develop spiritually in everyday life more so than if you cherry-picked principles that appealed to you from different systems.
- The human brain is structured to take in large amounts of information, discover patterns, and define principles that will provide the basis for future decisions. When you adopt a coherent set of well-established principles, you take maximum advantage of the way your brain works and optimize the rich associative network that connects it to your soul.
- Principles provide concrete reference points that not only help you decide what to do in a given situation but enable you to apply what you learn from that situation to other different situations in the future. As you analyze your own and other people's experiences with a coherent system of principles, your spiritual intelligence becomes increasingly astute.
- Although most of us start with a tendency to apply principles in a black-and-white way because we lack the experience to apply them in any other way, with practice you can learn to apply them in situation-specific ways that take into account the shades of gray in everyday life.
- When you are in a situation where you're not sure what to do, it's good to find several principles that suggest different courses of action. By thinking of your situation from the perspective of each principle, making the best decision you can and looking for the feedback of your messages, you'll gain experience in how to apply principles in the challenging, complex situations you commonly face.
- There are many ways of keeping principles active in your mind. One way is to choose several principles that seem

relevant to a situation in your life right now. Write them on an index card and carry them around in your pocket. Read them several times each day for a week, and see how your understanding of those principles grows.

ۍ ۍ ۍ

For Your Reflection

Spiritual principles play an invaluable role in the development of spiritual intelligence. They allow you to take advantage of the wisdom that others have accumulated by decoding their messages. Use the following points to examine your own relationship with your own principles:

1. Systems of sound principles exist in every tradition to guide our spiritual development. Do you have such a set of principles? If not, how would you go about finding one from a source you trust that seems relevant to your everyday concerns?

2. To learn how your principles apply, you will need a clear understanding of the context in which they are meant to work. My principles work best, for example, when applied in a normal life in society. Find several principles in your own system that establish the context in which they are meant to apply. Do they agree or disagree with the principles I have quoted in this chapter about the importance of a normal life in society?

3. How do you verify that your set of principles is spiritually active? Can you see spiritual effects similar to those of messages when you apply a principle? How does applying them change what you learn from a situation?

4. Go to decodeyourmessages.com to find out how others learned to access the power of their principles.

5. Take out a sheet of paper or turn to a blank page in your notebook and entitle it "The Power of My Principles." You can also go to decodeyourmessages.com to download these points for reflection to your computer or log into your online notebook. Write a paragraph on the principles you use: Why you've chosen these principles, how regularly you consult them, how they have helped you, and how important they are in your spiritual journey. Once you've written your summary paragraph, write in as much detail as you'd like about the evidence that demonstrates the advantages that using your principles has brought you.

6. Go to decodeyourmessages.com to add the experiences that demonstrate the power of your principles in your life.

CHAPTER 10

Increasing Your
Spiritual Emotional Intelligence

E motions are vital to our functioning in both everyday and spiritual life. Aristotle, in his *Nicomachean Ethics*, defined wisdom as being able to consistently feel an emotion at the right time toward the right person for the right reason in the right manner. More recently, Daniel Goleman, in his bestseller *Emotional Intelligence*, called our attention to the particular abilities needed to achieve wisdom: to be self-aware, manage our emotions appropriately, motivate ourselves in the directions we choose, feel empathy for others, and build mutually satisfying relationships. If, in doing so, we at the same time invest our emotions in time-honored virtues—like compassion, courage, zeal, and integrity—Goleman tells us that we actualize the truly human parts of our nature and ensure our greatest happiness. If we can align this basic level of psychological emotional intelligence with our spiritual principles and messages, we will develop *spiritual* emotional intelligence, a healthy emotional intelligence directed toward our spiritual goal, and actualize the deeper potential of our souls.

Goleman made us more acutely aware that our goal is not the absence of struggle but the actualization of our potentials that only comes through struggling with our emotions. The key to developing emotional intelligence on both the psychological and the spiritual level, then, is struggling in the right way with our passions and their demand for immediate gratification, in line with the wisdom of our principles. As we do this, we learn to use their energy to achieve realistic levels of the virtues Aristotle and Goleman define, working with a spiritual intention under the guidance of our messages.

To show you how spiritual virtue differs from everyday virtue, let's start with the case of Frances. Frances is a seasoned high-school science teacher, happily married, with many friends. I've known her for many years, and she has often given me good advice about the spiritual elements in situations in my own life. One evening, at a weekly discussion group she attended, she was listening to a presentation on spirituality. The speaker was trying to explain a certain point, which Frances couldn't even remember when she told me the story several months later. But she clearly remembered that she didn't like the way it was being presented. Since she was a teacher herself, she felt entitled to say to the person next to her, "She doesn't know how to teach. This is terrible."

Frances really believed that the talk was terrible, and she was sure that she could have done a much better job. She felt justifiably proud of what a good teacher she was. However, although her analysis of the presentation might have been correct, her emotions had hijacked her thinking so that she became unnecessarily critical of the presenter. She could have responded in other ways instead. She could, for example, have talked privately to the speaker and made positive, tactful suggestions as to how she might improve her presentation. In talking with her friend after the lecture, she could have brought up some positive points about the subject of the talk, even if those points weren't touched on in the lecture, so that she and her friend would benefit from considering the topic of the talk for themselves. At other times, she had been able to do these things, but not tonight. Tonight her emotions were in charge.

Am I making something big out of something quite small? Frances doesn't think so, and the end of the story proves her right. "The next day, I went to work and had a big surprise," she continued. "I had been teaching for about twenty-six years and nothing like what happened that day had ever happened to me before. The head of the school called me in and said, 'Frances, we have a problem. This is very surprising and very embarrassing, but a few students complained to me that the last class you had was terrible. They didn't understand anything. They said that if this is the way it is going to be, they won't go to your class.'

"I was stunned and furious. As I started to defend myself, however, the secretary came to me and said, 'Somebody is calling and says that it's urgent.' When I went to answer the phone, it was the friend I had complained to the night before. She was calling me at exactly that moment to tell me something that had been bothering her so much that it couldn't wait. 'That was a terrible comment you made about the lecturer last night,' she said. 'It was a very negative remark.' It was only then that I realized that my students were treating me just as I had treated the lecturer."

Her friend's unexpected call came with the impact of a message that helped her realize what happened to her. "I apologized to God," she continued, "but the matter was not finished. The next week, I had such a terrible backache that I couldn't move, so I missed the discussion group where I had criticized the presenter at the last meeting. When the following meeting came, I had another serious problem and I couldn't attend. When I finally made it to another meeting, three weeks after that episode, I parked the car in my usual place, but when I came out of the meeting it wasn't there. My car had been stolen."

Frances believes that these other incidents were like the aftershocks of an earthquake. They were so harsh because the spiritual dangers of giving into excessive pride were so great, and that's because pride undermines our ability to act ethically and greatly weakens our soul. Unless guided by reason and reality, our emotions all too often drive us toward self-centeredness and excessive pride. And it is by struggling to correct weaknesses like this, in situations that occur naturally in everyday life, that we develop emotional intelligence. Although both psychology and spirituality put excessive pride at the root of many problems, spiritual principles raise the bar higher—as Frances's message makes clear—because the harms of excessive pride are even greater in our spiritual life than in our psychological life.

In the Jewish, Christian, and Islamic traditions, pride's destructive power can be found in archetypal stories like the fall of Satan or Adam and Eve's expulsion from the Garden of Eden. Ostad Elahi puts it this way in one of the principles I draw on: "So destructive is [excessive] pride that more than any other sin it weakens the soul and strengthens the imperious self." What does Ostad Elahi mean by the "imperious self," and why does he call pride a sin and not just a weakness? Spiritual traditions focused on the danger of excessive pride far before modern psychology existed. Each religious and spiritual tradition has a slightly different way of describing the concerted inner resistance we all feel to acting on our principles and the consequences of giving in to it. In the Islamic tradition in which Ostad Elahi lived, the source of the resistance is called the *imperious self* because it arrogantly and tyrannically tries to counter our efforts to act on our spiritual principles that point us in the direction of our highest good.

You can substitute your own word to name the part of you that opposes your efforts to develop spiritually. Try to clarify in your own mind the nature of this force as you read so that when you get to the points for reflection at the end of the chapter, you will be ready to describe how it manifests in you.

The first step in getting to know our imperious self is to know its manifestations, beginning with how it induces the kind of excessive pride that leads to so many malfunctions in our thoughts, feelings, and actions. If people have had a problem with excessive pride since the beginning of time, as Frances did, I probably have it too. So her story pushes me to reflect on the harms of excessive pride—even in its mildest manifestations—and look for signs of it in my own life. It pushes me to look for any negative reactions that my displays of excessive pride may elicit and compare them to the consequences Frances experienced. It pushes me to compare the harms of pride in everyday life to those in spiritual life. It forces me to reexamine my idea of what humility is.

Seeking Emotional Balance

How do we get ourselves in the best possible position to prevent this imperious self from getting between us and our principles? Simply by bringing our emotions into balance. That's because our imperious self is able to take control more easily when we get caught up in everyday problems in our habitual ways. Any emotional imbalance that interferes with our everyday life makes it harder to act in line with our principles and be attentive to our messages. By bringing common imbalances like anxiety, fear, anger, or sadness into balance, we make it easier for ourselves to keep our imperious self in line. If we apply a spiritual principle along with our psychological efforts, our efforts will build spiritual intelligence.

Here's how a spiritual message compelled Martha, a successful physician, to develop her emotional intelligence and spiritual intelligence in tandem. "I had finished a written examination for my medical boards," Martha told me, her voice trembling as she recalled the experience. "Unbeknownst to me, somebody had copied my answers and both of our exams were disqualified. I was told that I had to take the exam over. I cried. My dad said that if I fought this decision, I would never win. I was close to the head of the general medical clinic where I was working, and he knew how the board worked. He too said, 'You are not going to win. Nobody is going to listen to you. Are you joking?'

"At the time, I was just getting interested in spirituality, and a friend who knew far more about spiritual matters than I did encouraged me to fight for my rights. She explained that it was important spiritually for me to defend myself when I was in the right. She said that although it was right to trust in God, I shouldn't think that God would always take care of me without my trying to take care of myself. Because of this advice, I decided to find a lawyer, go against the odds, and fight the decision. I just wanted to show that I hadn't done anything wrong. But I was also very scared."

When I discussed this with Martha, we agreed that the principle of mine that captured what she had in mind at the time was "Place your hope in no one but God." That was the only thing that kept her going through her ordeal, a desire to act on her faith and truly place her hope in God. After several agonizing months, Martha and her lawyer went to Chicago and met with the examination board and their lawyers. "My lawyer proved everything to their satisfaction," she told me. "They quickly apologized to me and released my grade. All of my professors at school were surprised. I learned from this that I should always say something in the face of a wrong, not just go away and hide. It was my right to win the case, but I had to take action to assert that right."

Martha's message was written into a *material situation* (the conflict with the medical board), gained force through a *heightened psychological state* (her fear of confronting authorities and her desire to rely on God), and was announced by an *unexpected external event* (her easy success) that drew her attention to an *inner spiritual impact* (a new feeling of inner strength). Her message confirmed that she had been right to put her hope in God, not passively, but actively, by speaking out in her own defense. There was no reason to be as fearful as she was. As a result of this experience, she felt encouraged to take more stands to promote her own interests and leave the results in God's hands.

We don't develop the virtue of courage merely by meditating on courage, but by acting with courage in situations that are difficult for us. That's exactly what Martha set out to do—develop more courage by putting her hope in God in those situations that filled her with fear. Each morning, she would think about what she might be afraid of that day, plan a way to assert herself, and remember to put her hope in God. What are some of the actions she took? She prepared herself to speak in a group, assert herself with colleagues, and not be intimidated by patients who were demanding. She pushed herself to ask for a raise, confront a coworker who was taking advantage of her, and voice her opinions with friends. Her efforts over the months and years that followed led to greater self-awareness and a greater overall emotional competence. She also developed a greater understanding of what she had a right to expect from putting her hope in God and what she didn't. She was developing her spiritual intelligence and improving her everyday life at the same time.

Reading Martha's example, we can see how some of our everyday emotions can divert us from our principles as much as pride does, not by causing us to rebel against them but by distracting us so that we don't even think about them. These emotions make it extremely easy for our imperious self to take over and get us to act impulsively to satisfy their demands instead of acting on principle. When we can use a combination of good common sense in conjunction with sound psychological and spiritual principles, each challenge that we face sets in motion a positive ripple effect that improves us both psychologically and spiritually.

A Modern Understanding of the Imperious Self

In both religious literature and the popular imagination, the reflex resistance to acting in line with our principles and messages is often depicted as a cunning devil inside of us because that is the way it can feel: The devil made me do it. But it is actually a function of how our brain is organized—we're wired to seek the satisfaction of a drive that is unfulfilled and causes us to feel, for example, hunger or sexual desire.

The brain has powerful built-in mechanisms designed to ensure our physical survival and that of our species in an environment that is constantly changing. It drives us, through our desires, to do all that is necessary to satisfy them. In our evolution, as humankind discovered the benefits of cooperation, each individual learned to postpone his own immediate demands for satisfaction and take on a role that would contribute to the collective good so that he could get his share of the collective reward. Our ego or self is the controller of these drives, managing them in a way that brings our greater benefit—more pleasure at a future time.

The imperious self is the part of us that resists this control and continues to reflexively insist on the gratification of our drives, pushing us to act against the spiritual principles that propose we act otherwise. The imperious self isn't that part of us that resists controlling our eating—other parts of us are responsible for this behavioral lapse—but it does work on a similar mechanism: our brain's inability to properly modulate our drives.

I am talking as if we were made up of all different, discrete parts, but of course we aren't. Each part of us is part of a larger whole and has access to one basic pool of abilities. So your imperious self is unique to you—and connected to the rest of you—because it draws upon the resources of the highly integrated emotional and intellectual centers of your brain that coordinate things in relation to your own temperament and experience. If you are strong-willed, then your imperious self will be strong-willed right back. If you are intelligent, it will be intelligent. If you are creative, then it too will be creative. If you use principles to fight it, it will do its best to turn those principles against you. Each of your assets, however well you have developed it, becomes a potential tool of the imperious self. This is why the resistance it puts up can seem conscious and cunning even though it's largely reflexive.

If we think of the resistance to our spiritual efforts as simply the result of different networks of neurons going about their job as they've learned to do it best based on our nature and nurture, we can demystify the opposition that we feel to acting on our spiritual principles. We can focus better on the job of reeducating those brain cells by reworking their interconnections over time so that we harmonize our emotion and our thought and bring them in line with common sense, the principles of sound psychology, and our spiritual principles. We can approach our resistance intelligently as we would work to break any other bad habit, giving greater priority to areas of spiritual importance.

Seeing how this struggle is built into our nature and how much time and energy it takes to keep our emotions in line so that they help us reach our goals, we soon understand that the conflict between our imperious self and our soul is the primary means by which our soul develops. It is no accident. We are here in this classroom in this particular body with its particular drives and its reaction to its environment in order to learn how to control our imperious self, and it is up to us to use the struggle with our own unique imperious self for our own development. To get started, you might even imagine that you are a boxer and your imperious self is your sparring partner. By fighting against it, you develop your spiritual emotional intelligence and become strong.

Developing Better Attitudes

Our emotional drives are constantly seeking our material benefit and trying to avoid the material dangers in everyday life. They keep us on our toes and provide the motivation for our efforts at psychological self-improvement. A major part of emotional intelligence is self-awareness, in which we are conscious of our feelings, our mood, and our thoughts about the mood, and use this understanding to function better. One of the goals in becoming spiritually emotionally intelligent is to become aware of the influences of the imperious self even when it isn't getting us into trouble. We can do this by pushing ourselves to act on our principles in more subtle ways in everyday situations and observing the reaction we get.

For the past two years, I have taken five to ten minutes at the beginning of every day to think about how I can keep my imperious self in check. Then, every night before going to bed, I take another five to ten minutes to think over my day and what I've done. These few minutes at each end of the day form a routine that helps me keep my emotional reactions to everyday situations in spiritual perspective. During these periods of reflection, I write down several key words that represent different aspects of the attitudes I want to develop. These words change as different things become prominent in my mind. Sometimes I only have one word, sometimes six. Here's a sample of what one day's morning review might be.

1. **Purpose**—My imperious self does better when I forget my purpose in life. During the day, I am swept along by the demands of everyday life and find myself thinking and acting in ways that can be contrary to my beliefs. I can feel myself attaching too much importance to the material aspect of life and not enough to the spiritual elements in the situation. In the morning, I set my intention: to try to recall at least three times during the day that material life really is a classroom and to look at what is going on at that moment in my life to see what I need to learn of spiritual value. I commit myself to examine at the end of the day what I learned that day.

2. **Integrity**—My imperious self is happy when I ignore my principles for any reason. I find it particularly demoralizing to walk down the streets or sit in a subway and catch

myself criticizing others, as if I am clearly superior. It's a certain sign of excessive pride and very humiliating to me. It feels beneath my dignity to react in this way, for I know better. So I plan to correct my critical thoughts about others at least three times that day—not just push them away so that they come back a minute later, but consciously and forcefully reject them so that they don't come back for at least a half an hour. If the thoughts don't go away, I force myself to consider how I would explain my thoughts to the person I'm thinking about, or to someone who loves that person, or even to God. Even the idea of doing this changes my perspective enough that my feeling of superiority soon vanishes.

3. **Gratitude**—My imperious self does better when I forget that God has given me everything and start to think that I deserve what I have and more. When I was a child, I would never forget to thank God for a meal. Now it's hard for me to feel grateful. So I try to think consciously about why I should thank God for meals, or for my health, my spiritual beliefs, my consciousness, or my very existence, at least three times a day and to focus on that thought until I feel grateful. When I have trouble doing this, I think of the people whose material help I do feel grateful for and push myself to think why I shouldn't then be grateful to God, who gives me even more.

4. **Focus of attention**—My imperious self is happy when I approach my spiritual life ritualistically without paying much attention. So I commit myself to being as focused as I can be during my prayer times. When my attention slips in my prayers, I go back and repeat the part where I drifted.

I carry out these plans in the spirit of CBT and emotional intelligence, with a goal of becoming more self-aware, motivated, and self-controlled, and in line with the feedback of my messages, for the satisfaction of God. The routine helps me remain aware of the constant inner pressure of my drives pushing me to be so engaged in the drama of everyday life as to forget my spiritual priorities. When I remind myself that this struggle is the means of my development and not a diversion, it motivates me to do my best to stay on top of it and keep my emotions working in line with my principles.

ॐ   ॐ   ॐ

Emotional intelligence is more important than our intellectual IQ in determining our success and fulfillment in life. Factors like self-awareness, self-discipline, and empathy make us smart in a completely different way. A purely psychological view of emotional intelligence, however, ignores another crucial range of potentials that matter—those of our spiritual nature. Like our emotional intelligence, our spiritual emotional intelligence is a potential that must be constantly nurtured and strengthened. With carefully planned efforts guided by our system of principles, however, we can use our emotional intelligence as the basis for developing spiritual emotional intelligence.

The emotional intelligences encouraged respectively by psychology and spirituality work well together. Spiritual principles, however, raise the bar for true happiness a bit higher; for example, they call on us to bring our pride and our emotional conflicts down to lower levels than psychology finds necessary for balance and well-being, and they give greater importance to finding the benefit in whatever happens to us. By drawing on the methods of psychology and the wisdom of our principles, we can, under the careful guidance of our messages, use a vital material life as a springboard and turn our passions in directions that are good for us spiritually as well. In the next three chapters, we will examine several of the numerous ways of developing spiritual emotional intelligence.

Keys to Chapter 10

- To achieve emotional intelligence, you need to be self-aware, manage your emotions appropriately, motivate yourself in the directions you choose, feel empathy for others, and build mutually satisfying relationships. You will want to develop more of time-honored virtues like compassion, courage, zeal, and integrity. This requires effort. As Daniel Goleman shows us in his book *Emotional Intelligence,* our goal cannot be the unrealistic goal of the absence of struggle; it must be the realistic goal of actualizing our potential by continually struggling to direct our emotions in ways that conform to our values.

- If you can achieve Goleman's basic level of emotional intelligence while applying your spiritual principles and decoding your messages, you will develop spiritual emotional intelligence: a healthy emotional intelligence directed toward your spiritual goal that actualizes the deeper potentials of your soul as well as your brain.

- Part of us—a part that I refer to as our *imperious self*—seems to actively oppose our own efforts to think, feel, and act in line with our principles. The resistance is not a devil inside of you but a product of the drives of your body and the associative systems of your brain.

- Although the imperious self manifests most obviously in excessive pride, it can influence you through an excess or deficiency of any emotion, whether it be desire, anxiety, fear, anger, or sadness.

- One of the goals of becoming spiritually emotionally intelligent is to help us be more aware of how the imperious self operates. A good way to do this is by pushing ourselves in everyday situations to consistently act on our principles in whatever way we can and overcome any resistance we encounter. This will prevent us from making more significant mistakes.

કુ   કુ   કુ

For Your Reflection

Spiritual emotional intelligence invests our emotions in ways that help us both live a satisfying material life and reach our spiritual goal. Use these points to help you clarify your views on the nature of spiritual emotional intelligence:

1. There is a force in each of us that resists efforts to act in line with our principles. Ostad Elahi calls it the *imperious self*. I think of it as the force of my emotional drives that cause me to act contrary to my principles. By what name do you call this force, and what are its defining characteristics?

2. Do your emotions get you into trouble in everyday life—whether it be through too much pride, anxiety, fear, or courage—so that you don't act in line with your principles? Do you feel psychological pressure that makes you overly reactive to the demands in your life? Try to identify any negative impact that your emotions have on your spiritual growth, as underscored by any messages you might have received.

3. Go to decodeyourmessages.com to find the strategies that others have used to battle their emotional drives and learn the results of their efforts.

4. Take out a sheet of paper or turn to a blank page in your notebook and entitle it "Increasing My Spiritual Emotional

Intelligence." You can also go to decodeyourmessages.com to download these points for reflection or log into your online notebook. Write a paragraph on the main ways in which *your* emotions keep *you* from acting on your principles. Mention the best strategy you have found to counter this tendency. Once you've written your summary paragraph, write in as much detail as you'd like about your struggles and what you have learned from them.

5. Go to decodeyourmessages.com to share with others the best ways you have found to increase your spiritual emotional intelligence.

CHAPTER II

Building Spiritual Willpower

The key to developing spiritual emotional intelligence is having the ability to stop ourselves from acting on emotional impulses that might lead to instant gratification but ultimately drive us in directions that are self-defeating. To illustrate the importance of impulse control for our psychological well-being, Daniel Goleman in *Emotional Intelligence* pointed to a classic study of four-year-olds. Each was left alone in a room with a marshmallow and told that if he refrained from eating it, he would be given two marshmallows when the teacher returned. The children who could stop themselves from eating one marshmallow in order to get two a little later grew up more socially competent, self-reliant, dependable, personally effective, assertive, and confident. They coped with frustrations and embraced challenges better.

The ability to control our impulses to act on the material value of things and take into account our spiritual principles in even simple situations in everyday life is just as essential for us to increase our spiritual emotional intelligence. Emotional drives exert a kind of pressure on us, and we experience the relief of these pressures as pleasure. Although all human beings have the same basic drives, there is great variability in how strongly each of them pressures each one of us. Taken together, our drives determine the intensity with which we engage the world around us. There is even more variability in the ways we end up satisfying them based on the options available to us. We might prefer money to admiration or a good sex life or advancement in our job. We might like one kind of person and not another or develop one potential or interest and not another.

Although it feels to us as if we are attracted to one thing and repelled by another because of something in the objects themselves, the truth is the pressure comes from inside of us and the choice of object is determined by a combination of our nature and our nurture. We develop spiritual emotional intelligence by managing this pressure and directing it in ways that are in line with our principles. To do so successfully requires self-knowledge and willpower.

To give us a basis to discuss the nature of the spiritual willpower we need to manage the pressure of our emotional drives, let's consider the story of Donald. He is a successful real estate broker who is happily married and has many good friends. During a slump in his sales, he found himself getting envious not only of other realtors when they made big sales but also of potential clients who could afford to buy homes that he could not. The longer he went without a sale, the more his feelings of inadequacy and envy grew.

Rationally, Donald knew that his business had good periods and bad. He even knew that being negative would only make things worse by affecting his demeanor with clients and dampening their enthusiasm for the properties he showed them. He also knew that being envious wasn't spiritually intelligent, as envy is recognized by all traditions as a spiritual defect. In Judeo-Christian parlance, it's one of the seven deadly sins; in one of Ostad Elahi's principles, its harmful effects are recognized as well: "The acid of jealousy first attacks its beholder and then permeates the surroundings."

As his slump worsened, so did Donald's inner state. The pressure began building. His attempts to stop his growing envy and bitterness now only seemed to speed his downward spiral. No matter what he tried, he couldn't get his emotions under control. The pressure was too great. His spiritual beliefs even fueled his descent as he started heaping negative judgments on himself for not being able to control his emotions.

Donald couldn't stand feeling powerless against it, so he told his imperious self, "If you don't stop, I'm going to hit my head against the wall until you do." His imperious self didn't believe him, but he was serious. So that no one would see him, he took an elevator to a quiet and secluded place in the basement of a building where he was trying to sell an apartment. There, he hit his head against a wall. He hit it harder and harder until the envious thoughts finally stopped. His mind was so focused on the fear that he would continue that all thoughts of envy just melted away.

Donald had a headache for the rest of the day, but his feelings of envy had disappeared and didn't come back that day. Donald had asserted his willpower in a very concrete way and refused to give into the emotional pressures that sought to dominate his thinking. Whenever they threatened to return, he threatened to hit his head against the wall again, and they backed off because they had learned that he was serious. Once he had reduced those pressures, he could again get his thinking into line with his principles and keep his emotions at bay.

Although I certainly wouldn't advise that you try Donald's method, I do advise a variation of it. I've often recommended to patients that they put an elastic band around one wrist and snap it harder and harder until the emotion that controls their thinking gives way to a stronger emotion—the desire to avoid immediate pain. It's a form of conditioning that links those negative thoughts to the physical pain that they cause us and makes us want to avoid the source of pain. It works because we hate discomfort in any form and we'll stop such negative thoughts when we are afraid of retaliation. It also reminds us that the negative thoughts are harming us far more than the snap of the elastic band.

A large part of the power of our imperious self comes from the constant pressure our inner drives exert on us as they seek their satisfaction, the objects of our desire. The pressure of the imperious self can become so strong that you might think the best thing to do would be to kill it off instead of just snapping an elastic band on your wrist. Yet thinking of killing off your imperious self, as mystics of old seemed intent on doing with their extreme asceticism, is like wanting to cut off your right arm because it makes a gesture you don't approve of. Yes, your right arm will never do that again, but you've lost something quite useful in the process.

The internal urge that we feel toward the objects of our desire is not an enemy but the means for our spiritual development. Once you understand how your imperious self gains its power from your basic drives invested in your heart's desires, you can formulate better strategies to stay on top of its antics and direct your vital energy toward spiritual goals while moderating those desires in line with common sense. You can then benefit from using those parts of you—like your right hand, above—for your material and spiritual betterment.

What Is Spiritual Willpower?

From the perspective of science, our brainstem is the origin of all our innate drives—like hunger, sex, and aggression—that are necessary for our own survival and that of our species. Each drive is geared toward a certain aspect of our life and creates a state of inner tension that can be satisfied only by its particular object. Hunger is satisfied by food and not by shopping. When a drive is satisfied, we feel pleasure. If it is put off, it gets more and more insistent. Our drives are not organized and have no collective will that integrates them well enough to ensure our survival. They just want what they want and that's it.

As we grow up and learn to deal with external reality, we learn how to integrate and direct our basic drives so that we act on each at an appropriate time in an appropriate way. This process is a function of our cerebral cortex. To see how important it is, imagine what a child would be like if each and every one of her drives was satisfied instantly. She would never develop the ability to manage her emotions or herself.

From Freud's perspective, we learn to partially inhibit or repress one drive so that we can act on another drive that is more important to us at that moment. Each time we successfully repress a drive, it's as if a part of its energy is stored to be used by our will-power to control that particular drive in similar situations in the future. The total of our appropriately repressed drives becomes the source of psychological energy for our willpower.

Once we have achieved a basic level of self-regulation and integration with material reality, our parents send us off to school, where we are further trained for the more complex task of living in society. We now learn not just to repress our drives in order to have an orderly life and please our parents, but to invest our drives' energy in "higher" activities, like learning to read, write, and think as our teachers tell us. We become increasingly oriented to the greater rewards of a future job with a good position in society, which promises far greater pleasure than going it on our own and taking up subsistence farming. Freud called this shift *sublimation*. We selectively invest the energy of our drives, and thus our will, into constructive activities of our own choice.

With this admittedly simplified view of willpower based on the early observations of Freud, we can form a clearer idea of what spiritual willpower is. Just as our everyday willpower is derived from the emotional drives of our body, our spiritual willpower comes from the emotional drives of our soul. It first manifests in our motivation to undertake a spiritual search. At times, this can drive people into ecstatic states where all they want is to experience divine love, as Haley did in chapter 5. If we are not to be carried away in our love of God, our spiritual drive needs to be repressed and directed toward the goals that our spiritual principles point us to. The energy of our spiritual drives thus becomes the basis of the force of our *spiritual* willpower. As we develop basic control of our spiritual drives so that we don't give up our whole life for spiritual love, we can sublimate the energy of our spiritual drives into the "higher" task of developing a spiritual will with which we more consistently strive to develop our spiritual intelligence.

The ideal is to get our psychological willpower and our spiritual willpower going in the same direction. We can do this by finding the right blend of common sense *and* spiritual principles. When we do, we will be able to contain the emotional pressure of all our drives and invest it into thinking, feeling, and acting in line with our principles.

Emotions and Spiritual Life

Being able to control our inner drives and the pressure they create requires discernment. Our emotions that help us act in line with our drives need to be shaped carefully. Their instinctive aim, after all, is to ensure that we do the things that feel good and avoid what feels bad. This is as true in our spiritual life as it is in our material life. Our emotional drives are quite content with our pursuing spirituality, as long as it brings emotional pleasure in some form. They don't want to hear anything about spirituality if it adds extra constraints on us on top of those that common sense and psychology have already imposed. In short, they don't want to hear about applying spiritual principles.

To remind myself of the need to make sure that my emotions are driving me in ways that are in line with my principles, I often think about the experience of Samira, a writer, who was just as interested in spirituality as I am. I met Samira when I was traveling to a small village in Iran to meet a blind, elderly woman, Malek Jan Nemati, who I had heard had a mature spiritual intelligence. I'll tell you more about her in chapter 18. Samira, who lived in Tehran, picked up my wife and me to visit a mutual friend who just happened to be in Iran at the same time that we were. We talked about spirituality as she drove through the busy streets, where the heavy traffic gave us plenty of time to discuss my favorite topic, spirituality.

"I had been interested in spirituality for about fifteen years and was very upset by the periods of inner turmoil that I constantly went through," Samira began. "One week I felt so very close to God, and then I was back in turmoil for the rest of the month. I asked Malek Jan Nemati what I could do to hold on to that state of peacefulness and inner contentedness. She patiently replied, 'You know, my dear, that those times when you felt so spiritually secure were the times when your soul was asleep. Now that you feel in so much turmoil and far from God, your soul is awake and struggling to get closer.'"

Samira had initially been drawn to spirituality because she had experienced some strong states of emotional connection and deep feelings of peace in the midst of a personal crisis. These experiences were wonderful, so she naturally thought that they were the telltale sign of spiritual connection. What had actually happened, however, was that Samira had become so focused on the feelings—which felt so good in themselves—that she lost sight of her goal of being better connected to God. Her imperious self was quite content with this; it enjoyed the feeling of deep peace too. So it constantly pushed her to pursue spirituality for this reason.

Malek Jan Nemati's surprising interpretation—that the times when Samira was feeling farthest from God were the times when she was actually closest—turned everything on end for her, and for me as well. Samira had thought that she knew the meaning of Ostad Elahi's principle "To find God, delve within your heart: then you shall see that he is everywhere and in everything." She had thought it meant that her heart would be filled with love and peace. Now she realized that it was just as easy for her to make a mistake in her spiritual life by blindly trusting her strong feelings as it was in everyday life. She would have to become more self-aware to be sure that her emotions were driving her at the right time toward the right aim for the right reason in the right manner, while at the same time fully appreciating that wonderful feeling of closeness to God when it came. It was difficult at first to maintain her zeal without seeking the emotional reward that had seemed to her synonymous with a state of spiritual connection. As she learned more and more about the complexity of her emotions, however, she was able to maintain her motivation and seek to apply herself in directions that her messages indicated.

Treating Faith as a Feeling

Faith is a feeling that arises from our connection with our soul, not just the beliefs of our mind. It brings with it a certain sense of rightness that is usually far greater than our evidence can justify. It is therefore just as subject to the triumphs and failures of emotional logic as any other emotion is. As faith will sometimes lead me to act correctly and other times not, depending on my own interpretations, I treat faith as I would any other feeling and make certain that it doesn't lead me in ways that are contrary to my principles.

Theresa's experience stands out in my mind as emphasizing the need to question the things we do out of faith, because of her very zeal for spirituality. She had been raised in a spiritually oriented family and felt very confident in her faith. "I thought that I understood the meaning of this word *faith*; I thought I had faith in God," Theresa told me, looking down as she spoke. "I was always telling myself that whatever happened to me, it came from God. When a more spiritually mature friend told me that my faith was weak, I dismissed what she told me as being off the mark. Several months later, an experience began that showed me how wrong I was."

Theresa would have done well to have firmly in place Ostad Elahi's principle: "More ignorant than the ignorant is one who says 'I know'—a true human being always seeks to learn from others." If she had, then her very confidence in her own opinions, rather than those of someone else who she admitted knew more than she did, might have set off a warning bell and led her to examine the facts more closely. But her excessive pride in her own faith made her vulnerable.

"I was four months pregnant with my first child when the doctors found that the fetus had a rare cardiac anomaly," Theresa went on. "The child would have to have surgery as soon as it was born and might live or die. I didn't want to see God's will in this, and I didn't want to accept whatever God wanted for me and my child. My heart was not calm. Because I believed that God acted in these situations through doctors, not through miracles, I did my part to try to get his help. I looked around to find all the ways and means that are available to mortals—the best hospital, the best doctors, and the best surgeon. I found a top surgical team in town that specialized in this type of problem.

"After finding all the 'bests,' I started to feel more comfortable, more secure. But this serenity was not a sign of faith and trust in God. I had put my trust in those doctors instead, and I was subtly relying on a totally human solution to the problem. Then two days prior to the date fixed for my C-section and my baby's corrective surgery, my water broke. I went to the emergency room. It was Christmas, and all the experts I'd lined up were out of town. I felt alone and abandoned. An intern performed the C-section. A second intern who was new on the cardiac surgery service did the corrective heart surgery, and everything turned out beautifully without the baby having a single problem."

From a psychological point of view, Theresa had handled the whole situation admirably. She had made a difficult decision based on her values, mobilized her resources effectively, and stayed far less anxious than most mothers would have been in that trying situation. She started off well from a spiritual perspective too, placing her hope in God. She had strong faith and great zeal. However, under the pressure of the situation, her attention gradually slipped and her emotions became fixated on the doctors who were going to help. She didn't even realize it until her water broke and the doctors she had put all her confidence in weren't there. Then she knew, for if she had truly been relying on God to the extent that she thought she was, her heart would have been much calmer. She would have known that whatever happened was for her own good and that of her child.

To develop her spiritual emotional intelligence so that she could direct her faith and zeal in more discerning ways, Theresa put together a program to increase her ability to rely on God in difficult times, using the principles of CBT. Every morning, she would spend five minutes thinking about the challenges she would face that day and planning how to handle them while remembering that the outcome was in God's hands. She would bring to mind how she had forgotten God at the difficult time of her child's birth and remind herself how she wanted to do the opposite now.

She would then spend five minutes every night reviewing the events of her day. She would try to find potential benefits in incidents like being late for work because of traffic, having her boss snap at her over a mistake she made, or finding a coworker trying to steal her project. She might see these incidents as important reminders, for instance, to always make her best effort but not to forget that God was in charge, or to always look to God and not her boss for approval, knowing that then she would do the best possible job, or to defend her own rights rather than assume that some divine force would miraculously step in to help her. By diligently following her program and disputing any inner voice that threatened to undermine her effort, she would refine her faith and her willpower so as to be more alert to the spiritual elements in more difficult situations in the future.

If Theresa can ignore what others tell her and be overly confident in herself, so can I. I remind myself of how "ignorant" I am when I think that I know better than others, and I remember why I need to make certain that I learn from what is happening to me in everyday life. By recalling how faith slipped from Theresa's hands, I am reminded to check out what my feelings of faith and zeal make me think I "know" and to examine how I might make small efforts in everyday life, as Theresa did, to improve my faith and maintain my zeal so that I will be prepared when larger tests come along. When I work on remembering to put my hope in God and see the benefits of it, Theresa's experience becomes a reference point in my own experience and lends weight to my own conclusions that are organized around my own set of principles. It helps strengthen my self-control and solidify my will.

Fighting Back

So far, most of our targets for emotional intelligence and spiritual intelligence have been quite similar from a psychological perspective. Spiritual emotional intelligence, however, will eventually encourage us to go beyond the levels that being successful in material life requires. Michael, who explained how he cultivated honesty in chapter 7, gave me a good example of "going beyond" in a way that I would find hard to do. It's a good example of zeal of the best order, zeal for fighting against our imperious self. "If I envy somebody," Michael told me, "I push myself to go and do something that will make that person happy. It is just like exercising. I started off doing very small things, like offering to help the person I envied with a task that he was doing or pick up lunch for him when he was busy. I gradually worked my way up to bigger things."

As an example, Michael told me of a situation at his workplace in which management was looking to promote one of his coworkers instead of him. "I felt the irresistible urge to let them know in some way that she really was not trustworthy," he said. "I felt that I had good reasons to give them. But from a spiritual point of view, I knew that I had to stop myself from acting on such a thought when it came, because it certainly didn't come from my good intentions.

"At first, I didn't feel that I was strong enough to take the next step, which would be to say things that would improve her chances for the position. I thought that I would end up conveying my negative opinion in spite of myself. So, when I got home and could relax, I tried to focus on her good points and even pray for her. I asked, 'Would I want to change places and be her?' I found I didn't." Michael just wanted the promotion for himself. Who wouldn't?

The ability to control our impulses and read our own emotions leads to self-knowledge; the ability to control our impulses and read the emotions of others leads to compassion and altruism. Michael wanted to be more altruistic and get the spiritual reward that he felt certain would be his if he passed this test. To do so, he identified the erroneous thought in his mind—that this promotion should be his—and substituted for it what I call *spiritual logic:* the idea that his coworker too was entitled to have good things happen to her, just as he was, and that if God wanted to give this to her, he had no right to object. "After a few days, even though it was an uncomfortable feeling to act against my own self-interest, I could finally force myself to say something good about her to the person in charge," he said. "That act of kindness gave me a very satisfying, rewarding feeling almost immediately. In fact, I didn't feel negatively about her anymore after that because I could very clearly see her strong points. She got the position, and I was happy that she might have benefited in even a small way from my good words."

Michael was able to act against his feelings of immediate self-interest and greed for someone else's good because he was really sure that doing so would benefit him even more than getting the job he so desired. He had worked on himself enough to build the spiritual emotional intelligence and willpower to dismiss the thoughts generated by his imperious self so that he could act in line with his spiritual principles, even if it took a few days. In so doing, he understood more deeply the pleasure of controlling his imperious self. It made him happier to be acting in this way than it would have to get the job he wanted, and he never had a moment's regret.

Through many small efforts over the years in many different aspects of his life, Michael's spiritual emotional intelligence grew until he began to feel differently about everything. "One day you see that you don't feel insecure or envious of anybody," he said. "How can you feel insecure when you see a very strong power that orders everything according to justice? You just can't feel insecure anymore."

Using Our Emotional Drives to Improve Ourselves

The more self-aware we become, the more we can use our emotions to stimulate different aspects of our spiritual development. For example, we can find that envy isn't all bad. The desire to have the good things that others have is a natural feeling that, when under control, becomes a motive for us to do what we need to in order to get the things that we want. You can see how it works in everyday life. If a friend has more money (or a better apartment, car, friend, or spiritual life) than we do, we might feel a twinge of envy, but instead of eating our heart out and just making ourselves feel worse, we can become motivated. We can try to get a better job, for instance, so that we can have more money ourselves. When we use our envy to improve ourselves, our desire for what others have actually becomes beneficial. Then we're using the emotional manifestations of that drive quite intelligently.

It can help us spiritually too—for example, if we can use a twinge of envy for other people's positive points as a stimulus to develop those qualities in ourselves. Philip gave me a good example of this: "I've always been self-centered by nature and quite content with myself. As I became interested in spirituality, I saw others who were much kinder than I was. They paid attention to people who weren't their friends and were eager to help out whenever they could. They didn't even have any spiritual beliefs and still they acted so much better than I did. I began to feel a little ashamed of myself, always looking out for number one but feeling a little empty and unfulfilled. In particular, I found myself thinking more about one friend who went out of her way to help others without any resentment. I began wishing that I could be as kind as she was. After a while, I found that I was beginning to become a little kinder and it felt very good. I felt closer to my friend too." This is a good example of using our feelings of jealousy and the drive to have good things for ourselves in a *spiritually* intelligent way.

ॐ ॐ ॐ

Our drives create psychological pressure and the relief of that pressure gives us pleasure. Our emotions help us seek to satisfy our drives in particular circumstances. To use our emotions in ways that motivate us toward the higher goals that our principles set, we need to develop spiritual willpower that draws its force mainly from the drives of our soul. As in everyday life, in our spiritual life self-control and zeal are both important. Self-control is like the brakes of a car and zeal is like the gas pedal. Used properly, they enable us to apply our principles and reach our goal by decoding the signs of our messages.

As we become more successful at maintaining the right balance between our emotional drives and our spiritual intelligence, we begin to feel the same peace of mind and certainty that we will reach our goal that a student enrolled in a university feels. We know that everything is laid out for our success and that if we just make the recommended effort, we will reach our goal. We may be stressed out by the tests that we face, but we can be sure that we will graduate and be in a far better position for all that we have learned. This makes us more content, energized, and optimistic about what we gain by our struggles. We feel a different kind of happiness, one that satisfies our nature in a deeper way that we wouldn't give up for the simpler emotional pleasures we used to seek.

ッ　ッ　ッ

Keys to Chapter 11

- Emotional drives exert a kind of pressure on us, and their satisfaction brings us pleasure. To develop spiritual emotional intelligence, you need to stop your automatic tendency to act on the purely material value of things in order to find out how your spiritual principles would have you act.
- Spiritual willpower has a different origin and different aim from psychological willpower. Just as your everyday willpower is derived from the emotional drives of your body and has a material aim, so your spiritual willpower is derived from the emotional drives of your soul and has a spiritual aim.
- Being able to control the emotional pressure of your drives requires careful discernment, for emotions are tricky. Your emotional drives will be quite content pursuing spirituality, as long as it brings emotional pleasure in some form. They will resist applying your principles if acting on them puts any kind of restraint on you.

- Faith is just as subject to the triumphs and failures of emotional logic as any other emotion is. It is a good idea, therefore, to treat faith as you would any feeling and make certain that it doesn't lead you to act against one of your principles.
- The more you can use your zeal as Michael did to fight against any manifestation of your imperious self that you find, the faster you will develop your spiritual emotional intelligence.
- The more self-aware you become, the more you can use your emotions for your spiritual development. You will then discover that the real purpose of your drives has been to stimulate different aspects of your spiritual development.

ॐ ॐ ॐ

For Your Reflection

To develop our spiritual emotional intelligence, we need to have sufficient willpower to stand up to our emotional drives and sufficient zeal to fight every manifestation of our imperious self that we can find.

1. Do you think, as I do, that spiritual willpower is different from psychological willpower? Is it a product of your brain, or does your soul contribute as well? If you think that your soul contributes, what does it add? Choose several examples where you either acted or failed to act in line with a spiritual principle, and decide the extent to which your willpower was coming from the contributions of (a) your brain and (b) your soul.

2. Zeal is important for a successful and satisfying life. The more passionately you can apply yourself in the right direction, the better the results you are likely to get. Yet those same passions can be diverted too easily and get you into far greater trouble than if you were content with the status quo. Think about your own level of zeal in both your material and spiritual life. Find several instances where either excessive or insufficient zeal has caused you to have greater or lesser successes or take too many or too few risks.

3. Go to decodeyourmessages.com to find the strategies that others have used to develop their spiritual willpower and zeal.

4. Take out a sheet of paper or turn to a blank page in your notebook and entitle it "Building Spiritual Willpower." You can also go to decodeyourmessages.com to download these points for reflection or log into your online notebook. Write a paragraph on the nature of your own spiritual willpower and zeal. Once you've written this summary paragraph, write in as much detail as you'd like about the evidence on which your conclusions rest.

5. Go to decodeyourmessages.com to share with others the best ways you have found to build willpower and cultivate zeal.

CHAPTER 12

Deepening Commitment

Intimate relationships with our partners, children, and friends form the nucleus around which most of the other aspects of our material lives revolve. Good relationships make us healthier, happier, and more complete. They bring out the best in us. They provide the center. Our relationship with the source of our messages occupies a similarly central place in our spiritual life. In this chapter, we will explore some examples of how the two—our material and spiritual loves—run parallel and see how we can discern and learn the spiritual lessons our most intimate human relationships can teach us. Since relationships—both with significant others and with the source of our messages—come in many forms, you will need to substitute your own kind of support system for the examples drawn from the more traditional ones mentioned in this chapter and add those experiences to those on decodeyourmessages. com to help others who might have a similar kind of relationship to yours.

Intimate relationships are wonderful, but they take work. They challenge us and force us to grow in very different ways than other aspects of our lives do. As my Iranian friend C.J., who escaped from the airport in Spain in chapter 1, put it, "When you are living on your own, you put a good face on everything you do. You tend not to see the devious things you do, so it takes longer to catch on to your own tricks. But when you have a good friend or a partner who is on the same wavelength as you are, he or she can just pick up on the things that you are doing wrong and tell you. It awakens us from this dream world that we create when we are on our own."

We are most ourselves in a close relationship, and that makes it an excellent mirror in which to see ourselves as we really are. So we can use these human relationships as means to improve our relationship with the source of our messages and develop our spiritual intelligence. For example, if you can't take constructive criticism from someone close to you, how likely are you to hear and correctly interpret the constructive criticism of your messages? So whenever one of your close, trusted friends criticizes you, consider that this might be a way of bringing to your attention something that you really need to work on. Make your best effort to improve it, and then look to see whether your efforts were indeed sufficient to meet the criticism. The skills that you develop will very likely help you forge a better relationship with the source of your messages as well.

Bridget, a thirty-three-year-old French woman, described how an impulsive first marriage became a painful but useful lesson in spiritual intelligence. "Ten years ago, I had a dream," she told me. "In that dream, somebody asked me if I wanted to marry Milos. I said a rapid yes, but then immediately I started running and screaming 'No, no, no!' A voice said, 'Too late.' Much to my surprise, six months later, Milos suddenly asked me to marry him.

"I had no feelings for Milos," Bridget recalled, "but he was a good person, and we had similar spiritual beliefs. Because of my dream, I thought that, like it or not, my destiny was bound to his. I also told myself that since passionate love disappears after a while, it was not such a bad thing to get married without love. So I got married."

Bridget had wanted to put her love of God above everything else, but despite her lofty intentions, her marriage didn't work. "After five months, love hadn't come, nor had any feelings of affection," Bridget said. "We were unhappy. I kept telling myself that this was a test from God and that I had to endure it. But I couldn't bear it. After six months, I got a divorce."

A commitment is meaningful only to the extent that we have knowledge of the situation in which we plan to act and the ability to act the way we intend. Bridget had thought that she was very sincere in her intentions to put God's satisfaction above her own and that this would make everything work. She made a leap of faith, thinking that her marriage to Milos would succeed because of their shared beliefs and that God would be happy if she did this for him. Instead, she created a mess that taught her an unforgettable lesson.

Why didn't everything work out? Why were her commitment and her intention so fragile? It was because she didn't know herself, Milos, or God very well. She didn't understand what went into forming a close relationship, with a man or with God.

Loneliness, like anxiety, can cause us to act in ways that are often impulsive and poorly planned unless we have learned how to respond to it correctly. When we are under its spell, something feels like it is missing and we are driven to fill in the space with emotional intensity, companionship, or some other form of human connection. Most of us learn what works for us as Bridget did, by making mistakes. Similarly, in our relationship with God, we are drawn to seek to be closer to him by a feeling of deep longing that is only briefly satisfied by moments of intense connection. The better we understand our need for others and the role of love in everyday life, the better we will be able to understand what we need to do to draw closer to God and forge a solid relationship that works.

Fortunately, Bridget learned her lesson. The next time she found someone with whom she shared her spiritual interests *and* had good chemistry. Today, she is happily married with three children. Her experience helped her improve her relationship with God as well. She hadn't realized how strongly her relationship with God had been built on her desire to have God do whatever it took to make her happy. She saw the kind of discernment that had to go into having an intimate relationship with another person and with God. Both relationships required a similar set of skills, yet each needed attention specific to that relationship to make it work. By living in line with her principles and decoding the feedback, she would develop the skills that would enable her to become proficient in both.

Looking Within

To sustain our commitment and reap the benefits of a close relationship, we need to combat our natural human tendency to be self-centered and, in particular, to blame others for the difficulties that we have with them. Close relationships—where it is in our best interests not to blame the other—are excellent places to assimilate the wisdom of one of the basic principles of Ostad Elahi: "The reason for everything that happens to you is within."

That's a slightly more radical statement of a basic truth I was introduced to in my studies of family therapy and learned about firsthand in my own relationships. When we look more closely at problems in our intimate relationships, we can always find ways in which we contribute to any problem that arises. If we behaved differently in some way with the other person, the problem couldn't exist in its current form.

The ability to find what you contribute to the problem is closely linked with another, more practical truth about relationships that I also learned from family therapy and my own experience. Since you can't change the other person very much, no matter how much you would like to, you are better off putting your efforts into changing what you contribute to the problem. If you do, something will have to change in the relationship as well. And if you do this by applying a challenging spiritual principle like looking for the cause of everything inside of you, you go beyond psychology and learn to see everything that happens as a spiritual lesson for your benefit.

Nowhere is this skill of finding a lesson in everything that happens to us and focusing on correcting our own contribution to a problem more crucial than in relationships between parents and children, where we can't give ourselves the option of just walking away. Penny found that the naturally humbling experience of raising two children, approached with a spiritual intention, helped her develop her spiritual character and intelligence better than any other scenario she could imagine. "Raising children is very hard for me, because I am not a diplomat," she told me. "I really want to say to my daughter, 'Just do what I say and shut up.' Although that would satisfy me at the moment even if she cried, a few moments later I would regret it, because I know that God hates it when I act that way. God is disgusted with me when I get angry with Daphne and talk to her like that."

After Penny's mother pointed out for the umpteenth time that the children were very well behaved with *her*, Penny finally had to face the fact that she might be doing something wrong. She really wanted her children to be happy, but she also wanted everything to magically fall into line with her own vision of how things should be, and her love and commitment only seemed to magnify the harm this desire was doing. So she started reading the latest parenting guides to see what the authorities considered the best child-rearing practices. When she tried the techniques the authorities recommended, however, her results were limited and temporary.

This made it even more obvious that the problem was inside of her.

One thing was for sure. It wasn't working for her to think that because she was the mother, her children should do what she wanted. The more she insisted that they obey her, the more they rebelled. She could see this was counterproductive, so, as she was very interested in spirituality, she tried to bring her approach to child rearing into line with her beliefs.

"Looking at my children from a spiritual perspective," Penny continued, "I consider them souls put in my care. I now try to view them not as being mine to do with as I please or use to fulfill my dreams, but more the way I view adults, as having their own separate destiny. I don't consider that I have the right to dominate them, as I used to, just because I'm bigger and stronger physically. I believe that I should respect them and speak to them in such a way that I don't get angry and they don't get upset. I should talk to them so that they do what is good for them without my having to resort to punishment. I need to help them develop a sense of their own dignity so that they won't want to do something wrong. When I talk to my children now, I always try to be diplomatic. It's tough, because it is not at all my nature to be this way. So I constantly have to look for spiritual help."

With this change in perspective, Penny saw that her job of raising her children was far more important than she had considered it before. It was important *spiritually*, and she could commit to it more fully than she ever had. Doing all the menial things one does to raise a child didn't feel demeaning anymore. She no longer envied her friends who were getting ahead in the work world or resented her children because they held her back from a more exciting life. God had given her these children, and raising them properly was now the most important thing she could do, for her own spiritual development as well as theirs. It wasn't that she had to give up everything in her life for her children. She just had to find a better balance. She had to try to be more accepting of her situation as the right one for her, a lesson in looking within for the reason that something was "going wrong" in her life because it wasn't the way that she dreamed.

Penny's love for her children motivated her to accept the complete program of psychological and spiritual self-improvement that came in the form of her children's constant but changing demands. In it, she would be challenged in every possible way and have to draw on every one of her principles at one time or another. By accepting this assignment in the spiritual classroom of everyday life, she put herself under consistent pressure to change so that one understanding would build on another until she grasped the main point.

Penny maintained her focus by keeping a small notebook. Every morning, she took two minutes to write out the problems she anticipated that day, along with a line or two about how she planned to address them. Every evening, she spent two more minutes reviewing how well she had carried out her plan. Whenever she had trouble with the children, she would try to remember that God was there, putting her in this situation to improve her patience, self-control, and sensitivity to others. She would discuss her problems with him in an intimate conversation, reviewing either the latest theories of child rearing *or* the spiritual work she was trying to do. In this way, her relationship with her children became a mirror in which she could see clearly what needed to be done to develop her spiritual intelligence.

When we don't accept that there is a lesson to be learned in a situation and don't look for the cause of our problems within ourselves, we are in effect complaining about God and resisting the system that he has set up for our development. We are seeing only the material aspects of our situation. This cuts us off from the feedback of our messages and gets us into more and more trouble, the kind Penny had originally.

As Penny kept at it, her children behaved better and felt calmer, and she became happier and more optimistic. She was even grateful for the constant demands her children placed on her, for they kept God more present in her mind than if everything were always going well. By establishing an intimate relationship with God in the very center of her everyday life, she was developing a sense of bi-dimensional identity and laying a solid foundation for her spiritual intelligence. Her heart was warm. She never felt alone.

Becoming More United at Heart

As we get better at finding the cause for our problems in ourselves, our close relationships become a mirror that becomes increasingly reflective of our faults. To see how this might work, let's look at the example of Jean, a twenty-five-year-old graduate student. Jean was relaxing at home one evening when Al, the man she had been living with for six months, came in from work and accused her of having too much wine at a party the night before and flirting with another man. The scene was all too familiar, and Jean felt a wave of anger welling up inside her. Al seemed to get jealous whenever she was enjoying talking to someone else. A thought flashed through her mind: Attractive woman, jealous man. Don't take his false accusations. Stand up for your rights!

Jean was about to launch a scathing counterattack by throwing Al's insecurity and his jealousy back in his face when the voice of her conscience stopped her. Jean was familiar with the principles of Ostad Elahi, so she thought of the maxim: "A true spiritual traveler does not feel hurt by, or complain about, the behavior of others." Having effectively halted her emotional logic with a sound principle, Jean still struggled to contain her anger, for she could easily have justified putting Al in his place. All her friends would have encouraged her not to tolerate his controlling behavior.

But rather than striking back, Jean reassured Al that she hadn't been flirting with anyone at the party and suggested that they talk about it later when she had had a chance to calm down. Al knew better than to press her. As she started to cool off, she thought about her situation from every conceivable angle, looking for a way to make sense of Al's attack and her own response, until suddenly a buzzer went off in her mind—a potentially meaningful connection. "The day before our fight, I actually *had* flirted with a very sexy guy in the library," she told me. "I knew that I wouldn't do anything, but I really enjoyed the attention. I even took down his number, getting off on the fantasy of it all. Now I saw that Al's reaction was a kind of poetic justice."

Jean hadn't thought anything of the incident at the time because she often entertained such "harmless" fantasies. They gave a little spice to life. But now the connection she'd made started her thinking. If the incidents in the library and at the party were indeed linked, she wanted to understand why her harmless fantasies and her pleasure in flirting were such problems. After all, she wasn't a nun, and these days fooling around seemed so common. But she forced herself to examine the evidence and decide what she really wanted.

The bottom line was that she had done a lot of experimenting in the years before she had settled down with Al. She'd liked the freedom, but in reality, it had brought her as much pain as excitement. Seeking out her pleasure might have been right for her then, but she had moved in with Al because she loved him and believed that ultimately she would be happier being with him. She wanted children and the security of a monogamous, committed relationship. That was what they had agreed to. She certainly wouldn't like it if she found out that Al was fooling around with someone else.

Then Jean took the next step: to see if this situation was a message pointing out that she had a commitment problem with God as well. When she examined her relationship with God honestly, she had to admit that she remembered her spiritual principles mainly when she was in some sort of trouble or when it was convenient for her. In the heat of the moment, she had conveniently forgotten about her commitments to both Al and God, rationalizing that everything had occurred in the privacy of her own mind. Since she knew that in spirituality her thoughts were almost as important as her actions, she could be certain that the source of her messages wasn't happy with what she had done.

To strengthen her commitments to both Al and God, Jean decided to set a program. First, she would spend two minutes each morning thinking about her level of commitment to both Al and God. She would think what making a commitment meant to her and what the advantages of greater commitment were. She would see whether there were any situations in the day ahead in which she might honor her commitments to Al and God in her mind. Not that her thoughts had to be puritanical; she just had to keep in mind what was best for her in her life and what she wanted most: a deep love with both Al and God.

Second, she would keep Al's vulnerability in mind when they went to parties and remember to touch base with him periodically to make sure that he was feeling comfortable and not getting jealous. Third, she would do one thing each week to make Al happy—for example, graciously going to the movie he wanted to see rather than fighting for her choice. This would remind her to see things from the other person's perspective and not turn her preferences into the way things *had* to be.

These steps would help to confirm her in the ways of thinking, feeling, and acting that support good relationships. She was committing to a set of principles that would undermine her self-centeredness and guide the way she and Al would work together. Our commitment to that the source of our messages works in the same way; it means that we commit to honoring that relationship not just in our actions but in our thoughts and emotions as well. It means being very attentive to messages for feedback as to how well we are doing. We can then measure our closeness to God by the extent to which we honor our spiritual principles in thought, feeling, and deed, just as we need to honor our commitment in our close friendships. The more we approach our relationship with God in this way, the more deeply we understand the fundamental principle of an intimate *spiritual* relationship: "Alone or in the company of others, awake or asleep, in motion or at rest, to delve within we must never consider ourselves alone and must always be aware that God is omnipresent, watching over our every thought and action."

Over the Years

A close relationship is characterized above all by our level of commitment to resolve problems and to remain close through the natural ups and downs of everyday life. To make a relationship work, we need to be able to put ourselves and our needs into perspective so that we can make compromises between what seems right to us and what seems right to the other. The more you apply your spiritual principles in your closest relationships, the more you discover their value. However, the full benefits aren't apparent in one or another incident; they emerge through your firm commitment to apply your principles as consistently as possible and turn to your messages over years until that relationship becomes the crucible in which you integrate what you have learned in every other area of your life into a coherent, functioning whole.

The center of my material life is my relationship with my wife, Susan. We have been married for almost twenty years. We love each other deeply, and our relationship holds everything else in our lives together. Susan and I have good chemistry and common interests, including psychology and culture. But the major factor in our connecting was our shared interest in spirituality, the core of both our lives. At first, it felt a bit awkward that God came first for both of us, as if that somehow meant we must not love each other as much. Gradually, though, the awkwardness was replaced by a sense of incredible relief that we could have more reasonable expectations of each other. We didn't expect the other to make us fulfilled in the same way that we had expected other relationships to fulfill us. Our deepest fulfillment would come from our respective relationships with God.

Over the years, we established a kind of spiritual triangle or three-way relationship, much like what you'd find living with a child and a partner or a partner and a very wise mother. It changed the way things worked and added another level of richness to our life. In the beginning of our relationship, for example, our spiritual beliefs made it easier for both of us to make the kinds of compromises that we all have to make when we partner with someone else. For example, if Susan didn't particularly like being out in nature as much as I did, I spent less time in nature. If she wasn't as intellectual as I was, we found topics that were less intellectual to talk about. She helped me rein in my hippie tendencies to live a more mainstream life, while I helped her to develop professionally and be more independent. I created and maintained the nest while she created the affectionate, caring atmosphere in it. Because our material interests were not the most crucial to us, these adjustments came naturally.

These arrangements were easier to make because we both saw each compromise asked from us as a kind of spiritual lesson—a reminder not to give undue importance to that area, for in truth it was less important to us than having a sound, loving relationship. When we looked closely at each compromise and put it in the perspective of our whole life, the individual thing we wanted usually seemed less pressing. Yes, nature remained important to me, but not so important. Intellectual discussion remained exciting, but less essential. Whenever we had any problem finding the balance that would work, we looked for the cause within ourselves first. We looked to see if our attachment to this preference kept us from relating to God as well as to each other. It worked for both of us, creating an atmosphere in which we could both be more focused on the lessons that came out of situations in a way that made us more attentive to the other's needs. In the end, the hundreds of deals we made left both of us with a sense that we got more than we gave. We both felt God's presence in some way helping us. Our triangle was working. It had resonance.

Of course, there are points of friction that arise because of differences in our essential characters that will probably never go away completely. I tend to be a perfectionist and overly serious. I get rigid and controlling at times, wanting things my way. I will talk and talk about an issue, for hours on end if need be, to try to hammer things out. But when I do this, Susan feels that I am just trying to beat her into line. So I try to lighten up and not beat issues into the ground, but it's hard to change a trait that is a part of our character. It's in the intimate context of our relationship that we are able to make the best progress.

To motivate myself, I wonder, "Am I with God the same way I am with Susan? Do I really decode his messages correctly, or do I just insist on hearing what I want to hear?" I see that I often tend to make my own analysis of a situation and set up a program for changing it without paying enough attention to the feedback of my messages. I summon up my energy and my willpower to try to force things to go the way I want them to go. I intentionally close off my inner objections to the plan, even though this closes me off to feedback at the same time. It's like putting my head down and pushing ahead, just as I do with Susan. I feel that if I am doing this plan that I think is right and that takes great effort, God will be satisfied with it. Sometimes it makes things go better, and other times worse. I can only be sure by the feedback that I get.

Finding similarities in the relationships that I have with Susan and with God makes it very clear that I tend to be overly self-centered and act as if they are both my servants. It helps remind me that I will do better in the long run remaining open to what both God and Susan might really want, not what I think they want. To combat this tendency, I push myself to remember that I am not the center of the universe and that I should be more grateful for the things both of them do for me that I tend to take for granted. I work on it by first being more sensitive to what Susan wants, for her feedback is easier to decode than that of a message. And because we live together, these issues continually arise and can remind me to be more mindful of the principles that will bring me closer to both Susan and God.

We can see the face of the person we live with, but we can't see the face of God. We can, however, learn to look at the face of the person we live with as a reflection of how well we are living by our spiritual principles. As we do, we can understand better what it means to always think of God being present and to take him into account in our thoughts, feelings, and actions. It fills that spiritual longing inside of us with a warm presence that helps us maintain our spiritual perspective so that we become more resilient to the stresses of life. Approached in this way, Susan's and my relationship has become an intensive classroom in which we both work to improve ourselves so that we can be closer to each other and closer to God.

༄ ༄ ༄

Love makes the world go round, and most of us need the love that comes in close relationships to feel complete. Our close relationships most clearly reveal our true nature, and they are an excellent context in which to learn the meaning of spiritual principles, like how to find a cause for everything that happens to us and what it means to consider God present at every moment.

Why do we feel so much better having someone with whom to share our life? It's the way that we are made, another aspect of the material system created for our spiritual development. And it is through our human relationships that we develop the skills that help us deepen our relationship with the source of our messages. Just as each of us will have to love in a slightly different way in our close relationships to make them work for us, so we will have to develop our own unique way of loving the source of spiritual messages in order for that relationship to work for us. It's in balancing these two loves that most of us actualize some of our most important potentials and achieve a sense of contentment with life.

و٦   و٦   و٦

Keys to Chapter 12

- Intimate relationships with partners, children, and friends form the nucleus around which most of our lives revolve. The emotional investment you make to form a relationship and the regularity of contact through which you build it make those close relationships excellent mirrors of who you are. That enables you to use your closest human relationships as a means of both improving your relationship with the source of your messages and developing spiritual intelligence.

- You can only build a truly close relationship with another person when you know yourself, the other, and what goes into making a good relationship.

- In our intimate relationships, we always contribute to the problems that arise, because if we were different, the problem couldn't exist in its current form. Since you can't change the other person, you are better off putting your efforts into changing your contribution to the problem. That will make the situation an excellent place for learning the deeper spiritual meanings of principles like "The reason for everything that happens to you is within."

- A spiritual perspective on a situation can often help you change your approach. For example, remembering that your partner or your child is a separate soul on a separate journey will help you to get a little distance from the self-defeating emotions driving certain situations so that you can find better ways of dealing with them.

- A close relationship is characterized above all by the level of commitment to resolve problems and to remain close through the natural ups and downs of everyday life. The more you apply your system of spiritual principles in your close relationship, the greater the benefits will be for both your psychological and spiritual lives.

- The more you commit to honoring your spiritual principles in your close relationships, the more primary your relationship with God becomes. This is good for your close relationships as well, because it helps you have more realistic expectations of your partner.

ॐ ॐ ॐ

For Your Reflection

The emotional demands and rewards of a close relationship touch us more deeply than other aspects of our lives. Such a relationship is the ideal place to discover the way your principles and the constant stream of messages that come through everyday events work together.

1. Choose one of your relationships that is important to you. Find one of your weaknesses that this relationship consistently brings to the fore. Consider it as the material situation that creates a heightened psychological state that is ripe for attracting a spiritual message. Select a principle that you believe might apply in the situation. As you pay more attention to this area of your life for the next few

weeks, see if the principle helps you solve the problem or receive a message or inspiration that suggests a solution or a new way of viewing the problem.

2. Review the spiritual lessons you receive via your close relationships. Think of things that you can do, the way Jean or I did, to improve one of your closest relationships and your relationship with the source of your messages at the same time. Try to find a way to motivate yourself to actually carry out such a plan and resolve to act on it during the next month. If you are able to do it, carefully observe what happens in both relationships after you do carry out your plan with a spiritual intention. Do you understand one or another principle better? If you can't act on such a plan yet, then simply imagine what might happen if you were able to do it and resolve to do so at some future date.

3. Go to decodeyourmessages.com to find out how others have used their intimate relationships to improve their relationship with the source of their messages.

4. Take out a sheet of paper or turn to a blank page in your notebook and entitle it "Deepening My Commitment." You can also go to decodeyourmessages.com to download these points for reflection to your computer or log into your online notebook. Write a brief paragraph about how you deepen your commitment to the source of your messages, noting whether you find any similarities between the way you relate to people close to you and the way you relate to the source of your messages. Once you've written your summary paragraph, write in as much detail as you'd like about what you have learned by applying principles in your close relationships.

5. Go to decodeyourmessages.com to add what you have learned in your intimate relationships that has helped you understand the deeper wisdom of your messages and principles.

CHAPTER 13

Achieving Balance

It's all too easy to get so caught up in seeking more satisfaction and pleasure in everyday life that we forget about our spiritual reason for being here. When we do remember, we often go too far in the other direction, increasing our involvement in activities that we consider spiritual and decreasing our involvement with material life. It's hard to balance our material and spiritual priorities. To strike that balance, we need our messages to help us discover the valuable spiritual lesson contained in whatever facet of everyday life is so attractive to us so that everyday life becomes the natural system in which to develop our character and intelligence both psychologically and spiritually.

We have already examined how to apply ethics and other principles in everyday situations and how to use our close human relationships to develop greater intimacy with the source of our messages. We have identified how to use the feedback that we get to improve our spiritual attention and form more effective spiritual intentions. In this chapter, we will explore how to bring the spiritual into areas of life that all too often seem completely material, and where our desires run high: areas like money, power, sex, food, fashion, love, family, and social status. I will show you how such desires give us an excellent opportunity both to increase our discernment of what makes something spiritual and to strengthen our soul's ability to influence our thoughts, feelings, and actions. I'll use the area of money as an example of how to find a balance that satisfies our material desires and promotes the development of our spiritual intelligence.

Let's start with the story of Venus, a forty-five-year-old public relations executive who both loves God and enjoys creature comforts. You already met her in chapter 4, where she was engaged in a power struggle with colleagues at work and learned how to control her anger by thinking about her spiritual immune system.

"I've been working to control my spending with a spiritual intention so that I won't waste the gifts that God has given me," Venus told me. "One day, I went on a shopping binge and spent an outrageous amount of money on face cream—more than $250 for two bottles. I really wanted them, and I didn't want to return them. But after about two days, I finally convinced myself that I had to, partly because money was tight but more because I thought I needed to learn how to act on the real value of things if I was ever going to develop a spiritual sense of value. So on Monday I returned the two bottles and decided to research the best creams on the market for the lowest prices."

I asked Venus how she could be sure that her action had any spiritual value. She eagerly told me about a message that she considered confirmation from the source of her messages. "That week, I went and had my nails done," she said. She was so excited by what had happened that she seemed to forget that it was a man to whom she was describing this. "I started talking to the woman next to me. I asked her if she knew any good creams that weren't exorbitant in price. She told me that she was working for an advertising company and that her research and development department had just analyzed all the moisturizing creams on the market. By working on a certain brand's account, she had learned that its expensive line of cream had the exact same ingredients as less expensively packaged products. She told me exactly where to find a very good cream for $14.99 and then walked out of the nail salon. I had never seen her before, and I've never seen her since. The whole incident showed me that when you put true spiritual principles into practice with the right intention, God helps you in ways that seem impossible."

For Venus, disciplining herself to return the expensive cream wasn't a matter of rejecting all extravagances in order to be more spiritual. She did so because she was working at the time on not letting her material desires eclipse her sense of value. It didn't make sense from a psychological perspective for her to spend that much money at a time when she couldn't really afford it and it made even less sense from a spiritual perspective to do it at a time when she had set a spiritual intention to be more mindful of the value of things.

Why did Venus form such a spiritual intention? It was to test her and be sure that her emotional desires wouldn't pull her over the line in more important situations. Her lapse showed that her desires could easily pull her over the line, making her not only go against common sense and moderation but also forget her spiritual intention. When she returned the cream, she increased her control of her emotional drives in this area of life ever so slightly so that she would do better in future efforts.

The amount of money we have is not in itself of much spiritual importance; neither is what we choose to spend it on, as long as we give a certain part to helping others and use the rest in a way that is in line with common sense for someone in our position in society. However, the weaknesses in our character that lead to lack of control in our spending give our imperious self a foothold so that it can get us to act first against common sense and then against our spiritual principles. So we are wise to exert our spiritual willpower to shore up areas—such as money matters—where we might be made vulnerable to the pressure of our emotional desires. In so doing, we increase our spiritual intelligence, for we learn to decide how to spend our money not by imposing formulas but by understanding the function of money in our own life and using it accordingly.

We have many different drives and even more desires that we need to integrate to create a healthy and vital character. We need to develop the kind of discerning control that is not just sufficient to help us meet our material goals but will also help us reach our spiritual goals. Messages teach us to do this not by dampening all drives and desires, but by keeping these drives vital and robust. By paying close attention to each of our drives and desires and finding the best way of satisfying them that also takes into account the long-term consequences of each action, we develop a more complete and well-rounded psychological character and intelligence. If we take our spiritual principles into account as well, we develop a more complete and well-rounded spiritual character and intelligence.

It's easy for me to forget that face creams and money are not my principles' direct objects of concern. What is important is to keep my emotional drives and whatever objects they attach to in my everyday life under the control of my will. If you have any doubt as to the spiritual value of Venus's effort, as I did when I first heard it, her message should make it clear that her effort had spiritual value for her, and this should make you more interested in the feedback that you might get in an area of your life that is attractive to you. Her message was just as useful to her in helping her balance her emotional drives as any other message, even one that dealt with matters weightier than face cream.

There's a traditional Sufi teaching story that underscores for me the need to focus more on the inner meaning of what we do than on its outward manifestation. A dervish who had long ago renounced all worldly things went to a king and invited him to walk away from all of his wealth and power to devote himself to God. The king, being very enlightened, agreed, for he heard the voice of God speaking to him through this dervish. They left immediately, detaching themselves from all material comforts in their journey to reach God. When they had journeyed into this metaphorical desert for a few hours, however, the dervish suddenly remembered that he had left his sole possession, his pipe, in the king's palace. The dervish turned back while the king continued on his way alone.

When I first heard this story, I thought that the king had walked away from his wealth and power in a supreme act of sacrifice to get closer to God. Now I understand it differently. The king had been surrounded by money and power but never attached to them. He was more attached to God, even if no one else knew it. He had no need to call attention to it. The dervish, who appeared so much more devoted to God by reason of his lifestyle, owned only his pipe, but he was so attached to that one thing that it held him back from getting closer to God. The king could live with or without money and power, depending on God's will. Only when God determined that it was right for him to walk away from the material comforts that God had earlier given him did his detachment manifest itself. Perhaps there's a lesson here for those of us who might be so attached to the external manifestations of devotion to God that we don't see what devotion to God really means. That's certainly what the story means to me now, and it encourages me to live with whatever financial situation God chooses to put me in. It helps me think, because of the seemingly positive feedback of her message, that Venus might just be trying to live with the situation in which God put her and so reach the same point that the king reached.

Applying one of my most useful equations, I ask myself (and I hope you ask yourself): If Venus's emotional drives push her to buy expensive face creams, do mine push me to excess in other ways? Venus's story encourages me to look for the equivalent of face cream in my own life—an area where I am prone to being self-indulgent in ways that don't fit the circumstances of my life—and see whether I can bring myself into better alignment with common sense with a spiritual intention. Does it help you find a corresponding area in your life?

The Other Side of the Coin

Dealing with our drives and desires is complex because imbalances in one direction affect us just as negatively as excesses in the other direction. I struggle with my emotional drives about money not the way Venus did, but from the opposite direction, for I tend to be overly self-denying, and I need to make certain that I don't equate that with being more virtuous. Whether we are self-indulgent or self-depriving, the result is very likely the same: We are more vulnerable to being distracted by our imperious self from acting in line with our messages and principles.

I was raised to think that it was easier for a camel to pass through the eye of a needle than for a rich man to enter heaven. Even as I developed a broader perspective on religion in college, I concluded the same thing that William James had underscored in his classic book *Varieties of Religious Experience*, in which he said as most recognized spiritual figures seemed to live a life of poverty, voluntary poverty could be seen as one of the major signs of devotion to God.

Since I considered frugal living to be a virtue, I looked down on people who valued money. I chose to work in a mental health clinic with the poorest people in New York City. The clinic salary didn't go very far in New York, so frugality was really a necessity. Yet it didn't take much to see that I had gone too far, even from a psychological perspective. My upbringing and my attempts to be detached from money had made me far more preoccupied with it than my friends, who freely enjoyed the comforts that life had to offer but attached far less importance to them than I did. They lived within their means without much worry, while I lived within my means with a lot of worry. But my worry didn't motivate me to go and work for more money so that I wouldn't need to worry about it. It wasn't a good balance.

As I began to decipher my messages, however, I became aware of what has become a central theme of this book: that the spiritual value of an action comes more from our attention and intention than it does from the material manifestation of the action. Each facet of everyday life, each thing we are attracted to, stimulates the development of a different facet of our character both psychologically and spiritually. Although it is possible to develop certain aspects of our spiritual character by renouncing material pleasures and connecting to the spiritual dimension as mystics did in the past, it is better in our spiritual life as in our material life to develop a well-rounded character that deals effectively with all our different drives and gets the best all-around benefit from the opportunities in our own life that are in line with our values.

It sounds very easy to do—just live a normal life within your means and discern from your feedback whether you are managing your money in the best possible way or not. In fact, doing so requires constant vigilance. It's easy to think that you're being more virtuous when you deny yourself pleasure, but such an idea misses the point. It is more difficult to develop the self-understanding to know how much of what kind of pleasure we need to achieve our goals most effectively. This we can do only by understanding what makes an action spiritual and decoding our messages.

Balance in Practice

One good way to test ourselves and see how well we are dealing with money is to look at whether our attraction to money makes us go against our ethical principles. C.J., whose stories we read in chapter 1 and the last chapter, gave me a clear example of how he thought about money in his profitable medical practice. "Because I spend the bulk of my time, say fifty hours a week, at the office," he said, "the best chance I ever get during the week to really practice the things I've learned about spirituality is at the office. If I don't do something nice for somebody at work, I won't get another opportunity."

I asked him how he did it. "I think that if you believe in spirituality, you do observe ethics," he said, "but ethics stop at some level. I try to go beyond that and do the best possible thing I can in a particular situation, as if my whole life depended on that one little action. Ethics doesn't really push us that far. Ethics would just say, 'You should do something decent and be nice to that person' rather than 'You should do something that is as good as you possibly can do.'

"While I am doing my professional work, I try to treat every patient as I would my mom or my dad or my wife. I try to care about my patients' welfare as I would care about my family's welfare. I do the best possible work regardless of whether a patient is paying me more or less than average. It just doesn't matter. And because I do it for God's satisfaction, I can keep myself working at that level."

Since C.J. had an essentially middle-class practice yet charged standard fees that would certainly be high for some patients, I wondered how he set fees in a way that was coherent with his spiritual ideals. C.J. explained that when determining what to charge, he set fees that were appropriate for someone with the kind of practice that he had. He didn't give away his services for free or at below-market rates in order to make his work "spiritual." Instead, he made his efforts spiritual by giving more committed and compassionate service to all and deciding on a case-by-case basis when to give discounts based on his assessment of a patient's genuine financial need rather than any emotional appeal that he or she might make.

He would analyze the different rights involved: his, his family's, his patient's, and society's. He didn't expect his family to give up the material benefits that other doctors' families might enjoy. He planned for his retirement as his colleagues would. He based exceptions to his fees on what balance felt right and then acted on his feeling and watched for any feedback that might indicate what he might have done better in individual situations. He balanced the material and the spiritual and combined his everyday and spiritual intelligences in a way that worked for him, as evidenced by the ongoing string of spiritual messages that came through his work. The challenge of being more mindful of this balance, he believed, gave him a more vital spiritual life.

Moderation in Practice

Moderation is a virtue, yet we need to be just as careful that achieving moderation doesn't lead us into complacency that will make us vulnerable all over again to the influence of our imperious self. Life is filled with ups and downs. Our goal is to achieve a moderation based on inner equilibrium rather than on temporary stability in a given area of our life.

To illustrate what I mean, let's look at the example of Jacob, whose attitude toward money is quite moderate in relation to that of his peers. "I work in a milieu where everybody is after money; it is hard for me to be detached," he told me. "Seven years ago, before I was interested in spirituality, I was spending a lot of money on things that were useless. Comfort was important for me. Now it is different. Money is not my objective anymore, but a means to get where I want to go. I have learned to stop following fashion and to find quality without having to spend a lot of money.

I used to be much more under the influence of those around me; I still work on my image, but in my heart I do not attach the same importance to the opinion of others as I used to."

Jacob works hard and makes even more money than he did when he had little interest in spirituality because now he is more diligent in everything that he does. He has moved up the ladder of success in his business. He dresses well and lives well, as suited to his position in society. He wants his children to have a good education and enjoy the same perks that their friends have. At the same time, he teaches them to love God.

Jacob believes that living a normal material life for someone in his position has made his spiritual life more vital. Holding on to his values in the business world in which he works keeps him on his toes—just as it did Giorgio in chapter 9. Although maintaining moderation isn't often a challenge for Jacob anymore, he keeps examining his relationship with money and renewing his spiritual intention, just as Venus or I might do, to make certain that he doesn't become complacent about his financial affairs. He might check, for example, to make sure that he doesn't feel superior to people who give money too much or too little importance, or he might check to see whether he looks up to people with more money than he has or looks down on those who have less.

Because Jacob has been successful, let's use his high standard of moderation to explore other attitudes that we might have about money and spirituality. Would Jacob be more spiritual if he lived a more marginal life, worked in an organization that helped others, dressed very plainly, didn't save for his retirement, or gave all his extra money to the poor rather than spending it on his children? When I first heard his story many years ago, my heart reflexively said "yes" even though my head knew better.

Although at the time I was beginning to understand that someone could be successful financially and still be just as spiritual as someone who deprived himself to give to others, I still hadn't fully grasped why. As I had spent most of my own professional career working with the poor for a minimal salary, thinking this was more noble, it was hard for me to accept that working with the poor and living modestly was not more beneficial for the development of my spiritual intelligence than Jacob's being a businessman and living very comfortably was for the development of his spiritual intelligence. Now I understand that we were each put in a different situation and that society needs people to do both jobs in order to function properly. Spirituality has far more to do with our attention and intentions than with the actual ways in which we earn and spend money.

Even now, though, my heart still struggles with living comfortably. Can I consider myself ethical, much less spiritual, if I live comfortably while thousands are dying of starvation in the world? Can I consider myself a true human being if I am comfortable and others are homeless in my city? Isn't it my duty to help others? What if Jacob or I made more money and gave it to help others? Would that make our choice better? How much should we then give? Should Bill Gates and Warren Buffett then be my models because of all the money they have given to help others?

Each of us will come up with different answers as to what to do to earn money and how to spend what we earn. We will each draw the line in a different place and make different choices in our own life to bring our drives into balance forceful enough to help us reach our goals but well enough under control that our imperious self can't use them to dominate us when we are under stress.

If I've chosen to tell stories of people with financially comfortable lives, it is because they help me undercut the stereotype I was raised with—that it's more spiritual to be poor. Of course, people can learn lessons from financial hardship too. What is important is how to keep the emotional drives that underlie our relationship to money and other material pleasures from loosening our attention to ethical and spiritual principles.

Striking It Right

Is it worth the effort of trying to walk this fine line? Wouldn't it be better to get control of our desires once and for all so that issues about money just didn't affect us? For my answer, I turned to the author of the set of principles that I use, Ostad Elahi, and an experience he had while serving as a judge in Iran. "There was a young man whose father had died when he was a child," he wrote. "His aunt, who had been appointed as his guardian, was in charge of his inheritance. When he came of age, however, his rather strict aunt would not relinquish control of his inheritance, so the young man came to court to lodge a complaint against her. In accordance with the law, we relieved the aunt of her guardianship and returned control of the inheritance to the young man.

"Shortly after this incident, I needed a pair of patent-leather shoes for a set of judicial robes I had ordered. Since there was no shoemaker in town, the shoes had to be bought from a shoemaker in the city. Since this young man happened to be going into the city, I gave him money to buy the shoes and bring them back. During the trip, he apparently ran out of money and spent mine. When I looked into the matter, I learned that he had bought the shoes, but had then sold them again. Upon his return, I asked him for the shoes. In response, he became angry and snapped: 'I suppose you're going to use your power now and throw me in jail.' I told him to leave.

"A few days later, he was brought into court on charges of publicly slapping a respected local merchant. Because this young man wanted to become a police officer, if I convicted him it would have resulted in a criminal record that would have made him ineligible for such employment. The merchant was adamant in his refusal to forgive the young man. I could have sentenced him from eight days to two months in prison.

"In short, I found myself in a state of inner turmoil. At times, my heart sought vengeance for what he had done, but I kept struggling internally and telling myself that I shouldn't take advantage of my power to seek revenge. After a great deal of struggle, I managed to overcome my imperious self. I turned to the merchant and said, 'So far, no matter how much I have insisted, you've refused to forgive this young man, but this matter will impact his future. Now, in the spirit of chivalry, will you forgive this young man for my sake?' The merchant paused for a moment and then forgave him. I dismissed the young man. Feeling ashamed of himself, he wanted to come and apologize. 'Don't spoil the moment,' I said.

"Had I sentenced that young man to prison, I would have always thought to myself, See how you stooped to revenge."

To understand the full importance of what Ostad Elahi is advocating in this story, you need to know a little bit about him. He had gone through years of ascetic deprivation during his spiritual training between the ages of twelve and twenty-four and had brought his thoughts, feelings, and actions in line with the source of his messages. He knew in every part of his being the ultimate insignificance of money and shoes. He had achieved complete control of his emotions. What did the loss really mean to him? Not very much.

So what was this impulse toward vengeance doing in him that could be provoked by the theft of his shoes and his money if he was spiritually mature? Why did this feeling even surface in him if he had banished every trace of attachment to material things from his heart many years before, as so many other mystics before him had done? It was because after overcoming all of his natural desires and reaching the goal of ascetic life—union with his Beloved— Ostad had deliberately given up asceticism so that the natural human urges of his body reemerged and attached to the things his psychological self naturally liked.

He described his conclusion to this experiment as follows: "God made me take up a public career despite my aversion to it. He forced me to become a judge and gave me sensitive judicial assignments, each of which I realized later contained a thousand pearls of wisdom. Before taking up government employment, I was unaware that my twelve years of devotional and ascetic practice had no more value than one year of public service. Official duties and sensitive assignments, rife with all manner of things which I would not have any dealings with, [...] each of the latter were as rewarding as the whole of the former twelve put together. That is why I say, be in society, keep your belly full, strengthen your constitution, but make sure that your soul is so fortified that it can resist any temptation."

Ostad Elahi lived a full life in society. He loved his children and was a good father. He enjoyed certain foods and certain activities. He took on the difficult responsibility of a judge to uphold the social order according to the law. He saved for his retirement. He proved to himself in so doing that it was more advantageous to allow thoughts like the desire for vengeance to enter his mind, and keep them from dominating him, than to stifle the emotions that gave rise to vengeance at their very root as ascetics in the past had done. Everyday life provided him with a constant stream of opportunities to practice, experiment, and learn from the results, for everyday life is full of just such incidents. That's why he considered it to be the natural system created for our spiritual development.

Ostad Elahi's example has encouraged me to make a vital material life the basis of my spiritual life, and I too have found it more rewarding than all of my previous efforts. Having a vital material life means investing enough of my emotions in everyday things like money or shoes so that the events of everyday life provide constantly changing challenges through which to apply my principles and develop spiritual intelligence.

જ઼ જ઼ જ઼

Each of our desires seeks to satisfy the pressure caused by one or another of our drives. Each drive exists for a reason—a material or psychological reason—and they collectively ensure that we pay attention to all of the important elements in life. Each reveals to us a different aspect of our own nature. Money is just one of these aspects, one window into our drives and ourselves. All that I've said about money in this chapter is true of all the objects of our desires. Although the ideal in each area is moderation, we don't need to be moderate in all things equally, but to arrive at an overall balance of our drives that creates a vital basis for our spiritual development.

Everyday life thus becomes a system of naturally changing challenges. Each aspect of everyday life is like a separate course that helps us develop different spiritual potentials. We can learn best by concentrating on gaining discerning control of the desires that make us most likely to forget our principles when we are under the power of their attraction.

જ઼ જ઼ જ઼

Keys to Chapter 13

- Spirituality isn't about the amount of money, power, intelligence, sex, fashion, love, family, or social status that you have—or the degree to which you deny yourself these things—but how well you use each of these areas to develop spiritual intelligence. It's about controlling the emotional drives that cause you to be attracted to these things well enough that they don't cause you to act contrary to your principles.
- Despite the fact that most recognized spiritual figures have renounced material pleasure, messages encourage us to build a successful and satisfying material life that is in line with the principles of psychology and common sense rather than to deny ourselves pleasure and comfort.

- It's challenging to both enjoy material pleasures and develop spiritual intelligence at the same time. It's easy to fool yourself as to the amount of pleasure that is good for your spiritual development, so you will need to continually look for messages that confirm or correct the balance you strike.
- In our spiritual life, there is no advantage to moderation in itself unless it is used to bring us closer to our goal—the development of spiritual intelligence. In the case of money, what is important is how well our attitude toward money reflects the wisdom of our principles.
- We all go too far in one direction or another. Nonetheless, our best advantage lies in directing our emotions' vital energy toward our spiritual goal, not simply suppressing that energy. A vital material life with our drives fully engaged is the best place for the development of spiritual intelligence.

꓿   ꓿   ꓿

For Your Reflection

Each aspect of our everyday life provides an opportunity for us to develop a different facet of our spiritual intelligence by keeping our emotional drives and desires in balance.

1. What do you naturally pay attention to or feel most attracted to? Is it money, power, sex, love, fashion, family, social status, or something else? Try to rate each of these, and any others that come to mind, on a scale of 1 to 10 that indicates how important each is to you in everyday life. Think of it as a psychological profile of your-

self, and make certain to include the areas that are most important to you.

2. Do any of your drives and desires cause you to think, feel, or act contrary to the ways that common sense might suggest? Which area do you think would benefit you the most if you brought it into better balance with a spiritual intention? Pay more attention to this aspect of your life, and try to think up ways to bring it under control with your best spiritual attention and intentions. Find a principle to support your efforts, and look for the feedback of a message to help you refine your understanding of that principle.

3. Go to decodeyourmessages.com to find how others have balanced their material interests with their spiritual understanding.

4. Take out a sheet of paper or turn to a blank page in your notebook and entitle it "Ensuring Balance and Vitality in My Spiritual Life." You can also go to decodeyourmessages.com to download these points for reflection to your computer or log into your online notebook. Write a summary paragraph about what level of material pleasure, deprivation, or moderation you consider ideal for your spiritual development and what messages have confirmed your conclusions. Then write in as much detail as you'd like about the actual experiences that support your conclusions.

5. Go to decodeyourmessages.com to add how messages have helped you find the level of involvement with everyday satisfactions and pleasures that promotes optimal spiritual growth for you.

CHAPTER 14

Resolving Dissonance

As we develop greater spiritual intelligence and begin to think more clearly about the spiritual elements in everyday life, we become more and more certain that our messages really are guiding us in an orderly way toward some goal that is for our ultimate benefit, even though we can't quite comprehend it yet. Nevertheless, the more confident we become of our messages' coherence and beneficence, the better the answers we expect to get to our questions and the more troubled we feel when we can't find them. For me, the most troubling issue was suffering. Although I could find good reasons to accept the misfortunes in my own life and learn lessons from getting sick, losing loved ones, and even facing my own death, it became increasingly difficult to reconcile my newfound confidence in the beneficence of the source of my messages with the all too apparent injustice and suffering in the world.

In this chapter, I will explain how I came to terms with this dissonance, this profound lack of agreement between the way I thought I should be seeing things based on my beliefs and the way I actually did see them. I hope that it will encourage you to seek your own answers in areas where you are troubled by a dissonance between what your beliefs tell you and the material realities that you perceive around you. Not every instance of dissonance deserves thoughtful consideration, but the more it interferes with your ability to follow your messages' guidance, the more important it is to seek to resolve it. As any solution is likely to be theoretical and beyond our ability to confirm it in our own experience, we can only validate it by seeing how it helps us bring our thoughts, feelings, and actions into line with the effects of our messages. The most valuable solutions will help us put our messages into better perspective so that we can decode them better.

The problem of the all too obvious injustice in the world bothered me for many years. When I listened to the news in the morning or went to work in a mental health clinic in the South Bronx with some of the poorest people in New York City, something in me rebelled. It couldn't be quelled by thinking of life as a classroom. I couldn't comprehend how God could be just and want our good, as religions say, when every second, somewhere in the world, innocent people were starving, suffering, and falling ill, while others were being tortured, raped, and killed. How could I make sense of innocent children born into unbelievable poverty suffering with terrible diseases and dying painful deaths? It didn't sound very merciful and certainly not a sign of a very intelligent design.

I wanted to think that God had come up with some system of spiritual compensation to make up for these people's physical suffering, but I couldn't imagine a system that made sense. If God were to compensate people in their eternal life for suffering now, it might make things seem more merciful, but it would be unjust to those who *didn't* suffer in this world: It would be better to have the momentary suffering with eternal gain than the momentary ease and comfort with no such long-term advantage. Yet if those who didn't suffer were somehow compensated for not having the opportunity to suffer, then nothing that happened during our life would make any difference and those who suffered would seem to be treated unjustly all over again.

Spiritual inequalities posed the same problem for me. If people were rewarded in eternity because they had a certain faith, it would be unjust to those whose life circumstances gave them no chance of getting to know that faith. But if these unenlightened people (children who died young or people born in places where no one talked about God or spirituality) were rewarded because of their lack of opportunity to develop spiritually, it would be unfair to those who *did* struggle to develop themselves spiritually but didn't make as much progress as they could have. Life would be absurd. The truly fortunate would die at birth.

If you don't question how a higher power can be just and loving when you look at the world in which we live, or if the question doesn't stop you from being in tune with the source of your messages, then you needn't look for a solution to this problem. You might, however, be troubled by your inability to understand something else about the spiritual dimension. If that's the case, you can compare my way of coming to terms with God's apparent injustice to your own and then share your feelings with others on the Web site decodeyourmessages.com.

Positing a Solution

In general, we turn to theory to extend the reach of our thinking beyond our own experience. In this case, I turned to one of Ostad Elahi's principles proposing that each of us has not one but many lifetimes in which to develop spiritually. Although not a part of my Christian upbringing, a belief in successive lives is a solution to the problem of injustice that has been held by millions of people in many different traditions over thousands of years. It was one I had intuitively believed in since childhood.

With a belief in many lifetimes, I could at least imagine that what-ever suffering someone endured and however little she seemed to learn from that suffering, it was a part of a larger plan in which everyone could easily have equal opportunities for spiritual edu-cation over the course of many lifetimes. Within a single lifetime, then, people might develop the personal qualities that the partic-ular lifetime drew into focus—perhaps just a little more patience or perseverance or kindness. They might also become a little more aware of the existence of their souls. This idea fit with the slow pace with which messages seemed to be teaching us and their focus on developing ethical virtues, for the main thing that we take with us when we go from one lifetime to another is the progress we have made in developing these qualities. It helped make sense of the fact that each of us seemed to have a different life lesson to learn that was a product of the body and the milieu into which we were born.

A belief in successive lives also helped me feel at peace with the world around me. If someone starved to death as a child or was killed in the prime of life by a flood or an epidemic, it was no longer as intolerable an injustice to me as it had been before, because I didn't see it as the person's only chance. It was tragic, but it wasn't unjust, since we had all probably starved, been abused, or suffered other injustices in the course of our lifetimes.

I still didn't understand why things worked the way they did and how a God of such a universe could be merciful, but by thinking of a law like karma, I could imagine how he could be just. From this perspective, the circumstances into which we are born aren't accidental, but a result of our actions in past lives. They provide the setting for us to develop one or more of the qualities that we need to develop to more fully engage the spiritual dimension. How we act in each life and whether or not we learn its lessons determine the circumstances of our future lives. We continue coming and going until we actualize our potentials to think, feel, and act in line with the guidance of our messages and principles. Then we under-stand the spiritual dimension and its benefits. There is justice.

Having briefly outlined the belief that offered a theoretical solution to my problem, let me say that, as a psychiatrist, I have a pragmatic attitude toward beliefs. Much of our material life is lived in a world of intentions and meanings that are beyond objective validation. We can't live without beliefs to fill in the gaps in our understanding and help us interact with others in our society. Beliefs provide us with meanings for situations we can't yet decipher based on our own experience. Rather than articles of faith, however, beliefs for me are more like hypotheses that are confirmed by their influence on our life.

So I don't think of spiritual beliefs as being "right" or "wrong," because I accept that I can't prove them to anyone else, but as being functional or dysfunctional, depending on whether or not they help us to think, feel, and act in line with our messages and principles. My new belief in successive lives was functional in just this way: In helping me take a major step forward in resolving the dissonance that had been interfering with my spiritual connection, it also put what I was learning from messages into a context that was rationally coherent.

Deepening the Belief

Though I had arrived at a satisfactory theoretical solution to the injustices of life, I was still bothered by them. As everything that I knew about life grew out of my experience in *this* life, a belief in successive lives naturally ran counter to everything that I knew. Thinking of successive lives was like a fantasy, and it had little power over my thoughts or emotions. I needed to find a way to come to a deeper understanding of this new belief—to make it more fully a part of who I was so that it would influence how I actually perceived the events in my life.

I turned for help to the work of Carl Jung, one of the few early psychoanalysts interested in spirituality. It was his essay on synchronicity that I was reading when the leaf fell in my hand, related in chapter 1. He had a deep interest in the mysteries of mental life and in spirituality. In his work, Jung explored and mapped archetypes—the set of images that reflect our basic human nature and have arisen independently in the minds of men and women throughout history in many different cultures, uninfluenced by the ideas of other cultures. Archetypes are the deep programming that determines, for example, our way of being a mother, a father, or a child in such a way as to ensure the survival of the human species and the growth of the individual. Although their expression is highly influenced by our nature, culture, and circumstances, archetypes are a basic imprint in all of us. They are what determine our most fundamental human nature. To live a rich and satisfying life, Jung believed that we needed to express all aspects of our deep programming in ways that fit our own circumstances and individual nature.

Much of his work, therefore, was concerned with how to connect to our inner programming and actualize the potentials in the deeper parts of our being. As a psychiatrist, he dealt mainly with the psychological level of the mind. However, he believed that the idea of God was itself an archetype, one particularly central to our understanding of ourselves. Further, he believed that God had put this archetype in us so that we could find our way to him. Unless we actualized this spiritual part of ourselves, Jung believed that we would never feel completely whole.

To help him understand how to connect to this deepest part of him that longed for God and bring its resources into his and his patients' lives, Jung studied the early Gnostic mystics and how they deepened their understanding of God. The Gnostics believed that the essential attribute of God was that of Creator. They argued that to understand our true nature, we need to understand where we came from, who our Creator is.

To help human beings activate this archetype and connect to the Creator, every religion had developed a story of creation. It was not enough for the Gnostics, however, to relate to the Creator through a generic myth formulated hundreds of years before. It was not even enough to rely on a myth formulated by another Gnostic, even one who they believed understood God better than they might themselves. Each Gnostic could connect with the Creator only by constructing his own *personal* myth that emerged from his own deep programming into his own unique consciousness. In a state of mystical absorption, he would write his own myth of creation—his own version of Genesis. He would transcend the beliefs that he had been taught in order to found the pillar of his identity on his own personal understanding of his Creator drawn from his engagement of this archetype. Inspired by the Gnostics, Jung too wrote his own myth of creation and found that it helped him feel closer to God.

Jung's explorations encouraged me to try to establish the pillars of my own identity and sense of self on a belief in successive lives. If I connected to the deepest levels in my own self, would I encounter details of my own successive lives, and if I did, what difference would this make? Would it bring a better connection and a better understanding of my messages, or not? I decided to give it a try.

The mystics entered trance states to make the myths that would connect them to their Creator; hypnosis is a more scientific and controlled way of working with such states. Because of my interest in hypnosis, I began to investigate the practice of past-life regression to help me see what I thought and felt about successive lives on the deepest level of my mind and emotions that I could access.

Past-life regression poses many theoretical difficulties that can be solved only by approaching it as the Gnostics did their myths. Even recovering memories of our childhood in this life can be unreliable, as has been made all too clear by cases where people recalled early abuse that was later proven not to have taken place. This means that to accept a memory as being completely factual, we need to have some objective validation; otherwise, we must treat it as one would a questionable memory of abuse recovered in hypnosis, recognizing that, regardless of its factual accuracy, it conveyed a true feeling that would still have to be dealt with for the person to find happiness in life.

When I began to investigate reports of past-life regressions, I found them unconvincing in this objective sense, for they couldn't be confirmed. Few people discovered their names, the towns in which they had lived, or details of lives that could be independently corroborated by birth certificates, photos, or old newspapers. Still, though hypnosis didn't yield the kind of detailed, rigorously examined evidence that Ian Stevenson, M.D., had reported in his book *Twenty Cases Suggestive of Reincarnation* (University Press of Virginia, 1974), it remained a plausible way of connecting to my deep programming. Since I believed in past lives by this point, I decided to proceed and judge the results not by whether they could be validated objectively, but by whether they helped me see life in line with the perspective that the source of my messages was teaching me. If they could, then that would be the best possible proof for me, just as in everyday life, the help a belief gives us in reaching our goals is sufficient for us to embrace it until such time as evidence proves it false or we no longer need it.

Being a psychiatrist interested in hypnosis, I found it natural to use hypnosis to connect to this deeper level of programming. Chances are you aren't a psychiatrist with an interest in hypnosis or the deeper programming in your own unconscious. Yet those deeper levels of programming are functional in each of us and we each access them in different ways in our everyday life. For many people, this integration just happens naturally and they don't have to think about it because it works. Others might talk with advisors who they believe know more than they do to align their thinking with that of the "experts" and so access those deeper levels of their being; still others meditate or enter into different states of introspection in which they examine their lives. There is no one way of accessing the deep programming that will connect you better with the source of your messages. In the pages ahead, I'll tell you how the process worked for me and why I believe it helped me. I hope that it will help you think about what means might enable you to connect more deeply.

Constructing My Myth

I underwent my first past-life regression in a workshop where I was learning how to do spiritual hypnotherapy from Michael Newton, author of the bestseller *Journey of Souls* (Llewelleyn Publications, 1992). He and his assistants taught us what to do and then helped us practice on each other. After I lay down in a comfortable position, closed my eyes, and did some relaxation exercises, the person I was working with guided me into a light level of trance, first suggesting pleasant scenes like walking in a forest and standing under a waterfall of light and then moving me on to remembering childhood scenes. At the end of an hour, I had drifted into a dreamlike state where images came into my mind spontaneously in reaction to what my colleague was saying with no conscious deliberation on my part.

My colleague then guided me through a long, dark tunnel in time as he counted backward from 10 to 1, telling me repeatedly that on the count of 1, I would be in a significant day in my last lifetime. When I reached the end of the tunnel, everything was black. I gradually realized that it was very early morning and I was lying in the mud in the dark. I had just about no energy and could barely move, so I couldn't look around. I only realized where I was when two men came to lift me up by my armpits. They dragged me to a nearby room. I saw that they were German soldiers and the room was a messy shack. I knew that this was the day they would finally kill me. One of them picked up an ice pick and waved it in front of my eyes. It was beautiful to me—one of the most beautiful objects I can ever recall seeing. It was my release. I was too weak to experience any fear. I was beyond fear. I was beyond anger. I was beyond pain. I even felt sorry for these men that they had allowed themselves to be induced to do such an inhuman thing.

My colleague froze the action right there by asking questions about who I was. I told him I was a German who had been caught trying to help Jews escape. My wife and children were killed, but I was taken prisoner. I was happy that my family had died quickly. We had all known the risk of helping others and had agreed to it. I was sad about what was happening in the world and didn't really want to be a part of it anymore. I had been in this concentration camp for a few months and been tortured so much that I wasn't really in touch with my body anymore. Maybe that's why they killed me, because I no longer cared.

I died that day as they drove that ice pick into my brain through my left eye. I felt no pain. I experienced that death as one of the most ecstatic moments in my life—soaring out of that body. It was incredibly real and powerful. I was smiling and laughing out loud. I was now a soul. I was free and going "home." I can't describe how good it felt.

In the schema of successive lives, most of the real learning happens after the death that ends one lifetime, as we begin to think as souls do. As I oriented myself to my new state, having left my body behind, and reflected on the lifetime just ended, I felt no residue of the trauma I had just experienced. I was surprised that, from this perspective, the lifetime looked like a relatively easy one because my choices had been easy to make. I just couldn't have turned my back on other human beings like an animal. Living with that would have been worse than what I went through. From this experience, I had solidified my inner commitment to being ethical by holding on to it in trying conditions.

My second past-life regression, done a few months later, took me to the lifetime immediately before my German life. I entered it on a very happy day when my son was being born. I was standing near the bed where my wife held him. My parents and a few other family members were there. We were a spiritually oriented family in which God was the center of everything. The house we were in was small and simple. Outside it was warm and sunny. The wheat was just about ready to be harvested. We lived a simple agrarian life. We were all completely in tune with God. It was as happy a life as I could imagine.

My colleague moved me ahead in time to the day of my death, and I found myself in that same bed many years later. My wife and children were around me. The whole scene was radiant and I was very happy. My family members were both happy and sad. They knew I was going to a better place, but they would miss me. I died quite easily; I was ready to go. I took in a deep breath and let it out. As I did, my soul easily left my body and floated up. In contrast to the ecstasy of my previous regression death, this time I felt hardly different from what I had felt in the body.

While I was in that soul state of mind, my colleague asked me questions to help me relate these two past lifetimes to my current life so that I would understand the purpose of the life I was living today more clearly. At first, I was a little disoriented by the order of the two lifetimes; I would have imagined that a life of noble sacrifice would be rewarded by a joyous spiritual life, yet for me, it had been the other way around. I was also surprised that after a deeply spiritual life, I had a life in which spirituality wasn't as central to me. My idea of what was important in life, of how the "system" worked, was clearly not correct. It was the development of different facets of my character that mattered, not the specific circumstances or setting in which I lived. I was also a little confused by the fact that both past lifetimes appeared equally easy to me in this soul state. Although one had been filled with suffering and the other with joy, the right choice in each situation had been equally obvious and easy to make because of the circumstances.

Again, to my surprise, I saw that the task to be mastered in my current lifetime was more difficult: to hold on to my spiritual and ethical beliefs in a context with less contrast, where things were neither clearly good nor clearly bad. The options that I faced in my everyday life weren't black or white, but shades of gray. It would never have occurred to me that it was more challenging to develop my spiritual intelligence and hold on to my values without such an obvious distinction between right and wrong. But here it felt intuitively correct and fit right in with what my messages seemed intent on doing: helping me develop enough spiritual intelligence to think for myself about the spiritual elements in the decisions of everyday life.

Changing Perspectives

To what extent these memories were objectively "true" or products of my own unconscious mind doesn't really matter to me. Either way, they helped me align the deeper parts of myself with my beliefs so that I could feel more in harmony with the perspective of my messages in everyday life. The injustice of life still bothered me, but for material reasons. It no longer disrupted my sense of spiritual connection. That part of my dissonance was gone, and I was left with justifiable outrage at the wrongs that we humans are capable of doing to each other of our own free will and sadness for those who die in accidents and catastrophes.

I felt less fearful of death and more certain that I was a soul. I was more than just Paul living this life. In each of those lifetimes, I had been the same person I am today. What tied the different bodies and lifetimes together were the personal qualities that all the religious and spiritual traditions emphasized—traits like kindness, compassion, courage, diligence, and dignity. They manifested slightly differently in each life depending on the circumstances, but there remained a common ground of who I was that stayed the same in each lifetime, with a slow, gradual progression in my understanding.

Once I grasped this, my sense of personal identity was no

longer as strongly tied to my current body, family, or role in life, for I now felt sure on a deeper level that I had had many different bodies, families, and roles. This understanding freed me in a wonderful way to be myself and be responsible for my own future. I no longer felt a lingering resentment of my mother and father for not being the perfect loving parents I wanted. Instead, I was grateful that my parents had taught me what I needed in this lifetime: that it was good to believe in God and to be ethical, honest, rational, and self-supporting. I hadn't given them enough credit for these important attitudes, which had laid the cornerstone for my spiritual progress in this lifetime without tying me to their beliefs. I was still their son, but their role in my far longer life history was now quite different, for I had had many sets of parents and many sets of children myself.

I had long believed that all religions were one—that is, from the same source. My regressions (the two I've described and a series of others that took me back many thousands of years) made this intellectual belief immediate and tangible. In other lives, I had been a caveman, a humanist, a Buddhist, a Jew, and a Christian, and all these different traditions had organically contributed to the beliefs I held in this life. And as I went forward in time, tracing the overall progression in humankind's thought from prehistoric times to present, I saw that the advances in my thinking and my ability to decode messages weren't a result of my own innate ingenuity, but of the collective progress humankind has made over thousands of years. God is different in our time because we are different and so relate to him differently. That's why our messages are guiding us differently today than they did in the past.

I continued assisting others in their regressions and found an interesting change in myself after each. On the subway or walking down the street, I found myself aware that each person was more than the material body that I saw. Each was a soul, as I was. Each had a long history of many lifetimes and had been born into her situation to learn a lesson and develop her spiritual character, just as I had been born into mine. I wondered how I would be different if I had been born into their circumstances and they into mine. Each set of circumstances provided the lessons that we needed to learn. Neither was better or worse. As a result, I judged people less and compared myself with them less. I felt more kindly disposed to them and kept my attention more on what I needed to learn in this lifetime, for I realized that I couldn't know what they had to learn.

These changes were all in line with the effects of my messages and helped me bring my thinking more in line with their source. This was the validation that I most wanted, and this is what I found.

ॐ ॐ ॐ

Despite all that we have learned, our knowledge of the spiritual dimension remains rudimentary. We are bound to sense some dissonance between certain elements in the world that we see and those of the spiritual world that we sense by decoding messages, developing attention and intentions, and applying principles. We can make progress, however, by approaching these areas of dissonance with the attitude of a student who values what he has learned and views the contradictions as problems to be solved someday, rather than as proof that everything he has learned is false.

To decide on the best approach, we need to know whether the problem we are wrestling with is one that we can currently solve with greater effort or requires us to set it aside until we have reached a sufficient level in our spiritual development to be able to understand this issue. Are you like an elementary student in physics who needs to content himself with learning the elementary lessons under the watchful supervision of his teachers if he hopes to one day grasp quantum physics? Or should you study, as I did, how others have reported being able to resolve their contradictions and see whether you can apply what they have found to your own questions?

An understanding of spiritual development is essential for deciding what effort to make and what results to expect in anything that we do. Therefore, in the chapters ahead, we will turn to the topic of how to assess our level of development.

ॐ   ॐ   ॐ

Keys to Chapter 14

- The more answers you find to your spiritual questions, the more questions you will dare to ask and the more courage you will have to expect answers. You are likely, however, to find certain areas of ongoing dissonance between what you think you should believe and the way you actually think. I myself was most troubled by the dissonance between my own belief, from decoding messages, of a beneficial force at work in my life and the blatant injustices that I could see all around me.

- For our beliefs to touch the deepest parts of our nature, we need to resolve such dissonances. A satisfying theoretical solution offers a good start, but it often isn't enough to overcome the grip that material reality has on our minds and hearts. We need to find a way to come to a deeper understanding of this theoretical solution if we are to develop spiritual intelligence.

- In everyday life, we turn to psychological theories to extend the reach of our thinking beyond our own experience and then judge the usefulness of the theory by whether or not it improves our life in some tangible way. To help me come to terms with the injustice in the world, I turned to a spiritual principle in my system of principles proposing that each of us has not one but many lifetimes in which to develop spiritually.

- A belief in successive lives helped me not only feel that there could be justice in the world but also put in context the slow pace of my own spiritual development. It helped me come to terms with the incremental approach that messages advocated because it gave me more time to master the conflicts that I faced.
- I used hypnotic regression to explore the idea of previous lifetimes; you will need to find your own ways to make your beliefs more tangible to you. You can judge how well you are doing by checking whether you are increasing your spiritual intelligence and can see the perspective of your messages more clearly in your everyday life.

ॐ ॐ ॐ

For Your Reflection

Even if you have made good progress in developing spiritual intelligence in certain areas of your life, it's quite likely that you still relate to everyday life largely through material eyes and that this creates areas of dissonance between the way you think you should be seeing things and the way that you actually do see them. To help focus in on any such areas that hold you back from developing your spiritual intelligence, think about these questions:

1. How naturally do you see the world around you from the perspective of your spiritual beliefs and messages? Are there any aspects of everyday life that bother you as the injustices of life bothered me? Do you expect to be able to resolve this conflict?
2. How do you diagnose the cause of your conflict? Is it a weakness in your faith to be addressed by trying to increase your faith? Is it a developmental issue that you'll

resolve by continuing to decode your messages? Is it because you have some erroneous belief that can be approached using the CBT methods I've described elsewhere in the book? Is it because you are anchored in the material reality that you grew up in and need an additional principle to help you gain a spiritual perspective on yourself?

3. Go to decodeyourmessages.com to find areas of dissonance that others have discovered and how they resolved them. You can also find on the Web site a link to a more detailed description of the other past-life experiences I've referred to here and how they helped me put my theoretical beliefs into better perspective.

4. Take out a sheet of paper or turn to a blank page in your notebook and entitle it "Resolving Dissonance." You can also go to decodeyourmessages.com to download these points for reflection to your computer or log into your online notebook. Write down the areas that challenge your beliefs and the way in which you have dealt with them or hope to deal with them. Once you've written your summary paragraph, write as much detail as you'd like about your experiences in coming to terms with those areas of dissonance.

5. Go to decodeyourmessages.com to add the ways you have found of overcoming dissonance between your beliefs and the way the material world works. Be sure to include the ways that your understanding of messages helped you validate your solutions.

PART IV

Charting
Your Progress

CHAPTER 15

The Milestones of Spiritual Infancy and Early Childhood

We've discussed how spiritual messages reach us and what they have to tell us, and we've explored ways of engaging with them to build our spiritual intelligence. But how can we conceptualize the goal toward which our messages are guiding us and see if we are making meaningful progress toward it? Every religious tradition has a model that describes our spiritual development from its own perspective and helps us make sense of the changes upon which it focuses. The same is true of the studies that try to identify the commonalities in spiritual experience across traditions. For example, Evelyn Underhill's classic treatise *Mysticism*, first published in 1911, examined Western mystics and defined the stages that they went through on the path to spiritual wisdom as *awakening, purification, illumination, the dark night of the soul (or abnegation of this world),* and *union with God.* More recently, James Fowler described in his book *Stages of Faith* six steps in the development of faith in ordinary people, from a superstitious level through conventional levels and ending in radical actualization of our individuality through faith and love.

The more I studied messages, the clearer it became that they are guiding us through their own series of stages—an orderly and sequential process of development that parallels what an infant goes through growing up—and that we can use an analogy with child development to put our own journey into perspective. Imagine a newborn and all the processes that she goes through growing up as she engages reality in ever more advanced ways until eventually she can interact with it as an adult does. The potentials that make this possible are encoded in her DNA and are activated in an orderly and sequential way. It's the same in our spiritual development. We start off engaging spiritual reality by becoming aware of our messages and then decoding them. By following their guidance, we develop the potentials encoded in what I'm calling our *spiritual DNA* that determine the orderly and sequential steps we go through in our spiritual development, moving toward gaining the more and more advanced rewards that are intangible to the infant.

Turning once again to psychology to flesh out the analogy, I found a particularly apt parallel between the development of rational thinking in children as described by Jean Piaget, the famous Swiss psychologist, and the development of spiritual intelligence. I found other parallels between psychologist Erik Erikson's descriptions of the ways we attain a sound character, by sequentially developing qualities such as hope, will, competence, fidelity, and wisdom, and the ways we attain a sound spiritual character, by developing ethical virtues with a spiritual intention. In each different facet of a child's development that I reviewed, I could find interesting parallels with other aspects of our spiritual development that put my own and others' experiences learning to decode messages into a perspective that made sense.

To fill in the outlines of this analogy would require a book in itself, so I'll just touch on several important milestones in each stage to give you an idea of how the analogy works. In this chapter, I will take several of the most important milestones a child passes through as she goes from birth to four years of age and show how we go through similar stages as we first notice and then engage our messages. I will draw parallels with how a child first encounters reality, discovers cause-and-effect relationships, develops object constancy, establishes a bond with her parent, and responds to an inner push to explore.

In the next chapter, I will show you how the fundamental skills that we master in school from the ages of five to twelve will help you learn from the guidance of your messages in our spiritual classroom. In chapters 17 and 18, I will show you how to use the advances we make in adolescence and adulthood to imagine what the later stages in spiritual development might be like so that you can appreciate the ultimate benefit of the skills you are building now.

By the end of this section, I hope that you will have a better grasp of the value of what you have learned by decoding messages, the assignment you need to work on now, and the rewards you can reasonably expect for your efforts. When you can assess your own developmental level, you will know more clearly who you are and why you are here and you'll be able to apply yourself to the developmental task before you now with greater vigor.

There's one way our spiritual development is different from a child's development: We do have to apply ourselves. A whole range of physical and psychological changes appears like clockwork as a child grows; most babies start to walk, talk, and develop object constancy according to a timetable that is programmed into their DNA. Spiritual changes only come about when we make the right effort over the right period of time. If we don't work to develop the spiritual skill to reach our next milestone, it will never just appear on its own. No matter how strong our faith is, we will be stuck at that level forever. But, like children, we have to master each skill in order; we can't get impatient with one and go on to the next because we find it more interesting. We need to follow the orderly sequence of developmental milestones required to activate the next part of our spiritual DNA that in turn makes it possible for us to move toward the next milestone.

Seeing and Believing

When we first start detecting spiritual messages, we are like babies who have just been born. It's as if a door has just opened to give us a glimpse of the world. Unlike babies, we have a choice: to pass through that door or to stay where we are and let it close. As we peer in, we contemplate all that we've been taught about spirituality and wonder whether it is worthwhile to go through that door. If we choose to seize the opportunity, we find ourselves in a spiritual space whose features and dimensions we can't yet fathom. No matter how well developed our material intelligence might be, in this space we are like infants, at a loss to explain what is happening to us.

To get a better sense of what it is like when we pass through that door, imagine what it must be like for an infant when he is distressed and mother with a bottle magically appears. Something tastes good; he feels a wonderful pleasure. In the womb, he had been constantly fed and protected; he never felt hungry and never knew the pleasure of hunger being satisfied. He certainly doesn't have any idea that it was his hunger that caused him to cry, which signaled his mother to get the formula, which had been developed by researchers, made in a factory hundreds of miles away, and delivered to a store where his mother had bought it last week. He simply identifies his feeling of satisfaction with this mother-with-a-bottle figure. He has no idea of hunger, another person, a bottle, or food. He just didn't like the distressed feeling that had arisen and now he likes the feeling of relief that has replaced it.

It's confusing at first to accept that we are spiritual infants when our material intelligence is mature and has so many good ideas about spiritual experiences based on what we have read and heard. But once we accept our status as spiritual infants and get oriented to the task that lies ahead of us, it is a tremendous relief. Now we can understand why we know so little. We can fully enjoy the rush of energy that comes with a message, as an infant enjoys the sheer simple pleasure of hunger satisfied, and then apply ourselves to the simple developmental task of engaging the source of our messages so that we can repeat this pleasure again and again.

Initially, we have no experience to draw on, only theory. To enter that spiritual space, we need to push theory to the side and respond instinctively. Our developmental task at this stage is to become aware of our spiritual hunger and what satisfies it. Although others' experiences can give us some direction, we have to identify our own feelings of hunger and find out what satisfies them in this strange new world that our messages introduce to us.

Appreciating what an infant goes through in her early encounters with reality, you will see why theory does so little good and can even slow your progress. The theory we need to know at this point is incredibly simple: Spiritual reality exists and we can engage it in our everyday life. Before we can understand anything beyond this, we need to establish a basic interaction with spiritual reality by getting our attention focused on what our own messages are trying to tell us and learning how to respond to their impact. We have a lot to learn to become alert, oriented, and ready to respond to the impact of messages in our everyday life.

What does it mean for a spiritual infant to be fed for the first time? Nancy's experience of being overwhelmed in nature by divine love, which you read about in chapter 10, is one very direct analogy to the experience of a human infant. But the spiritual energy in a message will affect each of us differently. Each of us needs to learn from our messages what our spiritual hunger feels like, what satisfies it in a way that suits our character and life circumstances, and what gives us the nutrients we need for the development of our spiritual intellect. When I received my first message, as I described in chapter 1, I had had an intuition and gone to the garden in Rio de Janeiro, where I had a completely different kind of experience from Nancy's. A leaf fell into my hand and satisfied the curiosity that had brought me there. I was happily confused, just like the infant experiencing the first satisfaction after the arrival of mother with a bottle. I didn't understand what had caused it to happen to me at that moment or how paying attention to it would change my life forever. It simply awakened a hunger in me to know more.

Action-Reaction

We need to pass many developmental milestones to be able to understand even the simplest messages. One of these is to recognize the spiritual reactions to certain of our actions. It's our first awareness of a cause-and-effect relationship, like an infant's associating his mother's appearance with his feeling satisfied. He uses the temporal relationship between the two events to establish a primitive understanding of causality, and so do we.

I gave an example of one of my earliest experiences of spiritual cause and effect in chapter 1, when I formed an intention to give money to the first person who asked me and then found that I couldn't bring myself to do it because he was a drunk urinating in the subway station. I recognized the situation as a reaction to my action because the events were so close in time. The experience had a very different effect on me from the whimsical flight of a leaf that had fallen into my hand and marked my spiritual birth. Instead of thinking that I had just witnessed an interesting example of synchronicity for which there was unlikely to be any good explanation, I began to believe that there was a cause-and-effect relation between my intention and the strange response. It gave me a different kind of satisfaction to ponder the meaning of the drunk's behavior than I had found in thinking about the leaf's fall. Looking back now from a developmental perspective, I see that I was wrestling with something more advanced than I had been in my experience with the leaf: not just to accept that a different dimension of life existed, but to understand the way it worked.

Just by noticing more and more instances of the kind of temporal causality that I call *action-reaction*, we soon recognize patterns that help us anticipate certain kinds of reaction in response to certain simple actions we take. This is an easy idea to accept in theory, but it's a big step forward in our development to actually see cause-and-effect relationships at work in our own life often enough that we can hope to understand how and why they affect us as they do. It can take years of active effort to understand the basics of causality in a meaningful way—that is, to understand why an action of ours has elicited a specific reaction in a given situation when similar actions didn't get that same reaction in other situations.

Jesse, an insurance salesman I met in a spiritual discussion group, told me how he became aware of simple cause-and-effect relationships in his own experience. "Action-reaction really got my attention," he said. "When I went to lectures about spirituality, I noticed that something would happen to me that week that seemed related directly to what the talk was about. If I heard about jealousy and started paying attention to my own jealousy, something would happen to make me very jealous. If I heard about the spiritual harms of being angry, something would happen to get me really angry. At first, I dismissed this as coincidence, but others I knew found the same thing to be true. They didn't think we were just noticing these issues more because we had discussed them; it seemed as though these situations actually arose because we had decided to work on a particular subject.

"After I saw these 'coincidences' five or six times, I too began to think that maybe they weren't really coincidences at all, but spiritual lessons for me. It seemed that as soon as I decided to work on a particular issue, a situation would arise to give me the opportunity to do so. I've gotten fond of these little coincidences. Now, when they happen, I think of them as evidence that God loves me."

When we first begin to note spiritual cause-and-effect relationships and discover patterns in how they work, as Jesse did, we have made a significant step forward. When we act on what we learn, we start to experience the benefits of our new understanding. Our positive results help us become more confident that we are not making the whole thing up but actually seeing a predictable spiritual reaction to something we have done or thought. We are sure it is spiritual, even though we don't yet know how it works. We feel compelled by our innate curiosity, encoded in our spiritual DNA, to try to understand what's happening and look for more examples of it. We are optimistic that we'll understand more in the future.

This stage is particularly difficult for people who are attracted by and satisfied by theoretical knowledge about spirituality, as I am. We have read so many different accounts of spiritual experience that we think we already understand what is happening. However, if we don't set this theoretical knowledge aside in order to have our own experiences that we can then analyze in the light of what we have read, we delay our development. We do better when we remember that we have the spiritual intelligence of small children, that we need to develop our understanding by actively decoding our own messages rather than trying to rely on what we "know."

Keeping the Spiritual Dimension in Mind

So many important developments take place in a child's early years, and each milestone has a spiritual equivalent that can orient us to what's going on in our own spiritual development. For example, in Piaget's schema, when an infant's mother leaves the room, it's as if she ceases to exist. If a child drops something and it falls out of sight, that object ceases to exist. Children just can't keep track of the things they can't see. As their brains mature, however, they develop *object constancy*—the ability to understand that things continue to exist independent of their needs or their perception. Only then are they able to think of their parents when they are out of sight.

Similarly, we notice the spiritual dimension at first only when something is happening in our field of vision, when a spiritual message is arriving. In the example we just saw, God was real to Jesse only in moments when he noticed an example of action-reaction taking place. When nothing was "happening," it was as if the spiritual dimension didn't exist. But when we can keep God's existence in mind even when nothing is happening to remind us of his presence, we have developed spiritual object constancy. We don't have to think about God every moment or expect him to anticipate our every need, but we can rest comfortably knowing that he exists and is there watching over our development, available whenever we need him.

Here's a simple example that demonstrates a basic level of spiritual object constancy. Mary proudly told me about a recent shopping trip with her husband. "I wanted my husband to buy a certain vase that I really liked, and he said that we couldn't afford it. In the past, that would have precipitated an argument, but this time I began to think about how God would want me to act, and I controlled my temper. Afterward, I felt really good and wasn't even unhappy that we didn't buy the vase. It was a strange feeling."

Mary remembered God, even when he wasn't pushing himself forward to grab her attention, and changed the way she acted because of it. Just as a young child thinks of how her parents want her to act even when they are not around because of the solid bond formed with them, so Mary thought of how God in that moment wanted her to act. At this point, it was more important to honor her bond with God, who was like a parent to her, than get the vase she wanted.

By the time we achieve object constancy, we have matured enough to start taking a more disciplined approach to spiritual development, as I outlined in chapters 7 and 8, and acting in line with basic principles, as we discussed in Part III. We start to control ourselves, as Mary did, because the pleasure that we get from honoring our inner bond with the source of our messages through actions that satisfy it is greater than the pleasure of simply feeling its love when we are in a state of devotion.

Bonding to the Source of Our Messages

Now that we've looked at some early milestones in the development of our spiritual intelligence, we can turn to Erik Erikson's work for an appreciation of our emotional connection with reality. From an emotional perspective, what is most important at the earliest stages of development is a child's relationship with an adult who can take care of him and gradually expose him to situations to which he can learn to cope. The adult compensates for all the things the infant cannot do himself. He protects and nurtures the infant by exposing him to age-appropriate challenges and giving age-appropriate rewards so that the child can develop confidence in himself, his parent, and his environment. Feeling safe in a caring world, he continues to flourish. Without this feeling, he becomes troubled and withdraws from reality.

Just as a child's emotional well-being in the future depends largely on his forming a loving bond with a caring parent figure, so our spiritual future depends on our forming the right kind of bond with the source of our messages by decoding the messages that we receive in the same spirit that a child accepts and plays with a new toy given to him. If we are to develop naturally, we must depend on the source of our messages to establish situations where we can learn the skills we need to engage spiritual reality. The initial bond that we form with the source of our messages is simple. It needs to be instinctive and originate from our soul, not from our psychological or material understanding of spirituality. It's the same kind of instinctive response that children have programmed into their DNA to do things like cry when they are hungry, smile when they are full, and bond to their parents; parents are similarly programmed by *their* DNA not only to respond protectively to the cry of their baby, but also to respond affectionately to the shape of their infant's smiling face and bond even more closely during feeding. It's an instinctive response on both parts that is essential for normal development.

The task of our earliest messages is to arouse our spiritual instincts so that we become aware that we have a spiritual dimension that is being activated. As we experience more messages, we bond with the source of our messages in a way that is programmed into our nature by our spiritual DNA, the unknown factors that determine the nature of our soul and its unique potentials. The only way our everyday intellect can help us here is by recognizing the importance of what is happening but staying out of the way of our instinctive responses.

To appreciate the importance of this step, remember that if a child doesn't form an instinctive bond with a benevolent figure, she will not develop normally. So at this stage, we must gather enough evidence to become convinced that behind our messages is a benevolent figure who wants to help and guide us, carefully exposing us to situations that are appropriate for the developmental tasks that we face.

What does it look like in real life to become aware of this pull, and how do we then form a bond with the source of our messages that gets us to take our messages seriously? Most of the programs that people set up early in their spiritual life are to establish just such a bond. Greta in chapter 3, for example, felt discontented with life and was searching for answers when she received a message on a plane in the middle of a thunderstorm. She recognized in that moment that she had been living a self-indulgent life and would have to significantly change her ways if she were to find her purpose. Although Greta didn't want to make the efforts that she needed to make, she couldn't ignore the drive that was programmed in her spiritual DNA. It had become too strong. As she responded by trying to be more ethical, as the book she was reading advised, she received more messages and began to feel watched over, nurtured, and cared for. She gradually bonded to the source of her messages and continued her development.

The Push to Explore Further

A child who is loved and cared for experiences an increasing desire to push beyond the boundaries of his world. Erik Erikson observed that at around five to nine months of age a child starts to explore the world around him. He is driven to do so because a program in his DNA makes him feel uncomfortable just sitting like a blob and waiting to be fed. This discomfort is relieved when he is active. His activity garners a reward, another kind of pleasure that comes as he sees that his actions affect what happens to him. Gradually, he learns how to avoid mistakes such as getting burned by something hot. He experiences *feelings of efficacy* by knowing how to avoid other hot things in the future. Seeing that he can affect what happens to him prepares the child for discovering the even more exciting possibilities that will come when he can finally walk. These new feelings of satisfaction are different from the feelings of pleasure that he gets from eating or being held close, or even the more intellectual pleasure he gets from observing simple instances of action-reaction. They push him to constantly seek to increase his field of operations.

So it is in spirituality. The more we know, the less content we are with the answers we get from theory and the more we want to know things for ourselves. Each little success encourages us to believe in ourselves and to seek better answers as we direct our spiritual attention and act on our spiritual intentions using the techniques I described in Part II. Messages direct us toward challenges that are age-appropriate for us on a spiritual level so that mastering them will advance our spiritual development in the best way possible. When we succeed, we feel a sense of efficacy that motivates us to detect and decode more messages and find better reasons for many of the things that seem to just happen to us. This is experiential knowledge that can't be acquired merely by hearing others' experiences and agreeing with their conclusions.

For a good example of how feelings of efficacy translate into better motivation, let's look again at Martha's experience, which you read about in chapter 10, when she successfully confronted the medical board. Martha had been fearful by nature but had already formed a good enough bond with God that she hoped he would help her in her time of crisis and was able to act on her hope. She felt an inner push that was strong enough to get her to trust that God would help her. It's like a child feeling that he really can trust his parents and so being encouraged to make more efforts in directions that please them. When Martha drew on her newfound confidence to make efforts to improve herself further, she noticed the positive results and solidified her feelings of spiritual efficacy even more.

When our drives that push us to explore the meaning of spirituality get stronger, it's both exciting and dangerous. We can easily make the equivalent of the mistakes children make when they begin to explore, like falling off a chair or poking a fork into an electrical outlet. We have already seen how Ernest and Jane ended up in cults, Haley was overwhelmed with divine love, and I became involved with spirits. Spiritual infancy is full of many such dangers. However, if we can follow good common sense, form a good bond with the source of our messages, and not wander too far beyond the limits that that source sets, we will avoid most serious trouble.

Think of yourself like a child who reads about what grown-ups do and feels motivated to do the things that are needed to become a grown-up herself, rather than one who suddenly starts dressing like a grown-up in the hopes that she will become one faster. No one knows you like the source of your messages, and so it is essential for your development to put your trust in those messages and learn to decode them in the sequence in which they appear.

ॐ ॐ ॐ

This early stage in decoding messages—our spiritual infancy—sets the foundation on which everything else is built. To benefit from it, we need to make many adjustments in our attitude toward ourselves. When most of us first detect messages, we are inclined to think that our soul is already wise, just hidden by the veil of our body, and that all we need to do is get in touch with its wisdom. That's because when we are under the influence of the effects of spiritual messages, they make us feel for the moment more competent than we actually are, like a child thinking that she has mastered a complex skill because she is following directions or that she understands a complex concept because she is repeating something an adult told her to say.

As we get used to thinking of ourselves as spiritual children, however, we lose our infantile grandiosity and can focus on learning the lessons that our messages deliver. Once we have established a basic sense of efficacy from our own experiences, we are ready to move on to the next stage, where we learn to reason about the spiritual dimension of everyday life in a more systematic way.

ॐ ॐ ॐ

Keys to Chapter 15

- The discoveries of developmental psychologists suggest a striking analogy between a child's process of maturation and your own spiritual development. This analogy provides a valuable framework that can help you understand the stages through which you learn to decode messages and develop spiritually.

- Even if you are a very competent adult with a highly developed material intelligence, and even if you have studied spiritual writings extensively, your first encounters with spiritual reality are likely to be analogous to a newborn's early encounters with material reality. They awaken instincts that are encoded in your spiritual DNA.

- When you first become aware of the spiritual dimension, you notice that certain of your actions elicit mysterious spiritual reactions. It's the first awareness of a cause-and-effect relationship, like the connection an infant makes between his mother's appearing with a bottle and his feeling satisfied.

- When you can keep God's existence in mind even when you are not receiving messages, you will have developed spiritual object constancy, the equivalent of another important milestone in a child's development.

- Just as a child's ability to communicate with his parents is profoundly influenced by the nature of the bond he has with them, so your ability to decode messages is dependent on your forming a solid bond with the source of your messages.

- Just as a child learns by exploring the material dimension with physical movement, so you learn about the spiritual dimension by exploring it with mental movement, by increasing the reach of your spiritual attention and spiritual intentions. The feedback you get helps you learn how to interact with the spiritual dimension more effectively and develop a sense of efficacy that motivates further efforts.

For Your Reflection

To apply yourself with patience and persistence to the demands of spiritual life, you will need a way of putting your efforts and the results that you get in perspective. Take this time to clarify your ideas about spiritual development and compare them to mine.

1. I've used an analogy with the milestones of a child's development as a framework for our spiritual progress. What schema helps you put your progress in perspective? What analogy to the material dimension is it based on? In what ways is your own schema for explaining the first stage in decoding your spiritual feedback similar to or different from mine?

2. The following questions reflect some of the milestones we pass through in learning to develop spiritual intelligence. As you reflect on them, try to pull together the concrete experiences you've identified in previous chapters that are relevant to the first stage of your spiritual development.
   - Have you ever detected a spiritual message?
   - Have you ever found a spiritual message to be a reaction to an action of yours?
   - Has a spiritual message ever proposed that you make a specific change in your life? Could you act on its advice and see positive results?
   - Do you have a good bond with the source of your messages and think about what that source wants from you, even if you can't always deliver on it?
   - How curious are you to know more about spirituality?

3. Go to decodeyourmessages.com to find out how others gauge their progress in engaging spiritual forces in their everyday life.

4. Take out a sheet of paper or turn to a blank page in your notebook and entitle it "Milestones in the First Stage of

Spiritual Development." You can also go to decodeyour
messages.com to download these points for reflection to
your computer or log into your online notebook. Write a
concise paragraph that expresses your perspective on your
early messages and whether you have found anything in
them suggesting a developmental process, as I have. Once
you've finished your summary paragraph, continue on and
write as much detail as you'd like about the experiences
that highlight the progress that you have made.

5. Go to decodeyourmessages.com to add your schema for
spiritual development and how your early messages illustrate the important milestones in this first stage.

CHAPTER 16

The Milestones of
Spiritual Childhood

O nce we connect with the source of our messages, what remains for us to do? Do we keep on maturing, and if so, in what direction? What skills do we build and what other milestones do we pass? Every model for spiritual development encourages us to focus on developing one or another skill that it considers most important in our journey toward spiritual maturity—capacities like love, compassion, virtue, or service. For me, spiritual intelligence is the defining characteristic of the journey.

In this second stage, then, we develop our spiritual intelligence further, building mental skills and personal characteristics analogous to those a child develops during the elementary school years. We do this by mastering the techniques I've outlined in Parts II and III. I have chosen three of the most significant milestones that occur during this period to give you an idea of the important changes that happen: forming images and words that convey useful meanings, recognizing how the material and spiritual dimensions work together, and learning how to serialize, order, and group our experiences into meaningful categories.

When we enter this stage, we realize that advancement requires effort in the direction our messages indicate. Much of the work in this stage involves controlling our emotional drives and getting ourselves to do the things that common sense and most spiritual traditions tell us to do. As we apply ourselves to these tasks in our own life circumstances, the rewards that motivate us shifts from the material and psychological benefits of our spiritual interest— help with our problems, greater peace of mind—to the spiritual benefits of thinking, feeling, and acting in line with our messages and principles. Although we continue to seek our material advantage, we develop a balanced bi-dimensional perspective where we use a healthy and vital material life as the basis for our spiritual progress.

Refining Our Ideas and Images

You can get a better idea of the kind of skills we build in this stage by looking at what in Piaget's theory of cognitive development children learn to do between the ages of five and twelve. One of the most important of these skills is imbuing mental representations (ideas and images) with the same meaning the children's teachers give them. Doing so allows children to organize and manipulate these ideas and images in their mind so that they can get the answers their teachers expect them to get and communicate their own thinking to them. Over time, children learn to think more like they do, read more like they do, and do simple math problems the way they do. They can even discuss what they have learned in class with other students, because they all share the same system of meanings.

At the same time that children are learning to form better ideas and images that help them solve ever more difficult problems, they need to develop the qualities of character required to act on these ideas even when they are not emotionally satisfying, as emphasized in the work of Erik Erikson. During this period, children become increasingly focused on reality and more interested in building their competence than in just playing. In the beginning, the child has to be forced to study, but then he starts to enjoy being industrious as he learns to appreciate a new class of rewards that his greater understanding brings him—greater autonomy in a far larger and more interesting field of operations.

The spiritual correlates of these basic thinking skills are important to our development because so much of our spiritual progress depends on our conscious thought. To think in a meaningful way about the spiritual dimension, we need our ideas and images to take into account all that has been discovered about that dimension so that we can engage it more effectively. We develop effective ideas and images by adopting the principles of our tradition and following the guidance of our messages so that we learn how to mentally "operate" in an age-appropriate way in the world around us.

We are a little like Helen Keller, who, though she was blind and deaf, formed ideas and images that enabled her to get around in a world that she couldn't see. She did this by capturing functional relationships among the various objects and events that she encountered, and between herself and those objects, through the senses she did have. For us, principles lay out the most basic functional relationships between the material and spiritual dimensions, compensating for our own limited experience of the spiritual dimension so that we can interact with it in simple ways just as surely as if we had eyes that could see it. Messages give us the feedback in a form that we can observe so that we can refine our understanding of what is actually going on. Principles and messages together enable us to form meaningful intentions that turn material reality into a kind of virtual reality we can use to develop our spiritual intelligence. As we improve our intentions with experience, the words that we use in thinking about the spiritual dimension grow in their meaning and their power.

To give you an example of how our words gain more meaning as we understand more, when we first hear terms like *spiritual*, *soul*, and *the source of our messages*, we don't have much of an idea what they mean. They give simple names to certain of our experiences, but they don't have much functional value for us because they aren't based on our own experiences. They are simply basic concepts that others have found useful and that we hope one day to be able to use in meaningful ways. So they can't influence our everyday choices very much. As we apply principles and decode messages, though, we begin to understand what these words stand for more concretely, as with Helen Keller when she first understood that the tracings of the letters w-a-t-e-r in one hand corresponded to the cool stream she felt in the other hand. Then step by step our understanding of words like *spiritual, soul*, and the *source of our messages* becomes more meaningful for understanding ourselves, because we have experience that makes them understandable to us.

Let me give you a more concrete example from my own experience. When I first thought of the word *soul*, what came to mind was some kind of light or energy field. It was both formless and in some way had my face. Now, after years of decoding messages, I think of my soul as being my mind or consciousness. When my body dies, what will remain is my personal consciousness, which has been shaped by my experiences and understandings. The more I can develop the perspective of my messages and principles in my current consciousness while I am in this body, the more my soul will have gained from my experiences. This has many functional implications that I can explore and validate or correct.

It helps me, for example, consider how my soul manifests in my current consciousness. It seemed logical to me that the soul most likely contributes those elements that make us distinctively human. One of these is the uniquely human part of our intelligence. Another is our moral conscience, which inclines us to judge things as right or wrong not simply because society tells us they are but because we sense their inherent rightness or wrongness in ourselves.

It helps me consider my purpose in being here, which I see as the development of my uniquely human intelligence and conscience. Thinking that my intelligence and conscience will come with me when I leave this body helps me think of them differently, as no longer being just products of my brain. It helps me think about which elements in everyday life will best develop the part of my intelligence and conscience that comes with me. It shifts the balance in my consciousness and conscience toward the spiritual values of my principles and messages, my only certain reference points for conceiving of the spiritual dimension and imagining my soul. As I validate these concepts through my own experience and see their usefulness, the words take on ever more functional meaning.

Each time we think the word *soul*, it has a certain effect on us. The more the meaning we give that word helps us to connect with the truth of our soul and how it is operating in a particular situation, the better effect it will have on us. But if it consists of a generic definition not connected to the actual experience that we are thinking about, it cuts us off from engaging the spiritual dimension. This is the struggle at this period—to shift the meaning of words like *soul*, or *intelligence* or *conscience*, from their ordinary sense to a spiritually resonant one. We start by trying to understand the meaning that others have given to the words and then gather our own evidence to see what the words mean to us. We first develop a basic understanding of our soul and the spiritual dimension that is the equivalent of an elementary student's understanding of himself and the material world around him and then gradually form better representations that enable us to "operate" more effectively in the spiritual dimension.

As you have seen throughout the book, developing meaningful

understandings of our spiritual nature can be a painful process. We often see that our favorite ideas and images are limited or wrong only when events in our life force us to. Marinka, for example, struggled to come to terms with the meaning of losing a house, in chapter 4, that she had naïvely purchased from a crook with false documents. Marie, in chapter 8, struggled year after year to come to terms with her in-laws, whom she was trying to keep away from her children. Both women had strong faith, but the meanings they currently held for their souls and the source of their messages did not help them connect to God. Eventually, however, they refined their ideas and images and made significant advances in their understanding of their souls, of the source of their messages, and of what they needed to do to develop their relationship with God.

Recognizing Spiritual Influences

Another milestone in child development that helps us grasp what we must master in this stage of our spiritual development is the ability to take into account two dimensions of an object simultaneously to solve a problem. In Piaget's classic example, if you pour water from one glass into a taller, narrower glass right in front of a four-year-old child, that child will insist that the narrower one has more water in it because it is taller. But if you repeat the same action in front of a seven-year-old, that child will easily recognize that the two glasses hold the same amount of water.

The younger child assigns meaning based on the one factor that is most immediately impressive to his mind (the glass is taller), whereas the older child can disregard what he sees and insist on what he knows (the amount of water is the same). The younger child sees that he is not getting the "right" answer according to adults, but he can't grasp why, no matter how hard he tries. It's as if some kind of trick is being played on him. He can describe many different aspects of the situation correctly—a glass, water, someone pouring it, the room he is in, the purpose in being there. The best he can do with the puzzle of the taller glass, however, is pretend that it is the way others tell him and hope that some day he will understand the reason why. His ability to think has not matured sufficiently for him to grasp how those two dimensions, height and width, work together. The older child, on the other hand, can consider both the height and the width of the glass without a second thought, so he is able to easily get the right answer for the right reason.

According to Piaget's theory, the child develops this skill automatically as his brain matures. We know that it is the right time for him to develop this skill because he has gone through all the other stages before this one. For us to master the comparable skill and understand how the spiritual dimension influences the material dimension that we see, we have to make a deliberate effort and repeatedly search for spiritual reasons for the things that happen to us. In a sense, that's the aim of this book—to help you gain the experience and develop the capacity to discern how the material and spiritual interact.

Realizing that it is a developmental process encourages us to patiently persist, as Theresa did in chapter 10, for example, after realizing that her faith had been weak in a difficult situation. If you persist, you too will make a transition like the one I underwent in chapter 5, when I was finally able to recognize spiritual influences where I had previously been unable to do so. As you may recall, I was attending a spiritual discussion group but frustrated by my inability to learn very much. I finally figured out how to get answers to my questions, not by asking my questions directly and having other participants with more experience answer them, but by attending with a better spiritual intention and then recognizing my answers in what others were saying about completely different topics. It wasn't a result of a merely intellectual understanding, but a result of all the work that I did outside the group in my own life to engage the spiritual dimension, which finally came together in that moment when I "got it." After this, I found I could take into account the spiritual influences in an ever wider range of situations.

As crucial as this connection is to make, there remains a great deal to learn at this stage. Although Theresa's and my experiences led to important advances in the development of our spiritual reasoning, they did not improve our overall spiritual functioning much more than taking into account the width and height of a glass would improve a child's ability to function in the material world. Our functioning on a spiritual level had increased to the equivalent of a seven-year-old, still not very mature or reliable.

Learning to Categorize

A younger child can accumulate information, but she can't draw upon her past experience to help her in situations that differ very significantly in appearance from the ones that she has already been in. For a growing child to go beyond her simple knowledge of how two dimensions, like the height and width of a container of water, interact in isolated situations, she needs to take an important cognitive step, one that will enable her to compare objects and organize them logically according to such criteria as size, color, or use. In Piaget's terms, the child must begin to *serialize, order*, and *group into classes* the things she learns from different situations so that she will be able to draw on relevant elements in her past experience to improve her choices in the constantly changing conditions of everyday life.

Piaget underscores, in the following example, how gradually we build the seemingly simple skill of organizing our understanding of experience into categories. If two balls of clay of the same dimension and the same form are presented to a child and one is then transformed into the shape of a snake, a seven-year-old will grasp that the matter of the clay is conserved in the transformation—

that is, that the snake does not contain more or less clay than the ball—but only at nine or ten will he be able to draw on experiences he has already assimilated to realize that the weight of the clay is conserved as well, and only at eleven will he realize that the volume stays the same too. (To realize what these distinctions mean at a practical level, just think of the huge difference in mental functioning between a seven-year-old and an eleven-year-old.) Though a child in this phase isn't yet capable of abstract thought, she can use simple principles like addition, subtraction, multiplication, and division in relation to concrete objects like pieces of clay or people. She can use other principles to adhere to the basic values of her society and get pleasure out of things like her schoolwork. She can organize not just her interactions with the world, but her complete range of thoughts and feelings, in ways that help her function better. By using commonly accepted principles to organize her experiences, she is able to effectively interact with others who use similar principles.

So, by analogy, for us to go beyond a knowledge of how the material and spiritual dimensions interact in certain simple, isolated situations, we need to be able to serialize, order, and group into classes our spiritual experiences in such a way that will help us decode our messages. We won't advance in our spiritual development by simply gathering experiences and organizing them in the way that comes naturally to us based on our everyday common sense. We need to organize them according to sound spiritual principles that help us know how things work in the whole range of situations. The more we use similar spiritual principles to organize our experiences, the better able we will be to learn from each other.

Right now, you're reading an example of what I did to try to master this milestone, for when I decided to write this book, I was sure that it would help me put all my thoughts and experiences into a coherent order. I wasn't prepared, however, for how long it would take. I expected that the "spiritual" elements would jump out at me, based on my understanding of my own experiences. I thought that because I had learned to take into account people's different nature, nurture, and life circumstances in psychology, I could use my knowledge to serialize, order, and group into just the right categories my own and others' spiritual experiences. Yet, it took me more than twelve years to be able to do this.

Let me explain what I went through in more concrete terms. Before I began, I had talked with many others who had come to a similar conclusion to mine: that it was possible to approach spirituality rationally. So, I began by trying to explain how this was possible as I would approach a similar issue in psychology that required more than introspection. I devised a questionnaire, sent it to everyone I knew, and asked them to send it to everyone they knew who might have had a spiritual experience. I was particularly interested in both the experiences that got people involved in spirituality and the ones that motivated them to continue, for I felt that I understood these fairly well in my own experience. I collected these and then personally interviewed more than fifty people about the experiences on which their beliefs rested.

This gave me a good pool of information from which to illustrate the points that I believed were true. I chose certain experiences and began to analyze them. Each time I reread what I had written, even the very next day, I saw it from a slightly different angle that seemed important to me. I hoped it would lead to this better way of integrating things. I couldn't ignore this new thought because it seemed better than the old one. Unfortunately for me, each analysis of each experience and even the main point of each chapter kept changing, while my overall understanding didn't seem to be growing very much at all.

The process was deeply emotional. Each time I had to change directions and reshape the chapter that I was writing, I became so emotionally drained that I could barely sit up. I would throw myself on the bed for half an hour just to recover enough energy to sit up and work again. So I would continue, up and down, often for twelve or more hours a day on weekends. I hired editors to help me to express it better. When one became frustrated with my constant changes, I moved on to another.

The problem was in my level of understanding, not in my ability to express what I knew. No matter how hard I tried, I just couldn't get the ideas to connect in a way that stayed stable in my mind for more than a few days. Yet, month after month and year after year, I pushed myself to continue, hopeful that I would eventually succeed. My situation reminded me of the classic Sufi tale of blind men describing an elephant, each one naming just the part he was touching, with no idea of the whole, only in this case I had the whole group of blind men inside my head; each day I saw a different aspect of an experience as I groped in the dark. I hoped that if I kept at it long enough, I'd figure out what I was touching.

Something gradually became clear to me that I was well aware of in theory: to progress, I needed to continue to write while at the same time working on myself in my everyday life and doing the things that I was writing about. I had to verify the truth of what I was saying in my own experience. I had to actually apply the principles that I was saying I used in these isolated situations in an ever more systematic way to ensure that the connections that I was making were sound and coherent. If I wrote about someone else's weakness, I had to not just see my own equivalent weakness but work on it. If I wrote about someone else's program and how it helped him, I had to see how my program helped me. Only by working on myself in this way could I serialize, order, and group my own and others' experiences into categories meaningful enough that I could complete this book.

What kept me going for all those years was that I noticed things coming together under the surface in a way that made sense by analogy with Piaget's description of development. Just as a nine-year-old doing her homework can have no real idea of how her thinking is developing, neither did I. Instead, I began to enjoy and value the process. It made me feel closer to the source of my messages. I became more and more convinced by my analyses of my own and others' experiences that life really did have another level of meaning and that there was a purpose to it. It was no longer just theoretical to me; it was real, for I felt that I had enough evidence to justify my belief. I became more optimistic about my future, feeling, like a student in a university, that everything was laid out for me in the right way and I just had to master the lessons that my messages put in front of me. It was hard work and I had to put aside other things to do it, but I felt determined to persevere by some inner drive that was being satisfied in a way I didn't yet comprehend. I was certain that I was advancing.

Although writing this book helped me pull together what I was learning from my messages and my practices into a coherent whole, you won't have to write a book, or be as systematic in your practices as I am in mine, to learn these same basic skills, any more than you would have to go to medical school and become a psychiatrist, as I did, in order to reach your own maturity and enjoy a full and satisfying material life. If I share with you my way of doing it, it's to inspire you to find the way to integrate your own and others' experiences that fits your nature and life circumstances. You need only to consistently apply effective spiritual principles over years, using the same kind of common sense and discipline that has worked to help you reach your material goals.

જ્ઞ   જ્ઞ   જ્ઞ

At the beginning of this stage, spiritual childhood, we realize how dominated we are by our spiritual ADD, and we see that if we are to overcome it, we must apply ourselves in a regular and consistent way. It's hard to bring ourselves to make the necessary efforts because we can't judge the ultimate value of what we are learning and each step forward requires greater discipline and effort, just as in school. Yet with each step forward, we understand the world around us from a more knowledgeable perspective, for only after we pass a milestone and set our sights on the next do we fully realize the value of the skill we have just acquired.

By the end of this second stage in our spiritual development, we are no longer blocked by our spiritual ADD. We have gained enough understanding to see the benefit of our efforts, so that now we are even more motivated to continue by the knowledge that this is best for us. We no longer need the material and psychological benefits of our spiritual efforts to motivate us.

To be sufficiently motivated to work on the intellectual skills and personal qualities you develop in this stage, you will probably need to be convinced, as I was, that others have followed a similar path, advanced beyond this point, and found it worthwhile. I can't describe my own journey on that path, for the next stages in my development are still ahead of me. So, in the next two chapters, I will turn to describing some of my contacts with spiritual adolescents and adults who have helped me understand what takes place in those stages and encouraged me to believe that my efforts in developing spiritual intelligence will be well worth my while.

$$\text{ॐ} \quad \text{ॐ} \quad \text{ॐ}$$

Keys to Chapter 16

- To be able to think about the spiritual dimension beyond the level of early childhood, you need to develop skills analogous to those you learned during elementary school years, starting with developing a set of coherent ideas and images that enable you to effectively engage the spiritual dimension. Because you cannot see the spiritual dimension, they will be more like the images that someone like Helen Keller, who was blind and deaf, might have formed in order to get around in material reality, capturing her experience of the functional relationships between various objects and events through senses other than hearing and sight.

- You will also need to make a developmental step similar to the one a seven-year-old takes that enables him to simultaneously take into account two material dimensions of reality—like the height and width of a glass of water—so that you can recognize what spiritual influences contribute to simple events in everyday material life.

- You will then need to serialize, order, and group into classes your own and others' experiences in relation to the spiritual elements that are active in a given situation in order to achieve an understanding of the spiritual dimension equivalent to an eleven-year-old's grasp of the material dimension in his psychological development.

- With each step forward, you will discover rewards that you hadn't been able to imagine, for they only become tangible after you develop the skill that enables you to pass one milestone and set your sights on the next.

ॐ   ॐ   ॐ

For Your Reflection

Organizing your own experiences into a developmental perspective helps you discover the pleasure of working at a spiritual task that is within your abilities, knowing that each step that you take brings you another step closer to your final goal. Nothing will make you more frustrated and stop your progress faster than always working at tasks that are too far beyond your abilities.

1. A developmental schema focuses our attention on those elements that it considers most crucial to our overall development. Which element in your spiritual experience

do you believe is most crucial in your reaching your spiritual goal in this second phase of learning to decode messages—faith, reason, ethical behavior, spiritual intelligence, or some other quality? How would the development of this quality manifest in your second stage of development, the equivalent in my analogy of the intellectual development of a child between the ages of five to twelve?

2. The following questions reflect some of the milestones we pass in developing spiritual intelligence. As you reflect on them, try to clarify equivalent milestones in your own development in relation to your own schema.

• When you use terms like *spiritual*, *soul*, and *the source of your messages*, what ideas and images come to your mind? To what extent are they the products of others' understanding, and to what extent are they enriched by your own experience?

• How often do you base your decisions in everyday life on a spiritual principle and find in retrospect that doing so improved the choice you made?

• Can you find concrete examples of the influences of spiritual forces in situations in your own life?

• Can you serialize, order, and group your experiences into classes in ways that take into account the spiritual forces that are at work in them rather than the psychological forces?

• Are you more motivated by the material or the spiritual benefits of your efforts?

3. Go to decodeyourmessages.com to find out how others conceive of the second stage in their spiritual development and how they gauge their progress in it.

4. Take out a sheet of paper or turn to a blank page in your notebook and entitle it "Milestones in the Second Stage of My Spiritual Development." You can also go to

decodeyourmessages.com to download these points for reflection to your computer or log into your online notebook. Write a paragraph describing your ideas about this period that I see as being analogous to the psychological development of a child between the ages of five and twelve. Make sure to indicate your own progress in this stage. Once you have finished this paragraph, write as much detail as you'd like about the experiences on which your theories are based.

5. Go to decodeyourmessages.com to add your theories and experiences concerning this second level of development.

CHAPTER 17

The Milestones of
Spiritual Adolescence

We have all experienced the sweeping change in everything
we think, feel, and do that comes with adolescence. A
powerful desire to have our own life, along with strong sexual
attractions, draws us into the adult world, where we now feel that
we can start to make our own way. As spiritual adolescents, we
are similarly pressured by new spiritual drives that spark a great
urgency for action. We become strongly drawn to the spiritual elements in everyday life and feel a powerful desire to make the most
of the new opportunities that we see before us in a way that is very
different from earlier stages, for we now have a level of competence that we didn't have before.

Tim, a twenty-nine-year-old philosopher, described how this felt
to him. "I was born into a family that was interested in following
the spiritual path; I never had to consciously choose to follow it.
The question of whether or not to be spiritual simply never occurred to me. I never went through a period of doubt or rebellion

or any crises' of that sort. Does that mean that I never had any kind of trouble staying on the path? That is another matter.

"Since spirituality was a kind of family tradition, there was a time when I was content letting myself be carried along by the comfortable beliefs I had been raised with. It made me feel secure and a part of things. And then there came a time in my early twenties when I suddenly saw that this wasn't enough. I had to actually take the responsibility myself to move forward. When that happens, spirituality is no longer that familiar familial background with its reassuring resonance. It is something you have to cope with. It is something you sometimes have to run after. It is something exciting and alive. I've found that the spiritual path does not simply stay the way it always was; it keeps evolving, and I am the one who has to adapt to it, to keep pace with its changes and reformations."

Tim felt new demands with greater immediacy. There were things to be done, and he wanted to be the one doing them. He sensed before him a larger world with real spiritual challenges and more tangible benefits in which he could take part. He could no longer be satisfied with the shelter and comfort that his previous beliefs had provided him. He could no longer just follow what he had learned from others and continue to approach spirituality in the way someone at an elementary-school level might. He had reached a point where he was ready to think for himself and make his own way. He was ready to try to keep up with the constant flow of real-time messages in his everyday life.

What suddenly fired this change that had previously been only a potential in Tim's spiritual DNA? It was that all the principles he had been applying in an elementary way suddenly came together so that the wisdom at the heart of them became apparent to him. He began to grasp his purpose in life in a way he never had before, much the way a burst of hormones had triggered his material maturation. He found that he could operate in this larger world with his own free will in a way that was distinctly different from the way he had used his will when he was a spiritual child. He still lacked the skills to engage the spiritual dimension in a mature way, but he was ready to take the next step.

It is this sudden increase in a person's ability to think, feel, and act in line with his principles and messages that marks his entry into spiritual adolescence. Everything he has learned seems to come together almost magically to enable a level of meaningful thought and action that just wasn't possible before. The spiritual adolescent is now at home in a bi-dimensional world, although he cannot manage with anywhere near the same facility an adult has, for he lacks experience. He has acquired enough ethical virtues that they begin to shine in him as he lives them more consistently. He has acquired enough knowledge that spiritual energy seems to determine his choices and help him guide others who are still in their spiritual childhood.

A spiritual adolescent might be an actual adolescent herself or she might be a wise elder. A world-renowned religious leader can still be a spiritual child, and an uneducated person can be a spiritual adolescent. Your child might be a spiritual adolescent, while you remain a spiritual child. Our level of spiritual intelligence is completely separate from our psychological maturity or our theoretical understanding of a belief system. For simplicity's sake, we will focus in this chapter on several of the ways that the more highly developed spiritual intelligence of the spiritual adolescent might manifest itself in a materially mature adult with good common sense.

More Effective Reasoning

From Piaget's point of view, the determining element in our development is our reasoning. The adolescent can use a more formal mode of reasoning than he could as a child, highly logical and systematic. He can reason deductively, make hypotheses, and draw conclusions. He can understand general theories and combine them to solve problems. He can evaluate his strengths, weaknesses, and possibilities to come up with a viable role for him in society that he can then work toward actualizing. As he strives to achieve his goal and actualizes the potentials in his DNA, he discovers who he is and sees more clearly who he can be.

So we expect that the hallmark of a spiritual adolescent will be that she can reason deductively, form hypotheses, draw conclusions, and think systematically about the spiritual elements in her everyday life. She will begin to naturally think and act in line with her system of principles. She will be able to evaluate her spiritual strengths, weaknesses, and possibilities so that she can start to form her own sense of personal spiritual identity and interact more effectively with the bi-dimensional spiritual/material world in which she is now at home.

I have a friend, Peter, a fifty-year-old cardiologist, whom I consider to be a spiritual adolescent. Since I was interviewing Peter soon after my father had fallen and broken his hip, I asked him to tell me how he would react to such a situation, and then to compare it to the reaction of someone who did not have a strong interest in thinking about spirituality (such as my father). Peter replied, "When someone who has no interest in spirituality falls and breaks a leg, he will say, 'I broke my leg. I'm stupid, clumsy, or unlucky.' When you are interested in spirituality, you ask yourself, why did this happen to me? You know that each action is a consequence of your prior actions, so you see the incident as a situation that was created for your benefit, to help you grow. But that is not enough. You must go beyond this point. You must try to learn the laws and the reasons that govern your fate."

To identify the most likely cause of such an incident and thus learn the most from it, Peter would have to know the kinds of things he was prone to doing wrong. "I would ask myself these questions: What did I do to someone else that might have resulted in this? Was it something in my past? Why did I break this particular leg at this particular time? Was I jealous of someone? Was I rude to someone? Was I angry with someone? Did I mishandle or break one of my possessions?" Any one of these errors could have been the determining spiritual cause for breaking his leg.

A spiritually aware and mature person, Peter explained, would ponder all the possible material *and* spiritual reasons for having broken his leg. After doing his best to choose a candidate for the determining cause, he would then step back to see what answer "felt right" based on everything he knew. He would somehow sense what answer fit the circumstances best, based on his experience and his understanding of the system of principles that describe how things work, whose synergy he can sense in himself as a kind of touchstone. In a similar way, we, as material adults, sense which of a number of options is most likely true based on our principles and experience.

Once he had an idea of the most likely cause, Peter would seek to confirm it by identifying the lesson in the incident and then imagining what might happen if he acted on that conclusion. If he thought it would be beneficial to act on his conclusion, he would do so and then watch for any feedback. If his analysis were confirmed by the feedback he received, he would gain experience that would help him make better decisions in the future. If it turned out to be incorrect, he would benefit equally by using this experience to avoid making the same mistake again. What distinguishes a spiritual adolescent from a child in this regard is the fact that his analyses are more often correct in more complex situations, reflecting a better understanding of himself and his life, a difference similar to that between the adolescent and the child in Piaget's theory of cognitive development.

You might wonder how being jealous, rude, or angry could contribute to someone's breaking a leg. Why would Peter even think of that? It's difficult to follow the basis of his reasoning if you are not Peter himself, and especially if you're not yet a spiritual adolescent yourself. The truth is that the spiritual value of an action is quite different from one person to another and often very different from what we might think. What we do wrong might be far more serious from a spiritual perspective than we imagine. And like in everyday life, things that are acceptable for a child to do aren't as acceptable for an adolescent.

The serious material repercussion of breaking a leg might be to make certain that we understand the spiritual gravity of what we have done. On the other hand, it might be that breaking a leg was not gravely harmful from a spiritual perspective—far less harmful, say, than losing our motivation to pursue our spiritual development for a few months. It's only when we reach spiritual adolescence that we start to understand the value of things to us individually so that we can make such judgments.

Despite this remarkable increase in her abilities to understand spiritual causes and effects, an adolescent is still an adolescent. She cannot grasp the complete picture, because she lacks experience. Just as a material adolescent is often idealistic and can commit herself totally to a group, idea, or cause in which she loses perspective on everything else, so a spiritual adolescent can get passionately involved in one aspect of her spiritual life or another to the detriment of others that might be more important in the long run. Her sense of purpose and her desire to fulfill it can't make up for her lack of experience and real knowledge.

Peter used an analogy from his own field of cardiology to explain why it is so easy in spirituality to think we know something when we really know so little. "To see the spiritual aspect of an event is like learning to interpret a cardiogram," he told me. "If you haven't studied cardiograms at all, you just see the regular pattern moving across the screen. If a person looks normal, you assume that everything—including his heart—is all right. As you learn the physiology behind what is going on in the heart to make this tracing, the line begins to mean something to you. Then you go on to learn how to recognize a heart attack or distinguish a potentially fatal arrhythmia from one that is benign. But you still don't know what to do with that information. Gradually, you learn which medication to give in relation to what sign. And when you master all this, then you realize that the heart is only one organ and all the organs have to be functioning well for a person to be healthy."

The spiritual adolescent can more accurately assess his own strengths, weaknesses, and possibilities so that he does well in most common situations that he faces. He can recognize one or another aspect of a situation fairly well, but he can't put it all together and know what to do in the same consistent way that a spiritual adult can. He can act in line with his principles even under stress, but not to the same degree a spiritual adult can. He has constancy of purpose that sustains him through the inevitable disappointments and setbacks. He feels good about himself because of all that he has learned; at the same time, he feels a new kind of humility, seeing how little he really knows and how insignificant his knowledge is relative to God's. He has lost his grandiosity but not his motivation. He sees the challenge and feels up to it, for he is certain, based on his experience, that everything that happens to him depends on God and is ultimately for his benefit.

Extending the Reach of Our Spiritual Intelligence

During this transition to mature spiritual reasoning, a spiritual adolescent can no longer trust her intuitions to guide her as they did in the past, for her old intuitions sprang from a child's view of the world that does not function well in the more complex reality of which she now perceives herself to be a part. As my friend Michael, whose stories I shared in previous chapters, put it, "There are a lot of people who say, 'I did this because I felt I should do this' or 'I believe this because it feels right.' But in everyday life, very few people are doing things correctly based solely on their intuition. It's like relying on intuition to pass a test rather than studying. If you have a multiple-choice test in front of you and you're not sure which answer to choose, it's good to have a strong intuition. But if you knew the right answer and you didn't have to rely on intuition, you would do much better. We can't go through school or life relying only on our intuition. We need to study to really be able to choose the right answer. Once you master what you need to know, you can count on your intuition again and it will be more reliable than it was before."

As Michael suggests, it's not that we put intuition aside for good. We just see its role better—to extend the reach of our reason, not to replace it. Dr. Rollo May very clearly explains the role of intuition in extending our understanding in his book *The Courage to Create*. One of the points he emphasizes is that the quality of our insights and intuitions is based on the knowledge we have of a given field. The better our knowledge, the more penetrating and fruitful our insights are likely to be. He offers the example of the French mathematician Henri Poincaré who struggled for years to come up with a solution to a complex mathematical problem. Unable to do so, he set it aside. Then one day the answer came to him out of the blue while he was stepping off a bus, not thinking of the problem at all. His intuition had provided a new insight. But then he had to work hard for months to prove that it was correct, using all of his knowledge. Someone without Poincaré's knowledge of math wouldn't have come up with that intuition or been able to prove its value.

By analogy, we can't expect our intuition to take the place of our spiritual reasoning, but to extend it. It is up to us to develop our knowledge of how the material and spiritual dimensions interact so that we can reason as well as possible. Then we can use our intuition to understand those things that are just out of our reach and return to our reason to prove the value of that intuitive insight. When we go from being children to being adolescents, it's like someone going from knowing basic arithmetic to learning calculus. The old information is still valid in its own way, but it doesn't solve these new problems. We need to first learn the fundamentals of calculus; then we will once again be able to use our intuition to extend our understanding.

The spiritual adolescent sees that his actions have greater consequences now. He aspires to rely on his intuition to extend the reach of his spiritual reason so that he can get more from the stream of constant spiritual opportunities that everyday life brings. As his spiritual intelligence comes more up to speed with his already mature material intelligence, the spiritual adolescent uses his material and spiritual intelligence together in an integrated way to take into account the important elements of both dimensions in the decisions that he makes.

May points out another factor that determines the quality of an insight—the degree to which we apply ourselves to it. Both the Sunday painter and the professional artist, he explains, may paint pictures, but the professional artist who devotes her life to creative expression in painting is more likely to create a masterpiece than someone who paints in her spare time. Similarly, our most meaningful insights will grow out of periods of deep reflection in which we commit ourselves as fully as we can to push the limits of our current understanding. The more deeply we commit ourselves to investigating the spiritual dimension, the more meaningful our answers are likely to be and the more our spiritual intelligence will grow.

Recognizing a Spiritual Adolescent

It's difficult for most of us to recognize a spiritual adolescent. He might not even talk about spirituality to someone that he doesn't know well, for spirituality is mainly a private matter. The best criterion that I have found is that he can help us better than one of our peers could. He knows what is important in a situation from a spiritual perspective and has good ideas about what we can do to master the step with which we are struggling.

When I talk to a spiritual adolescent like Peter or Michael about a problem I'm having—such as not being grateful or getting lost in my own head—it's clear to me that they have a better grasp of what is important in that situation than I do. They not only help me see other options that I hadn't considered but also encourage me to apply myself better, much as an older brother would a younger brother. They aren't threatened when I question what they say and they try hard to explain more clearly when I press them. They *like* questions. They know what is important and what isn't, so they can point out times when I am being overindulgent with myself and when I am being overly hard. They remind me of how kind God is while at the same time pushing me to do a little better. They know the goal and the steps that it takes to reach it, so they can see my struggles from a different perspective. Their advice has a different effect on me from that of my peers, for it seems to help me in the same way a spiritual message might—it changes my vision of the situation and motivates me to improve myself.

The spiritual adolescent can take into account the influences of his material nature and circumstances with greater precision than someone at an earlier stage of development. He uses his knowledge of both dimensions together in a fluid way to stay in tune with the spiritual forces that are active in his everyday life and can help others, even those who are quite different from him, come up with better solutions to their own problems. He isn't confused by the effects of people's different nature or life circumstances on the expression of their spiritual intelligence. He knows the general way in which the spiritual dimension works well enough to come up with sound advice for people in any circumstances, at any level of comprehension.

In this third stage, all spiritual paths become similar to him because he knows that they all lead to the same goal. He may choose one tradition to be affiliated with, but it is like choosing to be a citizen of one country: It's just one way to develop his potentials and express his individuality. As a result, he is less focused on the details of people's beliefs and more focused on improving himself. He is less interested in what others think about God than in improving his own private relationship to God. He is nonetheless ready to share what he knows with others who might be interested.

ᘒ   ᘒ   ᘒ

The spiritual adolescent's example inspires us to believe that our efforts to develop are worthwhile. She understands spiritual development, and she inspires us to think that if she can learn to interact more effectively with the spiritual dimension, why can't we? Her example encourages us to work harder and actualize our own potentials in our own life, whereas her greater humility challenges us not to make so much of ourselves for our efforts.

Adolescence is a time of transition. The real value of all the progress that we observe in spiritual adolescence becomes apparent only in adulthood, where the plan encoded in our spiritual DNA and activated by following our principles and messages reveals its true purpose. We'll get a glimpse of this kind of maturity in chapter 18.

ᘒ   ᘒ   ᘒ

Keys to Chapter 17

- Few of us are spiritual adolescents, yet thinking about spiritual adolescence helps us put our own efforts in perspective.
- Just as an adolescent perceives and reacts to the material world in a completely new way, so a spiritual adolescent perceives and reacts to everything differently, because he

has applied his principles in line with his messages enough for them to develop synergy and reveal the wisdom at their heart.

- The spiritual adolescent reasons deductively, forms hypotheses, draws conclusions, and thinks systematically about the spiritual elements in his everyday life. He thinks and acts in line with his principles in a systematic way. He is at home in a bi-dimensional world that is both material and spiritual.
- Spiritual adolescents rely less on intuition and more on reason in making their decisions. They use their intuition to extend their reason rather than supplant it. Their greater knowledge enables them to give better advice to others because they understand the real value of different choices.
- The spiritual adolescent understands many different aspects of a situation fairly well, but he can't put it all together in the same way that a spiritual adult can. He feels good about himself because of all that he has learned; at the same time, he feels a new kind of humility, seeing how insignificant he is in relation to God.

కో కో కో

For Your Reflection

What's the value of thinking about spiritual adolescence when the vast majority of us are still in our childhood years? It's to help us see more clearly the value of developing our own spiritual intelligence so that we are more motivated to strive to reach the milestone that is in front of us right now.

1. Have you ever met someone who could relate to the spiritual dimension in a way similar to the way everyday

adolescents relate to material reality? What were her outstanding qualities? If you don't know one, do you believe that such people exist? What do you think their outstanding qualities would be? How could you be sure that they were truly more spiritually mature than you and not just using their material intelligence in impressive ways?

2. What makes a spiritual adolescent able to engage the spiritual dimension better than you can? How do you see the roles of faith, intuition, reason, and will in this stage? If your schema of development differs from mine, think about what landmarks you would use in this third stage of decoding spiritual messages.

3. Go to decodeyourmessages.com to find others' views of how someone at this third level of spiritual development functions.

4. Take out a sheet of paper or turn to a blank page in your notebook and entitle it "Milestones in the Third Stage of Spiritual Development." You can also go to decodeyourmessages.com to download these points for reflection to your computer or log into your online notebook. Write your summary paragraph that reflects how a third stage of spiritual development helps you put your own experiences into perspective, and then write as much detail as you'd like about your own experiences with a spiritual adolescent that have motivated you to improve yourself.

5. Go to decodeyourmessages.com to add what landmarks you use for someone in this stage and how you would identify someone as a spiritual adolescent if you weren't one yourself.

CHAPTER 18

The Signs of
Spiritual Adulthood

What makes us adults in everyday life? It's not just the appearance of our bodies or even our greater ability to reason. We use much the same formal, logical, and systematic method of analyzing situations that a fifteen-year-old uses, but we can generally come up with better solutions because of the greater experience that we bring to bear.

What makes us real adults is being able to think as other adults do, feel as they do, and act as they do, but in a way that at the same time expresses our own potentials and preferences in our own circumstances. It's how we use those potentials to build the best life that we can for ourselves in our own society. It's how successful we are at establishing a family that fulfills our needs and a line of work that supports us and challenges us to improve ourselves. It's how well we use our strengths to compensate for our weaknesses. It's how fully we embrace time-honored values to achieve personal integrity and become good citizens.

By analogy, spiritual adults think, feel, and act as other spiritual adults have throughout history, but in a way that is uniquely their own and fits the circumstances of their lives. Spiritual adults may be quite successful in material life, but they are much more focused on the spiritual benefits of everyday life than on the material ones. They act ethically and have high levels of personal integrity. Nonetheless, it's very hard for us to recognize a spiritual adult if we are not at least spiritual adolescents ourselves, for we can't see the spiritual dimension in which their functioning so far surpasses ours. We can only see the material manifestations, and thus we can't know enough to judge their real capacity.

Nonetheless, I believe that if we look closely enough, we can find signs that spiritual adults do exist in all major religious and spiritual traditions. They are not all figures from the distant past, but men and women alive today who have established a mature relationship with God. All draw their wisdom from the same source and teach others to pay attention to the source of their wisdom rather than to them. Each is different from the others and manifests his or her maturity differently in relation to his or her own character, potentials, and circumstances.

As with the spiritual adolescent, I believe that the only reliable mark of a spiritual adult for the vast majority of us who are not adults is how these mature individuals relate to us. They will be strong enough to have mastered their material drives so that they do not seek material benefits from us in exchange for their spiritual guidance—certainly not admiration, sex, or financial advantage. They have no need for anything that we could give them. They help us in much the same spirit that teachers do their students, feeling a responsibility to help us without needing anything in return. Their compensation comes in a spiritual form that is invisible to us. The final confirmation of their status, however, is that their words and their writings have the effect on us of a spiritual message. It's not magic, but a result of their superior knowledge of how the spiritual dimension works, which they share with us.

You don't need to meet an Einstein to start learning physics, although it might be energizing to do so. You can learn in other ways. Although I feel fortunate to have met two people whom I consider spiritual adults, it isn't necessary to know one personally, for whether or not you do, you still have to establish your own relationship with the source of your messages and develop your own spiritual intelligence. And what we need to do to accomplish that is spelled out in most traditions and enforced by our messages: Apply ethical principles with a spiritual intention. Even more important than meeting a spiritual adult is therefore having a set of principles created by a spiritual adult to guide our development.

Spiritual adults do help out at certain points, but you can't rely on them to do your work for you or you will never learn to think for yourself. So regardless of whether you know such a person or not, you would do well to focus on applying the most basic teachings of your own tradition, particularly those teachings common to all religions, and gradually assimilate their wisdom into your own life in an orderly, step-by-step manner under the guidance of your messages. In fact, there may be a spiritual adult nearby whom you don't recognize because he has no need to call attention to himself. When you reach a point where you need one, regardless of your situation or your current level of understanding, you will probably find one.

In the meantime, what is important is to know that spiritual adults exist in our own time and aren't imaginary figures from history. Realizing this, you will more easily accept that the spiritual dimension is active and accessible today to those who seek it, and you'll be encouraged to make your best effort to connect with it.

Recognizing a Spiritual Adult

The first adult I met was Dr. Bahram Elahi, now a retired pediatric surgeon. He was born in Iran, received his medical training in France, and returned to Tehran, where he became the dean of several medical schools. He learned his approach to spirituality from his father, Ostad Elahi (1895–1974), the author of the spiritual principles I use, who had been a traditional mystic in his younger years but set aside his ascetic lifestyle to test his principles in the crucible of society. Most people who met Dr. Elahi didn't even know of his passion for spirituality. To them, he was a kind and attentive surgeon. It was not that he hid his beliefs but he only discussed them with others of all levels he knew to be sincerely interested in the subject.

I was introduced to Dr. Elahi in the mid-1980s after my spirit guide told me, as I related in chapter 5, that he couldn't take me any further because my pride was too great. To find a new approach, I started reading books and talking with as many people as I could about spirituality. When I heard about Dr. Elahi from a friend of a friend, I was interested in meeting him because we were both physicians. More importantly, when my friend gave me a translation of something Dr. Elahi had written, one sentence struck me strongly. Dr. Elahi said that his knowledge was like a drop in the ocean in comparison to his teacher's knowledge, a belief that he maintains to this day. I was deeply touched by this sentence. His genuine humility reached through the simple words, as if there were magic in that one line. I kept going back to it. Each time I read it, it affected me exactly the same way, and it encouraged me to feel that he might be able to help me with the excessive pride that my spirit guide had pointed out to me. I took it as a spiritual message, a confirmation that this was the right direction for me. Now that I am better attuned to such effects and have come across them in other books by other authors, I see them as the spiritual impact of a spiritual adult's written words that help and guide us in just such ways.

Several months later, I attended a weekend series of public lectures given by Dr. Elahi to an audience of about two hundred people. I wondered how I would know if he was a spiritual adult or just a good speaker. In fact, it wasn't easy. He seemed to have none of the special attributes that I thought would mark a spiritual person. He dressed normally and acted like a speaker at any professional meeting. He shared what he knew, much as a visiting lecturer might at a university. He answered each question thoughtfully and respectfully, and he didn't treat any question as too simpleminded. He related what he had learned from his own experience and didn't try to convince anybody of anything. He wasn't looking for approval, agreement, or admiration. He was more interested in explaining his ideas than in stirring our emotions. His feet were firmly on the ground, and most of what he said seemed like common sense, things that I had heard before. This didn't match my idea of spirituality at all.

After the lecture, I met Dr. Elahi briefly, and I described to him how my spirit guide had told me that he couldn't take me any further. "Why do we need them?" he asked. "We all know what we have to do. It's not complicated. We just have to do it." To him, spirits were real; they had often tried to contact him. He ignored them, because he viewed them as distractions that kept us from focusing our efforts on being kinder and more considerate of others in everyday life. What he was saying was in essence the same as what my spirit guide had said. I thought everyone who had contact with spirits and believed in them must nurture that relationship and learn to be naturally kind as a result of the love that came through from the spirit world. Dr. Elahi confirmed that this was not true.

A Spiritual Adult's Guidance

Over the years that followed, I attended a number of smaller gatherings where Dr. Elahi answered questions. For a long time, his answers struck me as rather superficial and generic. I felt like a child hearing an adult remind him to eat well, go to bed on time, and go to school if he wanted to get ahead in life. Dr. Elahi kept talking about our being more ethical and fighting with our self-centeredness. I would rather have heard him talk about more esoteric experiences that he had had. But these mundane matters, I would come to accept, are the heart of spiritual life.

Although I knew that Dr. Elahi knew more than I did, I didn't realize how much I had to learn. I thought that in a few years, I could master the simple things that he was teaching. I hadn't yet put myself in a developmental perspective, and I thought it would help that I had been religious as a child, a religion major in college, a psychiatrist for fifteen years, and in communication with a spirit for a number of years. All of this would, in fact, be a help to me later; at the time, it didn't dawn on me that I was a spiritual infant and that all I had learned was still more of a hindrance than a help.

When I first attended some small group sessions, I prepared my questions carefully in the hopes of getting Dr. Elahi started talking about things of real concern to me. I assumed that because he knew more than I did, he would get what I was alluding to and give me the perfect pearl of advice. However, when I asked my questions, he would look confused and say, "I don't understand your questions at all. What are you trying to ask?" This happened a number of times. When I finally asked him why I could communicate well enough with my friends and patients but not with him, he smiled benevolently and said, "It's because you don't understand anything about spirituality." It was as if he was pleased that I had finally asked.

It's hard to describe how someone can say such a thing without it being condescending or humiliating in any way. In fact, his answer came as a relief. It explained my problem to me in a way that made me feel that it was possible I might understand one day. To make any progress, however, I had to come to terms with the fact that right now I was a spiritual infant. Dr. Elahi's words helped in the process because they brought more than just an intellectual understanding. They affected me just like the influx of spiritual energy that comes with a message, altering my state of attention in a way that allowed me to see this perspective and be content with it. Being a spiritual infant, it was natural that I wouldn't understand. If I did the simple things he was pointing out to me, I could grow up. I felt humbled and cared for. I felt motivated to do what I saw needed doing.

A spiritual adult's words can have the effect of a spiritual message if we are receptive to them. It feels quite magical, but it's not really magic. It's just that the spiritual adult understands how things work. It reminded me of what I felt when I was eight-years-old and whatever problem I had my parents could help me solve it. When I followed their advice and approached the situation from their point of view, everything went so much better. That seemed like magic too. Over the years, I have heard Dr. Elahi answer questions from people of all ages, levels of education, and walks of life, without getting anything in return. He has helped many of us, always in ways that fit the details of our own life. This is what confirms him as a spiritual adult in my mind: his comprehensive ability to understand the spiritual forces that are active in a given situation and help very different people with very different problems to make choices that are both materially and spiritually beneficial to them.

He approaches spirituality as a science. I read in his book *Medicine of the Soul* a definition of love: "Without love one cannot reach any goal or persevere in any serious undertaking. Love translates into a feeling of attraction and gravitational pull toward something or someone. This attraction manifests itself in our consciousness in the form of a sentiment that either creates motivation within us or a strong pull. In spirituality, as long as this attraction translates into motivation, it is beneficial for the development of our spiritual intellect. If the intensity of this attraction exceeds our capacity, our reason is overcome and we will 'lose our mind.' Consequently, our spiritual intellect will stop developing, for it will no longer receive nourishment."

Although these words made complete sense to me, I had never read a drier description of spiritual love. It was hard for me to see why he would put it that way. How could it help me understand myself better? I wondered. Although I'm committed to pursuing spirituality in the rational way that I've outlined in this book, even after all these years part of me misses the emotional intensity that I used to have with spiritual experiences, in much the same way that

I miss the joys of childhood. Other people I know have emotional intensity in their relationship with God, but my messages have continually guided me toward a more purely rational approach. I could only assume that one way was good for those people and another was good for me, and that Dr. Elahi's description left room for individual expression. There were, after all, passionate scientists and dispassionate ones.

Reading this section in Dr. Elahi's book made me wonder once again whether I was balancing reason and emotion correctly. So I asked him whether he thought that I should continue as I was or do something to increase my feelings of love. I was hoping that he would encourage me to cultivate the latter a little more. Instead, he told me that I didn't need to focus more on love and then explained why in a way that took my understanding an important step deeper. He explained that there are as many different kinds of souls as there are kinds of people. I was an intellectual soul, he said. An intellectual soul is naturally determined to understand. He gets much greater happiness out of understanding a new point in something he is reading than out of other kinds of experience. This was certainly true for me. I really savored a new insight and was most motivated by understanding, despite my yearning for a little more emotion. If a time came where more love were important, Dr. Elahi went on to explain, it would arise in me naturally.

I had had the thought many times before that love manifested itself in different people in different ways depending on their nature and that my motivation to work on myself rationally as I was doing might be a manifestation of love. But now I could feel that Dr. Elahi's explanation had started a small ripple of change in me, helping me feel certain that there really was a greater value for me, given my nature, in the understanding that I was gaining. It was a surge of spiritual energy just like the surge that came with a subtle spiritual message.

Several days later, in my daily reading (this time of another book on spirituality), I noticed that when I read the phrase *spiritual dimension*, it no longer felt to me like a foreign place where I didn't fit in. It now read like "home." I understood my relationship to it better and felt that someone like me could be at home there being myself, just as someone who was more emotional could be at home there being more emotional. What was important was not our emotional state but how our emotions connected us as individuals to the source of our messages. Something inside of me had changed, just like the changes that messages bring.

A Role Model of Faith

Each spiritual adult is different. Dr. Elahi's scientific background and rational approach make his guidance particularly useful to me. The second spiritual adult I met—Malek Jan Nemati (1906–1993), the sister of Ostad Elahi—was quite different from Dr. Bahram Elahi. She had her own distinctive character and helped me in quite different ways. Although she had learned from Ostad Elahi how to approach spirituality in a rational way and was well informed about world affairs and modern advances in science, she led most of her life like a traditional mystic because she lived among people who looked to her for that kind of help. In her small village in Kurdistan, in Iran, she helped her fellow villagers with whatever problems they were worried about in the same way mystics had done in the past. She cured many people of illnesses, including blindness, even though she herself was blind. She gave lessons to those who sought lessons, encouraging them to approach spirituality rationally. In a male-dominated culture, this fragile and blind woman steadfastly advocated for the empowerment and equality of women.

Her own faith was tremendous. She had begun losing her vision at the age of fourteen and had become completely blind by the age of twenty, but this didn't upset her at all. "God took away my sight," she said, "but opened before me the door to the Kingdom of Heaven; no one can imagine what I have gained from this."

Dr. Elahi had mentioned his aunt a number of times during his talks as the person he turned to for guidance. This made me so curious about her that I traveled to a remote village in Iran to see her. At the time, I was still learning the ABCs of spirituality and adjusting to the fact that it was real and relevant to my life. I met her soon after the first conversation that I've described with Dr. Elahi and well before the second. On my way, I met Samira, who, as I said in chapter 11, told me how Malek Jan Nemati had shown her that when she felt closest to God, her soul was asleep. This primed me even more to expect more words of wisdom to help me overcome my own blocks.

When I met her, she was old and ill, lying in bed with an oxygen mask on. I was with about ten other visitors, and we talked with her for about twenty minutes on mundane topics. She asked about our trip and wanted to hear funny stories that we knew. I went back to the room where I was to sleep, a little disappointed that she seemed too ill to have a real conversation or give a real lesson. There had been nothing profound or magical in anything she said, unless I had missed it in translation, as she didn't speak English. If she had any special knowledge, it seemed that she wasn't sharing it that night. I couldn't help wondering what I was doing there in that remote corner of the world telling a sick elderly woman funny stories. Why had I expected something special?

Then, about ten minutes after I left her room, an answer to my question arrived. My perception of everything suddenly changed completely. I wasn't trying to meditate or concentrate on anything. It just came out of nowhere in the midst of my disappointment. I could actually hear a roaring in my ears from the spiritual energy I sensed flowing through me. It was as if I had had a small flame inside of me, like the pilot light on a stove, and now the burner was fully ignited. Everything I had read and heard about spirituality—and not understood very well—came into perspective. I had no question that this was her gift to me for coming.

Everything seemed so clear, and particularly clear was how

unprepared I was to benefit from this experience. I saw that this state of illumination would be temporary and that when the energy left, I would understand little more than I had before. I would only know that it was possible to know more. While the state continued, I sat pondering my life and all the questions about life that had seemed so difficult before but now seemed so simple; then I drifted into a comfortable sleep. When I awoke, the energy was still with me, but it faded over the next few hours as I rode away from her village, leaving me feeling quite empty.

Looking back on this experience, I saw it as a lesson about my desire for illumination. Despite all that I knew intellectually, I continued to think that the goal of spiritual practice really was this kind of illumination and that everything Dr. Elahi had said to the contrary in the first few years I knew him was just to help me to be patient. But the experience made it very clear how little value illumination had for someone like me who was unprepared to hold onto it. If I put my efforts into bringing my life into line with my principles, then my understanding would grow in a natural way and benefit more from the gradual influx of spiritual energy that came in response to these efforts. The experience was a kind of remedy for my longing, for now I knew how useless it was. I have never yearned for that "high" in quite the same way again.

A second experience with Malek Jan Nemati proved to me another characteristic of spiritual adults: Not only does their influence not depend on their physical presence, but their ability to help us doesn't stop after they leave their bodies. Several years after my meeting with her, she died. On the first anniversary of her death, I went on a pilgrimage to the place where she is buried in Baillou, France, a few hours by car from Paris, where a beautiful memorial now stands. By this time, I had been studying messages for more than ten years. I believed in a higher power that was the source of messages, but I still felt allergic to the idea of God because of all the connotations the word *God* held for me. I had too often seen it used as an excuse for every possible thing someone might do. I thought that I "should" feel more comfortable thinking about God, since I was trying to make sense of my spiritual experience the way that people in the past who thought of God struggled to understand theirs. In all honesty, I just couldn't. I was too much of an intellectual. My mind was unable to grasp what God might be and why I should believe in him at all if he was a being so far beyond my comprehension.

I can recall as if it were yesterday sitting in a field near Malek Jan Nemati's grave, going over my life and the issues I was facing in a kind of intimate conversation with her. Then suddenly I realized that I *did* believe in God. For more than thirty years, since I was twenty, I had felt repulsed by the idea of God, even as I became so interested in spirituality. Now I felt attracted by it. There was no emotion that came with the realization; it was more like a fact. Ever since that day, I have believed in God. I have felt an inexplicable, personal connection to him and not been bothered in the slightest by the fact that I can't understand him the way he really is.

ﮊ   ﮊ   ﮊ

Spiritual adults offer living examples of what it's like to have one's thoughts, feelings, and actions in line with the guidance of messages. In fact, that's what makes them spiritual adults: They live so closely in tune with the source of their messages that their guidance has the same effect as messages. The spiritual energy that passes through them isn't theirs, but is funneled in a way that reflects their own unique character, potentials, culture, and life circumstances. Seeing how they retain their individuality helps us value our own individuality more. Seeing that they can be agents who deliver spiritual messages—and that this is, in fact, what confirms their being spiritual adults—helps us grasp how central decoding messages is to our own development.

Knowing that spiritual adults exist puts our efforts and our development into perspective so that we can see what it means for the influences of our soul to be dominant in our mind. We can then imagine a path by which we may one day actualize our own potentials and become adults too. With each step, we become more confident that we can become more like them, in our own way.

శ్ర   శ్ర   శ్ర

Keys to Chapter 18

- Spiritual adults exist in our time, in all religious and spiritual traditions. They are not all figures from the distant past, but men and women who are alive today and have established a mature relationship with God. Although it is useful to know one, it isn't necessary. What is necessary is to have a set of principles constructed by a spiritual adult.
- Someone enters the fourth stage of spiritual development when he or she can think, feel, and act as other spiritual adults do, but in a way that expresses his or her own history, potentials, and preferences in the circumstances of his or her own life.
- If you're not a spiritual adult, it's hard to recognize one, for the most significant markers of their maturity are found in their private relationship with an invisible dimension. I rely mainly on two criteria: that they live an ethical life and that their guidance has the impact of a message in fostering the spiritual development of many different people.
- By realizing that what makes someone a spiritual adult is his or her ability to live in tune with a constant stream of spiritual feedback, we can better appreciate how central the task of decoding messages is in our own development.

శ్ర   శ్ర   శ్ర

For Your Reflection

Spiritual adults exist in every time and in every major spiritual tradition. They help us concretize the benefits of the efforts that we are making and motivate us to apply ourselves to the task of decoding the messages in our own lives.

1. Have you ever met a spiritual adult? How did you identify this person? How did he or she help you? If you haven't met one personally, do you believe that they exist in our time? How would you identify one? Is the source of your principles a spiritual adult? On what evidence do you base your answers?

2. Does thinking about spiritual adults or interacting with them help you put your own spiritual development into perspective, and if so, in what ways?

3. Go to decodeyourmessages.com to find others' experiences of spiritual adults and how they helped them actualize their own potentials.

4. Take out a sheet of paper or turn to a blank page in your notebook and entitle it "The Milestones of the Fourth Stage of Spiritual Development." You can also go to decodeyourmessages.com to download these points for reflection to your computer or log into your online notebook. Write a paragraph about how you would recognize someone who had reached spiritual maturity and how thinking about such a person helps you put yourself and your own struggles in perspective. Once you've finished your summary paragraph, write on in as much detail as you'd like about your experiences with spiritual adults.

5. Go to decodeyourmessages.com to add your criteria for spiritual maturity and the experiences upon which your ideas are based.

AFTERWORD

We have much to learn about the spiritual dimension. By reading this book and reflecting on the main points in each chapter, I hope that you have become more aware of the importance of the spiritual messages of everyday life—spiritual experiences that are confirmed by the kind of material and psychological effects that I have described—and how they teach us how to use our own character, life-circumstances, tradition, preferences, and even whims to improve ourselves both materially and spiritually. By continuing to follow their guidance, we develop the kind of personal sensitivity and discernment we need to engage the spiritual dimension in ever more effective ways so that they enrich our lives with greater wisdom and fill our hearts with ever-deepening joy.

In this book, I have presented my basic ideas for improving your spiritual common sense so that you can think more clearly about the spiritual implications of the choices that you face in everyday life. This is a good first step, and I hope that my experiences, those of others in this book, and your own—all of which are what science would call *anecdotal evidence*—will get you interested in reexamining the experiences on which your own beliefs rest, identifying examples of what I have been calling spiritual messages and expressing them in terms that people from backgrounds different from yours might understand.

The better we get at thinking about our everyday encounters with the spiritual dimension in everyday language, the easier it will become for us to detect the more subtle effects of our messages in relation to our everyday concerns. It will also make it easier to identify the similarities and differences between our own encounters with the spiritual dimension and those of others from around the globe, for our everyday lives express our common human nature and our common needs under different conditions.

It is an exciting and challenging time to be interested in spirituality, when great gains are possible with the right kind of effort. Everything is changing. Science has provided such good answers to so many of our everyday concerns that more and more people no longer even notice spiritual messages. It is a crucial juncture in the evolution of our understanding of spirituality. Will we go ahead or not? Can we build on the common sense approach of this book by making our inquiries more and more scientific?

If we can work together, I am certain that greater progress is possible. If progress has been made in so many other fields of knowledge by adapting the approach of science to the unique requirements of those fields of study, why should it not be possible for us to make similar advances in our understanding of spiritual experiences by adapting the methods of science to the unique requirements of studying the spiritual dimension? Why can't we use the mental tools at our disposal to go beyond the limits of past knowledge, transcend the limits of our current scientific mindset that excludes considerations of the spiritual dimension, and come to a better understanding of our common spiritual nature, at least to the same extent that psychology has helped us understand our common psychological nature? It is not unreasonable.

This, then, is my hope for the future—that the study of spiritual messages will lead to a more universal understanding of the truth that lies at the heart of all religious and spiritual traditions, and that this truth may inform and improve our spiritual choices in much the same way that our understanding of psychology has informed and improved our material choices. To ensure both your own progress and our collective evolution, I encourage you to continue to visit decodeyourmessages.com to add your experiences and reflections so that the rest of us can benefit from what you learn on your journey.